ONLINE PUBLICATIONS
A PRACTICAL GUIDE

ONLINE PUBLICATION CLAIMS: A PRACTICAL GUIDE

Edited by
Hugh Tomlinson QC and Guy Vassall-Adams QC

Authors
Darryl Hutcheon
Sara Mansoori
Ben Silverstone
Kirsten Sjøvoll
Hugh Tomlinson QC
Guy Vassall-Adams QC
Aidan Wills
Dave King, Digitalis

Contributing Editors
Gavin Millar QC
Lorna Skinner
Antony White QC

Publication Editorial Team
Anthony Fairclough
Pollyanna Cotterill
Mary Evenden
Becky Steels

First published 2017

British Library Cataloguing-in-Publication Data
A catalogue record for this book is available from the British Library

ISBN 978-1-99983-13-0-1

Matrix Chambers Limited,
Griffin Building, Gray's Inn,
London WC1R 5LN
+44 (0)20 7404 3447
matrix@matrixlaw.co.uk
www.matrixlaw.co.uk
@matrixchambers

TABLE OF CONTENTS

TABLES OF AUTHORITIES

Cases   *Page no.*

Legislative materials

INTRODUCTION

THE PURPOSE OF THE BOOK

I.1   This book is intended to provide a guide for legal practitioners advising or assisting in bringing or defending "media law" civil claims arising out of online publication. It deals with the private law tort claims in which claimants seek to assert their article 8 rights to reputation or privacy in the Courts of England and Wales: in particular defamation, harassment, breach of confidence, misuse of private information and data protection. The book does not deal with criminal liability for online publications, contempt of court or intellectual property issues, each of which could be the subject of an entire book.

I.2   Our aim is to provide a "road map" for what is an expanding but, for many, unfamiliar area of litigation. This is not a "textbook" – we have not tried to be comprehensive in our coverage but rather to provide an outline of the relevant law and procedure. Practitioners and the Courts are engaged in a constant struggle to keep up with technological developments that have, in less than a generation, revolutionised the world of communication – destroying a number of long established players and creating new ones, including some of the largest corporations in the world. We hope that this book will assist practitioners in advising their clients on some of the issues at stake in relation to online publication claims.

I.3   The book is a collective effort by members of the Matrix Chambers Media and Information Law team. The members listed as authors have contributed Chapters or parts of Chapters. Those listed as contributing editors have provided substantial additional input. Dave King of Digitalis was the main author of Chapter 1. He has great technical knowledge and expertise in this area and we are very grateful for his contribution.

I.4   In this Introduction we will give a brief overview of some of the issues that confront practitioners in this area and outline the contents of the book.

THE INTERNET AND THE LAW

I.5   The internet needs no introduction; everyone reading this book will know what it is and most readers will make daily use of it. It has been defined as "a global computer network providing a variety of information and communication facilities, consisting of interconnected networks using standardised communication protocols". Commonly used resources include the World Wide Web, email, telephony and file sharing.

I.6   There are a range of estimates of the size of the internet. According to Internet Live Stats there are now about 1.2 billion websites. It has been suggested that there are about 60 trillion web pages of which about 30 billion are indexed and so accessible via a search engine. These are approximate figures and the reality is that the internet is so large and is growing at such a speed that it is impossible to be definitive about such matters.

I.7   The internet has brought about a global communications revolution. An individual who wishes to communicate with others no longer needs a printing press or a broadcasting operation. Instead information can be communicated worldwide with a few keystrokes. Words, sounds, pictures or videos can, potentially, be communicated to the nearly 48% of the world's population – 3.2 billion people – who are now estimated to use the internet (see ITU figures).

I.8   Internet Live Stats estimates that every second there are at least 7,000 Tweets sent, 1,140 Tumblr posts posted online, 733 photos posted on Instagram, 2207 Skype calls, 55,364 Google searches, 127,354 YouTube videos viewed, and over 2 million emails sent. Gary Hayes' *Social Media Counter* gives daily, weekly, monthly and annual figures – for example, it is suggested that there are over 190 billion Tweets a year.

I.9   Within the space of 20 years, the internet has transformed the way in which people work, socialise, shop, seek entertainment and share information and ideas. In the traditional vertical model of publishing, publishers such as media organisations created their own content and sold their products to the consuming public. In the world of the internet, everyone can be a publisher, setting up their own blogs, or discussion groups, or posting their comments, photographs or videos online. Media law is only beginning to explore these significant developments, which raise many novel issues.

I.10   The internet is the realm of free communication, permitting individuals to express their own thoughts and opinions and to publish facts that traditional publishers do not know about or do not want to publish. But with freedom comes the risk of abuse. The traditional media is heavily constrained in what it publishes by the civil law. Media corporations employ in-house lawyers and are held to account for what they publish, by regulators or in the Courts. In contrast, those who publish on blogs or social media may not be aware of legal constraints or, if they are, may choose to ignore them. In addition, the great internet corporations that have made billions from the internet are, understandably, fierce defenders of the speech rights of users.

I.11   There are two particular areas where the "new communication world" of the internet can seriously interfere with the legal rights of individuals or corporations.

I.12   First, there is the right to reputation. The law of defamation is a powerful incentive to newspapers and broadcasters to check their facts and proceed in accordance with what the European Court of Human Rights calls "the ethics of journalism": checking facts, obtaining comment from the subject of articles and so on. Media corporations know that if they break the law in this regard they are liable to legal action and may have to pay substantial damages and costs. Of course, the incentive does not always work but every professional journalist knows the risks of publishing false and defamatory allegations and the law is a powerful constraint on the irresponsible publication of falsehoods.

I.13   The position can be very different for the vast majority of internet users who are not professional or even amateur journalists and know little or nothing of the law. The overwhelming majority of internet publications are not by professional journalists and are not subject to any legal checks. This means that the internet is a powerful vehicle for defamatory expression.

I.14   In addition, the internet creates many opportunities for users to publish under the cloak of anonymity. Such anonymity permits users to give vent to allegations and opinions that would never be published by any traditional publisher. By publishing such material anonymously users make it much harder for the victims of such abuse to hold them to account.

I.15   Of course, many internet communications are made to very small numbers of readers and do not therefore have the impact on reputation of publications in a national newspaper or on a television broadcast. Nevertheless, the impact of internet publications should not be underestimated. As Lyrissa Barnett Lidsky has put it:

> "Although Internet communications may have the ephemeral qualities of gossip with regard to accuracy, they are communicated through a medium more pervasive than print, and for this reason they have tremendous power to harm reputation. Once a message enters cyberspace, millions of people worldwide can gain access to it. Even if the message is posted in a discussion forum frequented by only a handful of people, any one of them

can republish the message by printing it or, as is more likely, by forwarding it instantly to a different discussion forum. And if the message is sufficiently provocative, it may be republished again and again. The extraordinary capacity of the Internet to replicate almost endlessly any defamatory message lends credence to the notion that 'the truth rarely catches up with a lie'. The problem for libel law, then, is how to protect reputation without squelching the potential of the Internet as a medium of public discourse".[1]

I.16   The phenomenon of "fake news" shows how easy it is for false stories to spread across the internet. Such stories are not always defamatory and may be invented for political or financial reasons rather than to damage the reputations of others. Nevertheless, whether transmitted knowingly or inadvertently, false defamatory material can be disseminated widely online in a matter of minutes or hours and then be extremely difficult to correct or remove.

I.17   A second and perhaps even more concerning threat to legal rights resulting from online publication is to the privacy of individuals. The internet presents a considerable challenge to those who wish to prevent the publication of their private information by the media. As is illustrated by the high profile case of *PJS v News Group*[2] even if an individual receives advance notice of a threatened publication of private information and obtains an injunction, social media "leaks", or publication outside the jurisdiction can lead to its widespread dissemination.

I.18   The online circulation of "intimate photographs" or "sex tapes" – often called "revenge porn" – has given rise to considerable litigation and has attracted criminal legislation in this and many other jurisdictions. But this is only the tip of the privacy-invading iceberg.

I.19   A huge volume of private information is now published every day on social media, much of it by individuals who believe they are communicating to a small group of friends and associates whereas, in fact, they are making their information potentially available to the whole world. Participation in social media almost inevitably involves the disclosure of personal information. For example, an individual's Facebook pages will often contain numerous personal photographs that may be generally available. Even those who restrict access to their pages cannot control the use that their friends make

---

[1] *Silencing John Doe: Defamation & Discourse in Cyberspace* (2000), 49 Duke L.J. 855, at pp. 863–64:

[2] [2016] AC 1081.

of their private information. Social media sites can be "misused as a medium through which to threaten, abuse, harass, intimidate and defame".[3]

I.20   The internet brings another new and important feature to publication. Traditional media publication was ephemeral. In the well-known phrase, "today's news is tomorrow's fish and chip papers". Old newspapers were only available in difficult to access library archives, while old broadcasts were not accessible after they had been made. Everything has changed with the internet. Newspapers now have "online archives" – some going back many decades. Postings on websites or social media may continue to be available for many years. There are web resources that enable old internet pages to be consulted – for example the Wayback Machine archives more than 299 billion web pages.

I.21   Search engines mean that old posts or articles can be accessed many years after they were first published. A link that appears on the first page of a Google Search against a person's name is a constant point of reference for all those who meet or deal with that person. Those with unusual names are particularly adversely affected. This means that, in contrast to traditional media publications, it is not safe simply to ignore false or private material published online. It is likely to remain available for many years into the future.

INTERNET INTERMEDIARIES AND THE LAW

I.22   The other side of the risks faced by individuals or companies who are subject to damaging online publications are the risks faced by those who provide internet services as a result of the misuse of their services by those who post damaging material about others.

I.23   The traditional media exercises editorial control over its offline publications: a newspaper editor can decide whether to publish a "letter to the editor" but if she does, then the newspaper takes legal responsibility for its content. However, the internet allows publication without editorial control. Twitter does not monitor the content of the 500 million tweets posted every day.

I.24   The common law takes a very broad view of responsibility for publication. Anyone who causes, contributes to or participates in a publication is jointly and severally liable for the publication of its contents. This covers not just the author of the material, the editor of a publication, the "publisher" (in

---

[3] *AB v Facebook Ireland* [2013] NIQB 14 at [13].

the sense of the owner of the publication) but also printers, distributors and vendors.

1.25   Application of common law principles to online publication could, potentially, result in liability not just for authors and webmasters but also for intermediaries such as broadband providers who enable users to access the internet, the provider of the website, social media or blogging platform, the owner of the servers on which the material is stored or the operator of the search engines that enable individuals to obtain access to the material.

1.26   As the internet developed through the 1990s, the ISPs were concerned to ensure that they were not be exposed to unlimited liability in respect of the communications that they were facilitating. The 1996 Communications Decency Act (US) 47 USC §430 granted providers of an "interactive computer service" immunity from most forms of liability in tort and this immunity was interpreted broadly.

1.27   The position was somewhat different in England and Wales. There was little relevant legislation and little or no "online publication" litigation in the 1990s. However, in the 1999 case of *Godfrey v Demon Internet*[4] the judge held that a service provider who transmitted or facilitated the transmission to newsgroup subscribers of a posting received and stored by them via the internet was a publisher of that posting at common law.

1.28   This decision, opened up the possibility of unlimited civil liability for the new internet service companies. However, that liability was restricted in two ways.

1.29   First, there was European legislation. On 8 June 2000, Directive 2000/31/EC on certain legal aspects of information society services, in particular electronic commerce, in the Internal Market (the E-Commerce Directive) was adopted. This requires member states to take certain steps in order to ensure the free movement of information society services between member states. This Directive was implemented into UK law by the Electronic Commerce (EC Directive) Regulations 2002. This provided so-called "safe harbours": ISPs were protected against liability for content that had been authored by third parties, provided that they were prepared to cooperate when asked to remove or block access to identified illegal or infringing content. It has been suggested that "safe harbours" proved vital in facilitating the growth of the emerging ISP, e-commerce and user-

---

[4] [2001] QB 201.

generated content industries.[5] They are considered in detail in Chapter 7 of this book.

I.30 Secondly, by a series of judicial decisions the English "media law" judges took steps to limit the liability of online publishers. These decisions showed the flexibility of the common law and the willingness of judges to adapt it to meet "freedom of expression" concerns. In particular:

- In 2006, in *Al-Amoudi v Brisard*[6] it was held that there was no presumption that an article placed on an internet website open to general access will have been published to a substantial number of people within the jurisdiction.
- In the same year, in *Bunt v Tilley*[7] it was held that ISPs were not publishers at common law if their role in the dissemination of allegedly wrongful material is merely passive and instrumental, and is undertaken without knowledge of the relevant words.
- In 2009 in *Metropolitan International Schools v Designtechnica Corp*[8] the operator of a search engine was not the publisher, at common law, of the search results.

I.31 A number of "policy" justifications have been advanced for the partial immunity conferred on ISPs by the E-Commerce Directive and judicial decision. These justifications include the role of ISPs as neutral conduits of information, the burden and impracticality of ISPs monitoring content, the chilling effect on free expression of any such monitoring and the economic case for protecting innovative online services and industries.[9] These arguments have been called into question as technology develops and the nature of online publication changes. Critics have highlighted the risks posed by online criminal activity and the (complex) phenomenon of "fake news", leading to threats of statutory regulatory action. It appears however, that in relation to civil liability the balance struck by the E-Commerce Directive is a stable one and there is no appetite for new European legislation in this area. Despite Brexit it seems likely that the United Kingdom will continue apply the EU rules on liability.

---

[5] Lillian Edwards, "The Fall and Rise of Intermediary Liability Online", in Edwards and Waelde (ed.), *Law and the Internet*, 3rd edn, Hart Publishing, 2009, p 61.

[6] [2007] 1 WLR 113.

[7] [2007] 1 WLR 1243.

[8] [2011] 1 WLR 1743.

[9] See generally, Jaani Riordan, *The Liability of Internet Intermediaries,* OUP, 2016, paras 1.18 to 1.48.

PRIVACY AND FREEDOM OF EXPRESSION

I.32   At the centre of the legal issues that online publication gives rise to is the balancing of the competing rights to privacy (which includes the right to reputation) and freedom of expression. Whilst the common law always sought to strike such a balance – for example, by the complex rules of the tort of defamation – it did not, until very recently, do so in explicit terms. However, since the coming into force of the Human Rights Act 1998 on 1 October 2000, the question has been formulated expressly as a matter of balancing competing rights. In terms of the European Convention on Human Rights these are the rights under arts 8 and 10.

I.33   In the English case law, the best expression of the "balancing exercise" to be performed remains Lord Steyn's "four proposition" in the case of *Re S (a child)*:[10]

> "First, neither article has *as such* precedence over the other. Secondly, where the values under the two articles are in conflict, an intense focus on the comparative importance of the specific rights being claimed in the individual case is necessary. Thirdly, the justifications for interfering with or restricting each right must be taken into account. Finally, the proportionality test must be applied to each. For convenience I will call this the ultimate balancing test" [17].

I.34   The European Court of Human Rights came to the problem slightly later but developed a number of "criteria" as relevant for the exercise of balancing of art 8 and 10 rights:

(i)   Contribution to a debate of general interest.
(ii)   How well known is the person concerned and what is the subject of the report?
(iii) Prior conduct of the person concerned.
(iv)   Method of obtaining the information and its veracity.
(v)   Content, form and consequences of the publication.
(vi)   Severity of the sanction imposed.[11]

The first criterion is said to be of particular importance and, in English terms, roughly equates to the question as to whether there is a "public interest" in the publication (see para 5.47ff below).

---

[10] [2005] 1 AC 59.

[11] *Axel Springer AG v Germany* [2012] 55 EHRR 6 at [88]–[95].

I.35   When considering the balancing exercise it is important to look at the nature and quality of the privacy and expression rights involved.

I.36   In terms of privacy, it is often useful to look at matters on two "axes": distance from core personal matters and distance from the most private space. "Core" personal matters would include, for example, medical information and information about intimate family relationships or sexual activity. Such activity has the most protection when it takes place at home, behind closed doors and lesser protection when it takes place in semi-public or public places.

I.37   In terms of freedom of expression, the case law suggests a "hierarchy" of types of speech, beginning with the most valuable and going to the least valuable:

- Political speech concerning the conduct of politicians in public office, including statements made at elections.
- Other speech concerning matters of public interest, including the private conduct of politicians, the conduct of large corporations and other powerful bodies, statements concerning the activities of individuals who perform a public function and statements about people who play a prominent role in public life, such as in business, finance, the professions, sport, society or the arts ("public figures").
- Statements concerning the conduct of private individuals.
- Artistic speech, including writing of all forms, painting, film and video.
- Statements made for commercial purposes, including advertising and "entertainment journalism".
- Pornography and other expression that undermines the rights of others such as direct attacks on religious sensibilities.
- Speech that promotes or is intended to provoke violence or attacks on the democratic order.

I.38   The "highest" categories of speech receive the greatest legal protection as does private information close to the "core". The balance is most difficult to strike when the "expression interests" and the "privacy interests" are of roughly equal value: for example, speech about the private lives of politicians. The exercise is a "fact sensitive" one, requiring considering of each piece of information and the precise "public interests" in play. This is dealt with in slightly different ways in the torts of defamation, misuse of private information and harassment but in each case a "balancing exercise" is being carried out.

THE MEDIA, NGOS, "CITIZEN JOURNALISTS" AND BLOGGERS

I.39   One of the key questions to be addressed by media law as it evolves in the internet age is whether non-traditional publishers should get the same protection in terms of free speech as that accorded to the traditional media.

I.40   The case law of the European Court of Human Rights has consistently recognised the "essential function the press fulfils in a democratic society". The special role of the media in a democratic society has been emphasised in many cases, particularly in reporting "information and ideas on political issues and other matters of general interest".[12] The Court of Human Rights has repeatedly emphasised that it is incumbent on the press:

> "to impart information and ideas on matters of public interest. Not only does the press have the task of imparting such information and ideas: the public also has a right to receive them. Were it otherwise, the press would be unable to play its vital role of 'public watchdog'".[13]

I.41   It has, as a result, been made clear that 'the safeguards to be afforded to the press are of particular importance'. The Court has often recognised and emphasised the importance of an art 10 right to protection of journalists' sources[14], which is given statutory effect in the UK through the Contempt of Court Act 1981, s 10. In addition, there is a special regime for the police when it seeks to get access to "journalistic material" under the Police and Criminal Evidence Act 1984.

I.42   The world of online publications has however greatly broadened the range of organisations and individuals who contribute directly to public interest debates. Non-governmental organisations, for example, may produce reports that involve investigative journalism in all but name and that may be as hard-hitting and carefully researched as any serious investigative journalism. So-called "citizen journalists" have come to the fore online, publishing on a whole range of public interest debates but outside the constraints of the traditional media. Beyond these categories, almost

---

[12] For example, *De Haes and Gijsels v. Belgium* (1998) 25 EHRR 1 at [37].
[13] *Observer and Guardian v UK* (1992) 14 EHRR 153 at [59(b)].
[14] For example, *Sanoma Uitgevers BV v the Netherlands* (App No. 38224/03), 14 September 2010.

anyone can now set themselves up as a blogger and publish their views online to anyone who is interested in reading them.

I.43 In their different ways, these publishers on public interest debates are each capable of making important contributions to freedom of expression. One of the issues that the Courts have to grapple with in future is to what standards such publishers should be held and what significance or weight should be accorded to the particular role that they play in contributing to public interest debates. These issues will assume increasing importance as the traditional media becomes less dominant, making way for an increasingly diverse range of online publishers.

STRUCTURE OF THE BOOK

I.44 The book is structured as follows

Chapter 1: The internet, site owners and takedown procedures
Chapter 2: Right to be forgotten
Chapter 3: Identifying the defendant
Chapter 4: Jurisdiction and choice of law
Chapter 5: Liability for online publication: defamation, malicious falsehood and harassment
Chapter 6: Liability for online publication: breach of confidence, misuse of private information, data protection
Chapter 7: Defences specific to information society service providers
Chapter 8: Remedies
Chapter 9: Bringing a claim, practical issues
Chapter 10: Defending a claim, practical issues

I.45 Chapter 1 provides a general introduction to the internet and the World Wide Web and the way in which websites operate. There is guidance on how to identify website owners and users and how to assess the extent of online publication through web traffic and user data. This Chapter looks at the community standards for a range of key internet publishers and provides guidance on the procedures that can be used, short of legal action, to have offending material taken down by website operators. There is also a section dealing briefly with search engine optimisation.

I.46 Chapter 2 is concerned with the "right to be forgotten", established by the Court of Justice of the European Union in its May 2015 *Google Spain* judgment. Following an analysis of the judgment, the Chapter reviews the guidance on the practical implementation of the ruling provided by the Article 29 Working Party. This Chapter provides an overview of Google's procedures and policies for "right to be forgotten" removal requests, before addressing a range of topical issues concerning de-listing. This Chapter then explores in detail the new "right to erasure" under the General Data Protection Regulation, which will supersede the right to be forgotten from May 2018.

I.47   Chapter 3 addresses two important preliminary issues that may need to be addressed before any claim can be brought against an online publisher. The first is the practical question of how to identify an anonymous publisher, which may require a claimant to invoke the *Norwich Pharmacal* procedure, in relation to which detailed practical guidance is provided. The second is the question of who is responsible, as a matter of law, for the publication of online material. The second half of the Chapter addresses this issue in relation to defamation (which gives rise to particular issues of publication at common law and different defences available to secondary publishers), misuse of private information, harassment and breach of the Data Protection Act 1998.

I.48   Online publication claims frequently have an international element, as many of the world's largest online publishers or ISPs are based abroad. Chapter 4 addresses the complex issues of jurisdiction and choice of law that may arise in online publication claims brought in England and Wales but which have a foreign connection. The Chapter starts by looking at the basis for jurisdiction in domestic law, which is service of the claim form in this jurisdiction. The Chapter then considers service of the claim form out of the jurisdiction on foreign defendants under CPR PD 6B, examines the impact of the Defamation Act 2013, s 9 and provides a detailed treatment of the jurisdictional rules created by the Recast Brussels Regulation. The second half of the Chapter addresses the issue of choice of law, namely whether English law, or the law of another country, applies to the claim and examines the distinction between issues of substance, and of procedure, the latter being frequently governed by English law even if the substantive law applied is that of a foreign country.

I.49   Chapter 5 is the first of two Chapters considering the operation of the various "tort claims" that can be brought in relation to online publications. The elements of the relevant causes of action and the available defences are considered. Chapter 5 provides an overview of these issues for claims in defamation, malicious falsehood and harassment, while Chapter 6 examines breach of confidence, misuse of private information, and data protection claims.

I.50   Chapter 7 is concerned with the defences or "safe harbours" available to ISPs under the E-Commerce Directive, which protect them against legal liability in civil claims for damages. This Chapter explains the background to the E-Commerce Directive, looks at the definition of "information society services" and examines the Directive's scope. There is a detailed analysis of the three "safe harbours", namely "mere conduits", caching and hosting, followed by an analysis of how safe harbour protection may be lost as a result of notification. The Chapter then examines the prohibition on the imposition of ISPs of general monitoring obligations. Finally, the Chapter reviews the case law of the European Court of Human Rights on ISSP liability.

I.51   Chapter 8 is concerned with the remedies available to claimants, both at the interim stage, when a remedy is sought to prevent an unlawful act from taking place or continuing, and at the final stage, following a trial. There is a detailed examination of interim injunctions in the context of each of the main media law causes of action, while delivery up and preservation orders are also considered. Final remedies covered include damages awards, final injunctions and the specific remedies available in data protection and defamation claims.

I.52   Chapter 9 provide guidance for claimants on the practicalities of bringing claims and the main tactical issues that arise. This Chapter starts by addressing the question of whether to bring a claim at all, or whether to seek to resolve a claim informally. Once it is decided to bring a claim, guidance is provided on how to choose the best cause of action. Online publication claims will usually involve a range of potential defendants and guidance is given on choosing a defendant. The Chapter then provides guidance on the practical steps involved in bringing proceedings, including pre-action correspondence, applications for anonymity, issuing claims, choosing the court, issues concerning service, the practicalities of obtaining an interim injunction, the main procedural issues that arise between issuing a claim and trial and enforcing injunctions and orders after a trial.

I.53   Chapter 10 concerns the same practical issues as Chapter 9, but looked at from the perspective of defendants. This Chapter starts by looking at the initial questions a defendant should ask when first presented with a claim, either in pre-action correspondence or just after proceedings have been issued. There follows a detailed section on how to assess the merits of a claim in defamation, malicious falsehood, harassment, breach of confidence, misuse of private information and data protection, looking at both the elements of the claims and potential defences. There is a specific section on the practical issues that arise for ISPs. Other issues addressed in this Chapter include interim injunctions, the settlement of claims through "without prejudice" and Part 36 offers and the use of interim remedies like strike out and summary judgment to bring about early disposal of weak claims.

CHAPTER 1: THE INTERNET, SITE OWNERS AND TAKEDOWN PROCEDURES

CHAPTER SYNOPSIS

- Provides general information as to the way in which the internet operates, outlines the nature of publication on the internet, providing a full overview of types of internet publishers and publications – from websites, blogs and social media, to hosts, ISPs and search engines. Briefly summarises issues relating to Search Engine Optimisation.

- Looks at the identification of site owners and the assessment of the extent of publication, as well as the procedures to have offending material taken down by website operators, short of legal action.

- Details categories of material subject to Notice and Take Down procedures, and outlines the relevant procedures, including links to forms etc, for major website operators – such as Facebook, Twitter and Google.

INTRODUCTION

1.1 The purpose of this Chapter is to provide general guidance as to the way in which the internet operates, the identification of site owners, the assessment of the extent of publication of online material and the procedures that can be used, short of legal action, to have offending material taken down by website operators. We will also deal briefly with issues in relation to "search engine optimisation".

1.2 Notice and takedown should always be considered before threatening or commencing legal action. The Notice and Take Down systems provided by operators of websites can provide a quick and effective remedy. These systems can usually be used by someone who does not have technical expertise but, in some cases, it will be necessary for lawyers to bring in expert technical assistance.

THE INTERNET AND THE WORLD WIDE WEB

1.3 The roots of the internet date to the 1960s when the US federal government conceived of a network of interconnected computers to provide secure communications. This led to the conception of the World Wide Web ("the Web") by Tim Berners-Lee in 1989.

1.4   The web was designed as an information space where documents and other resources could be identified using uniform resource locators (URLs). A website is a collection of related web pages, typically identified with a common Domain Name, and published on at least one web server. A website is accessible via a unique URL that identifies the specific site.

1.5   When, in the 1990s, businesses started to use websites to reach customers, new service companies came into existence to provide two things commercially. First, access to the internet and second, the hosting of websites. In this book, references to Internet Service Providers (ISPs) refer to companies that provide internet access and email services ("mere conduits": see para 7.19ff). References to Information Society Service Providers ("ISSPs") refer to all entities providing "information society services" (see para 7.4ff), including ISPs, companies providing hosting services like Facebook, and companies engaged in caching, such as search engines.

1.6   In the 1990s the internet was used as a communications tool, primarily for businesses in their efforts to reach consumers. In the late 1990s the internet moved into a new phase, often called Web 2.0 – where newer websites facilitated and published User Generated Content ("UGC"), providing ease of use and interoperability. Web 2.0 websites may allow users to interact and collaborate with each other in a social media dialogue as creators of user-generated content in a virtual community, in contrast to the first generation of Web 1.0-era websites where people were limited to the passive viewing of content.

1.7   The late 1990s also saw the growing importance of search engines. These use spiders or robots automatically to trawl the internet in order to identify as much as possible of the information that is publicly available. The search engine compiles an index that includes the content of the website and the URL. Algorithms are used by the search engines to determine the ranking of pages in advance of and upon a search query being performed, the weighting given to the individual factors determines how high in the returned listings a URL might rank. This ranked content – known as the "search results" – is provided through a single web page to a user searching for information.

1.8   While control of a website vests in the site owner or administrator ("the webmaster"), certain sites allow interaction with their users who can produce UGC. Such UGC may be moderated by the site owner, controller or editor; or it may be unmoderated. Moderated content is submitted, usually automatically, to the site owner for approval before it is published for universal access to the web page in question. Unmoderated content is published immediately to the web page.

1.9   Many news sites and weblogs (Blogs) allow and even encourage such multi-user participation. In particular, so-called "social media websites" developed user participation into user interaction. They usually allow the creation and sharing of content within a community or virtual network of users. These sites are diverse in their market, form and function and thus difficult to define comprehensively. A single social media site may boast many user accounts and pages, most of which are controlled by the users themselves. Pages on these sites may be accessible to everyone or restricted to certain users, often those users connected (virtually) to the individual publishing the information in question.

SEARCH ENGINE OPTIMISATION

1.10   The phenomena of social media and the digitisation and online publication of public records means an increasing amount of information about private individuals and organisations is available online. This means that the Web has become the default source of cursory research on or indeed due diligence into an individual or an organisation.

1.11   As a result of the dominance of search engines in directing traffic online, a number of new techniques have been developed to influence the ranking of particular websites in search results. The most important of these is search engine optimisation ("SEO"). This is the technique of optimising a website in order that it ranks more prominently for searches made on target phrases in key search engines in key territories. SEO targets the organic, or free listings, in search engines.

1.12   The early search engine spiders and algorithms were relatively unsophisticated and SEO practitioners devised ways to fool their systems. Although far from limited to a single sector, their activity within the adult entertainment and gaming sectors was significant. Underhand techniques were used to attempt to achieve ranking in search engines for phrases that were not relevant to their site content but which were well-searched online. One such technique, long since addressed by the search engines, was to use key words (for example "Disney" or "British Airways") in text on the target web page, which text was the same colour as the page itself. In this way, text was invisible to a human user, so not detracting from the experience of the page, but visible and read by the search engine spiders, which would consider the page to be of relevance to the phrase in question.

1.13   Search engine operators refer to such techniques as Spam[1]. They go to great lengths to combat spam and are open about the SEO techniques that they consider constitute spam (that the industry refers to as "Black Hat" techniques) and about those that they consider to be legitimate for the purposes of SEO ("White Hat" techniques).

1.14   Spam and Black Hat SEO contravene the terms of usage and promotional policies of most search engines and they tend to impose penalties on site owners found to be deploying such techniques. These penalties can include the temporary or permanent removal of a site from its search listings.

1.15   Search engine algorithms take into account many different factors in determining the relevance of one site relative to another for a specific search phrase. In recent years, the volume (and relative quality) of other sites that link into the site in question has been of increasing relevance. Essentially, the premise on which the algorithms are based is that if many people are linking to or referencing a particular article then it must be of more interest (and relevance) than an article that nobody mentions. Most recently, consideration of these "inbound links" – their quantity and quality – has been broadened to incorporate "social signals" such as likes, shares, votes or views, and the like.

1.16   As a result, link building has become a key pillar of SEO: the more links (natural or otherwise) into a specific site, the higher it might rank on search engine results pages for its target keywords. Creating the appearance of grassroots support for a news article or website can thus artificially enhance its ranking in search engines.

1.17   As the first page of search engine listings has become more important to the reputation of individuals and of businesses, many have turned to SEO and other techniques (including the building of links into desirable content), in order to promote positive content about them, to mitigate the risk of attack or to displace specific, negative content.

1.18   Such techniques are of some value in dealing with unlawful online content that is difficult to remove by using "takedown" processes (because, for example, the author constantly posts new material or slightly changes the URL). However, sophisticated abusers will use their own SEO techniques to promote their abusive posts up the rankings. They may also use content

---

[1] This word also applies to false or misleading content elsewhere on the internet, including in emails, and to other underhand techniques online.

spinning[2] and syndication[3] – techniques to proliferate their content. In such cases it is likely to be much more effective to use the "takedown" route or, if necessary, commence legal proceedings. The assistance of technology providers can help to ascertain the full extent of an attack and to pinpoint rapidly each new iteration.

IDENTIFYING SITE OWNERS

Domain Names

1.19   The Domain Name System (DNS) allowed the creation of memorable, text-based web addresses (that is Uniform Resource Locators, or URLs) that effectively direct visitors (collectively Traffic) to the information published at a particular IP address.

1.20   URLs are expressed in the format http://www.[DN].[TLD] where DN is the Domain Name and TLD is the Top Level Domain ("TLD"), for example, www.ft.com where "ft" is the DN and "com" is the TLD. The section preceding "www" is the Protocol (in this case and in all cases of a website Hypertext Transfer Protocol) and "www" might be replaced in a URL with an alternate subdomain of the primary named domain (such as news.[DN.TLD] or blog.[DN.TLD]). The URL structure as presented above may include a query string (such as /search?q=news) often containing a question mark that calls specific page content from a database or File Path (such as /materials/specificmaterial.html) that points to a particular page or file.

1.21   The Domain Name component of a URL can essentially take any form of letters and numbers that is unique to the particular TLD. Policies governing trademark and other IP infringement are overseen by ICANN, the International Corporation for Assigned Names and Numbers. This is a not-for-profit public-benefit corporation dedicated to keeping the internet secure, stable and interoperable.

1.22   ICANN coordinates all addresses within the DNS TLDs. ICANN assigns address blocks to Regional Internet Registries, each of whom maintain a WHOIS database (see para 1.30) that at the very least identifies the ISSP responsible for a particular website. ICANN has claims, complaints and dispute resolutions functions that may be considered alongside any relevant

---

[2] Rewriting existing articles, or parts of articles, and replacing specific words, phrases, sentences, or even entire paragraphs with any number of alternate versions to provide a slightly different variation with each spin.

[3] That is, republishing content on other sites.

legal remedy for infringement. Similar policies exist for dealing with cybersquatting (the registration of Domain Names including well-known names – especially of brands – with the intention of selling them at a profit).

1.23   There are currently more than 1,200 TLDs, falling into several types: Infrastructure TLDs that are essentially administrative; Generic TLDs (such as .com, .info, .net, and .org); "Sponsored" TLDs (such as .edu, .gov, .mil) and country specific TLDs (or ccTLDs) such as .uk or .fr. There is no TLD for the United States although, to all intents and purposes, .com performs that function.

1.24   The TLD .uk is the ccTLD for the UK, which is managed by Nominet UK, a not-for-profit entity that operates the UK Network Information Centre, with responsibility for the country's regional address block.

1.25   Although it is often assumed given its prominence that .co.uk is the ccTLD for the UK, in fact .co.uk (along with ac.uk, gov.uk and me.uk), is a Second Level Domain (SLD).

1.26   There are restrictions applied by ICANN, by regional internet registries and by governments to the registration of domains under specific TLD or SLDs. In the UK, ac.uk and gov.uk are controlled by government agencies with higher restrictions on their usage, whereas those typically registered by corporate vehicles or natural persons are subject to the following restrictions applied by Nominet:

- .ltd.uk: restricted to use by a corporate vehicle, registered with Companies House at the point of registry and maintaining such registration thereafter
- .co.uk: while designed for corporate use, in practice this SLD can be used by anyone, inside or outside of the UK
- .me.uk: restricted to natural persons and not permitted for use by a corporate entity.

Domain registration

1.27   Most registrations of Domain Names occur through an accredited domain registrar that often acts additionally as the ISSP. In registering a domain with a registrar, one must identify the registrant's name, postal address, telephone and email contact information.

1.28   The central registry (ICANN) and localised, region-specific registries (in the UK, Nominet UK) maintain a public log of Domain Names registered and the registrants thereof. In certain jurisdictions, evidence of legal residence and or a locally registered corporate entity is required in order to register a Domain

Name and details of the legally resident person will be recorded on the public register. No such requirement exists in respect of the TLDs .co.uk (in the UK) or .com.

1.29   Nominet UK allows the registrar (ISSP) to publish that information, or their own information, to their database. As a result, most registrars provide a privacy service whereby the information published to the database is that of the registrar rather than information that would identify their client (the ultimate registrant). As such, the details available publicly often only identify the registrar and further information concerning the identity of the registrant will require a *Norwich Pharmacal* order (see para 3.7ff).

WHOIS Look Up

1.30   All Domain Name data is held in a database system known as WHOIS. The Searchable WHOIS is the subset of the overall database that is available for public interrogation via a WHOIS query (being a database lookup on the WHOIS system). When looking to identify the owner of a Domain Name the logical starting point is to perform a WHOIS look up enquiry.

1.31   There are many Domain Name registrars, each of whom hold WHOIS data, so a WHOIS query, in order to be effective, must search the appropriate database. As a result, WHOIS proxy search providers are commonplace and a search online of "WHOIS query" will identify multiple providers, on whose website a WHOIS search can be actioned. ICANN, Nominet and many ISSPs also provide WHOIS lookup functions on their websites.

1.32   A WHOIS search does not provide historic data although there are providers who cache and provide historic information in relation to previous registrants. The data included in a WHOIS search result includes details provided (either by the registrant or by the ISSP on behalf of the registrant) of contact details of each of: the registrant, an administrative and a technical contact. In practice, these will often be the contact details of a single individual but this information is the typical starting point in identifying the owner of a Domain Name.

1.33   Most commercial sites will have contact sections that will provide identifying information in relation to the site owner or controller. Where this information is not available on the website a WHOIS query is the starting point for identification of the registrant.

1.34   In the case of blogs, while there may be multiple authors, the site itself will be controlled by a single owner. Where the blog does not publish details of its owner and where it has a URL that is not a Subdomain of a third party domain (such as those permitted by major blogging platforms, decribed in the next paragraph), a WHOIS query is the best starting point in attempting to ascertain the identity of the owner of the site.

1.35   Many blogs are published on blogging platforms, the most significant and best-known being WordPress and the Google-owned Blogger (hosted at .blogspot.com). While the software of these organisations can be used simply to administer a blog, which is then published at a discrete URL, many blog creators choose the easier and cheaper route of hosting their blog on a subdomain of the core WordPress or Blogger platform. Such blogs are findable via the URL [unique blog name].wordpress.com or [unique blog name].blogspot.com. As such, there is no record on the WHOIS database of the operator of the blog in question; meaning the only entity with identifying contact information will be the ultimate host (WordPress.com or BlogSpot.com).

Identifying a user and IP addresses

1.36   Any web-connected device is allocated an IP address, and those devices that are used to host information on the internet will maintain an allocated IP address indefinitely. In certain circumstances, an IP address can be used to acquire identifying information about a publisher to or user of the internet.

1.37   An IP address can be used to identify the network from which access was gained and/or the ISSP who provided an individual user's access. While this in and of itself does not identify an individual and their specific whereabouts it can identify the organisation who may be the subject of a request or application for further details on the individual in question (see para 3.7ff).

1.38   Some users seek to protect their anonymity by masking their IP address, which can be achieved with varying levels of technical sophistication. Virtual Private Network (VPN) or proxy providers sell solutions that enable the routing of web traffic through one or a number of servers in order to mask a user's own IP address. Where this includes servers in foreign jurisdictions it can make further data access difficult or impossible.

1.39   There are many reasons a user might use such services including maintaining privacy; avoiding being tracked by automated advertising servers; appearing to reside in a foreign jurisdiction in order to access content that is the subject of location restrictions (in China to access Google; in the UK to access American television subscriptions for example) and various other legitimate, nefarious or illegal activities.

1.40   At the more sophisticated end of the scale, users will operate via a proxy provider whose business and servers are in a foreign jurisdiction and who are likely to be unresponsive to English court orders.

AVAILABILITY, SOURCES OF TRAFFIC AND KEY ACCESS GATEWAYS

Introduction

1.41   While most information published to the internet is available to any connected user, access to some information is restricted through various mechanisms and for a variety of reasons. Some information can be difficult to find. As a result, most internet traffic is directed by search engines and a small number of other gateway sites.

1.42   In some cases traffic to a website will be the result of a user typing the URL or IP address of a web page directly into a browser. However, the large majority of traffic will be the result of a user clicking on some form of hyperlink. These will be found in sources including but not limited to: other web pages (either internally linking to a page on the same website or externally linking to a page on a different website); emails and other electronic messages. The most commonly used external links feature in the listings on search engines and within the content created on social media sites (where they may be referred to generically as social signals, or in relation to specific platforms, "Likes").

Search engines

1.43   Search engines are used by most users of the internet to find information and there are now over 6.5 billion searches per day on search engines. Major search engines at the time of writing include Google, founded in 1998, Baidu (founded 2000 and the dominant operator in China) and Yandex (founded 1997 and the dominant operator in Russia).

1.44   Google is the market leader globally, though statistics for its dominance vary between circa 77%[4] and circa 92%[5] of the overall search engine market. The consensus is that Google's share of searches performed on mobile devices is perhaps as high as 95%.[6] In the UK, market share is of the order of 89% of all search and potentially as much as 98% of mobile search. In the UK

---

[4] See https://www.netmarketshare.com/.

[5] See https://statcounter.com/.

[6] Ibid.

Microsoft's Bing and Yahoo! make up the majority of the remainder of the market.

1.45   While there are some differences in the modus operandi of the major search engines, there are many similarities and the discussion in this Chapter of their mechanics of operation applies to all current major operators.

1.46   The results presented by search engines for most search queries fall into two categories: sponsored listings (which are paid for, typically by the owner of the site referenced in the relevant listing) and organic listings, being a list of those web pages considered to be most relevant to the search query in descending order of relevance as determined automatically by the algorithms of the relevant search engine.

1.47   As to sponsored listings, their content and destination web pages are determined by the individual paying advertiser (but subject to the terms and conditions of the search engine). Where such paid content gives rise to legal issues then it is sensible to notify the search engine to the extent that it is in contravention of the search engine's terms of usage.

1.48   Organic listings in search engines typically comprise:

- A highlighted headline, its content derived automatically from the destination page in question and usually matching the title of that destination page;
- The full URL of the destination page and
- A snippet of information, copied from the destination page, again derived automatically from the page in question but cached (stored in memory for rapid recall from the search engine's own data storage without the need to revisit the page in question) and represented by the Search Engine.

Restricted access: walled gardens, closed networks, paywalls and the Dark Web

1.49   Early attempts by ISSPs to limit user access only to a "walled garden" of sometimes curated, endorsed or sponsored content have largely been confined to history. Most internet content is now either available globally or restricted to a specific subset of users, being either those who:

- Pay a subscription to access the site or area of a site in question or
- Are connected within some virtual, closed network to the author or creator of the content or page in question.

1.50   The term "closed network" is widely used but often misleading in the sense that on social media sites different sets of information will often be restricted in terms of its access to one of many different subsets of users rather than to the network as a whole.

1.51   Access to such content is usually controlled by user accounts. Accounts held by users with the requisite permissions (typically as a result of paying a subscription, being registered within a specific group or linked within the relevant network to a specific user) will enable access to the content in question, meaning a user must be logged into his or her account to access the information.

1.52   Information posted on closed or private networks, which cannot be accessed by non-members or non-subscribers, will not be identified by search engine spiders and thus will not feature in listings on search engines. There are exceptions to this rule, mostly within the area of subscription media as opposed to social media. Professional publishers whose sites require subscription and whose content is protected by access controls – commonly known as a paywall – will often take steps to ensure that search engine spiders can access and list a small section of their content only. This is so that they are not omitted entirely from search engines, which can otherwise be a valuable source of traffic.

1.53   Facebook (founded 2004, and now with over 2 billion monthly active users globally and 37 million active users in the UK), Instagram (founded 2010, now with 700 million active monthly users globally and 17 million active UK users), Twitter (founded 2006, now with 328 million monthly active users globally and 15 million users in the UK) and Weibo (launched 2009 in China, the dominant platform there and with a growing international user base) are examples of social media platforms with user access controls as described above.

1.54   Some social media platforms use the same communications network (the internet) as the World Wide Web but are essentially entirely closed networks, the entirety of their content residing elsewhere than on the public web. Examples include WhatsApp and WeChat and their function and content is outside the scope of this book.

The Dark Web

1.55   Unlike the so-called "deep web" – which comprises information on the internet that is unindexed by search engines and thus difficult to find – the "Dark Web" consists of servers, sites and information that are protected from public access, usually by way of encryption.

1.56   The size of the Dark Web is impossible to ascertain but it includes a number of individual, and in many cases significant, networks of sites such as those accessed through purpose-built browsers (such as Tor), peer-to-peer (P2P) networks and single sites with specific encryption. For the most part, networks in the Dark Web are designed to allow either anonymous posting of, or anonymous access to, specific information. As such it is the natural home of criminal activity on the internet but its use is not limited to this.

Web traffic and user data

1.57   In aggregate, the visitors to a website are described as its traffic. Most web servers maintain log files of information gleaned in relation to its traffic, which information will typically include IP addresses and data on each individual interaction made with the server (such as every image on a page that was downloaded, not only the page visited). Log files are controlled by a website owner or administrator and their data is typically visible only to those individuals with administrative access to the web server in question.

1.58   As a result of the volume of data that might be accrued by a log file, most servers are set routinely to purge data; often monthly but sometimes much more frequently. As such, in the event that the relevant data might be valuable to a claim, time can be of the essence in securing access, whether directly or by way of an order for disclosure.

1.59   A claimant who identifies content that might be the subject of a civil claim will wish to assess the extent to which it has been published both in the jurisdiction and around the world.

1.60   It is sensible to identify all publicly published iterations of the content in question. Search engines can be used to quantify with a high degree of accuracy the extent of republication and to identify the original source of the offending content.

1.61   Taking key, short, exact phrases from the offending content and searching on a search engine with the use of inverted commas to encapsulate the phrase will return only exact matches of pages that contain the phrase in question. As such, exact replicas can be identified individually and quantified in aggregate. Using multiple phrases or groups of words together as a search string, each encapsulated by inverted commas, enhances the likelihood of identifying edited versions of the content and mitigates the margin of error.

1.62   Search engines record the time each page was identified by their spider and while this will not be identical to the time of publication, in most cases the time lapse between publication and discovery by a search engine is minimal.

1.63   It should, however, be noted that this approach will not identify iterations or republications that are published on closed networks, except to the extent those iterations are themselves available for viewing beyond a restricted group.

1.64   There are, in addition, commercial sites that analyse website traffic. For the most part, such services acquire and aggregate the data of ISSPs, typically in order to determine market trends, key traffic sources and the overall traffic of specific major websites. Their data is extrapolated to take account of those ISSPs from whom they do not acquire data in order to give an estimate of the overall position. In particular:

- Alexa.com[7] – which provides "traffic ranking" information, and
- SimilarWeb[8] – which also provides traffic analysis, but with a lot more detail.

1.65   These services can be a good guide as to the likely audience of a specific website although the smaller the website the less reliable their statistics tend to be. It should also be noted that statistics acquired in this way will often give a good estimate of overall site traffic but not site traffic at a specific page level. That data will be accessible by the webmaster of the target site within the log file.

INTERNET PUBLISHERS AND PUBLICATIONS

Introduction

1.66   There are a great many types of website and various categories overlap as a result of differing aggregation of functionality and use. We will give a brief overview of different types of sites that are likely to give rise to civil claims. It is important to understand the categories do not have rigid boundaries and overlap. For example, Twitter is both a "micro blog" and a "social media site".

Blog

1.67   A blog is typically a diary-like monologue or dialogue, often on a specific subject. The individual posts on a blog appear in reverse chronological order (the most recent post first). Early blogs were typically created by single authors, but there now exist many multi-author, multi-subject blogs, which in many cases are professional businesses (such as the Huffington Post).

---

[7] www.alexa.com.

[8] www.similarweb.com.

1.68 Twitter is a microblogging site with a limit to 140 characters for each post (on Twitter referred to as a Tweet). This limit does not now include photographs, videos or polls and a large percentage of Tweets now contain such material.

Forum

1.69 Discussion forums and message boards (collectively forums) provide the opportunity for multiple users to engage in discussion around a specific subject. Some forums are moderated, meaning a site administrator must approve a comment before its publication. Others are unmoderated so users can comment freely as they wish.

1.70 In some cases users must log in to post a comment to a specific discussion ("a Thread") – in which case the Forum moderator or owner will hold data relating to their access and potentially their identity. In other cases users can post freely without holding a user account, thus achieving a greater degree of anonymity.

News site

1.71 A site that hosts news and is owned and operated by a company whose business is to provide news is referred to as a news site. A news site will typically be transparent about its ownership and the identity of its (often employed) contributors.

1.72 In recent times, "fake news sites" have appeared. These typically exist to generate revenue (normally from advertising or from selling outbound traffic to a commercial site) as a result of the volume of traffic, which can be created by sensationalist stories that are entirely fabricated or grossly exaggerated.

Review site

1.73 This term refers to sites that exist for the purpose of collating and publishing third party (typically consumer) reviews of products, services and brands, review sites allow moderated or unmoderated submissions by either anonymous users or registered users. Perhaps the best known example of such a site is TripAdvisor.

Social media site

1.74 The terms "social media" and "social networking" cover a wide range of different types of site and no comprehensive definition is possible. In general terms, social media sites are those that enable users to create and share content or participate in social networking. Such sites usually allow users to establish connections with each other and to see the connections of those they connect with.

Wiki site

1.75   A Wiki site allows content to be generated on a particular subject or subjects by the collaborative additions and editions made by a community of users. They differ most notably from blogs and forums in that there is no single owner or controller on a Wiki page or site. Like blogs and forums, some Wiki sites will require active user accounts whereas some do not. The most notable Wiki site is Wikipedia, the online encyclopaedia, the content of which is created by its users.

Attack site

1.76   An attack site, also known as a flame site, is a single site established for the purposes of publishing disparaging content about a person or organisation. These sites may be small scale and target an individual but there are many notable examples of successful attacks by groups of consumers on single corporate entities using attack sites. www.IhateRyanAir.com and www.dellhell.com attracted significant attention at the time of their publication and use. So successful was www.dellhell.com in attacking the brand that the comments, content and links it received from disgruntled consumers were sufficient to propel it to significant prominence in search engines for a search for the brand Dell. An attack site may additionally be a blog, forum or fake news site dependent on its form of operation. These sites will typically be established in an anonymous fashion, which can see differing levels of sophistication.

CATEGORIES SUBJECT TO REMOVAL

Introduction

1.77   There is much debate globally around the responsibilities of and capabilities of the major technology firms in relation to managing the content that is made available publicly via their respective websites. Regional legislation, localised pressure from individual regimes and media opinion mean the status quo is nuanced by territory. Except where explicitly stated otherwise, the focus of this section is on the UK position.

1.78   Typically content that might form the subject of removal will be illegal, inappropriate, offensive, or a matter of IP infringement or privacy. This book focuses only on those categories of content (excluding copyright and other IP claims) that might give rise to a civil claim, including those for defamation, privacy, data protection, harassment and theft or misuse of confidential information. This section therefore omits any detailed consideration of other types of content for which hosts might provide systematic removal processes and/or forms for submission and review.

1.79   This section focuses on the relevant categories of content that are included in those stated by the operators of some of the main technology platform websites as being the potential subject of a valid removal request.

Google

1.80   Google Search provides forms to apply for the removal of what it describes as being personal information including credit card, bank account numbers, images of signatures, nude images shared without consent and confidential information such as medical records.

1.81   The search engine also provides for notice and takedown of content falling within the scope of the *Google Spain* judgment (see para 2.3ff).

Facebook

1.82   Facebook has a "Community Standards" page that provides forms for Notice requiring removal of:

- Direct threats;
- Bullying and harassment;
- Attacks on public figures;
- Nudity;
- Hate speech i.e. racism, homophobia, anti-religious, anti-disability.

1.83   In cases of "direct threats", Facebook states that it will remove credible threats of physical harm to individuals as well as specific threats of theft, vandalism or other financial harm. Facebook explains that it may consider factors such as a person's physical location or public visibility in determining whether a threat is credible.

1.84   In cases of "bullying and harassment" Facebook states it will remove content that appears to purposefully target private individuals with the intention of degrading or shaming them; content that it explains may include:

- Pages that identify and shame private individuals;
- Images altered to degrade private individuals;
- Photos or videos of physical bullying posted to shame the victim;

- Sharing personal information to blackmail or harass people; and
- Repeatedly targeting other people with unwanted friend requests or messages.

1.85   There is no express reference in Facebook's "Community Standards" to defamatory posts.

Twitter

1.86   Twitter provides forms for Notice requiring removal of:

- **Violent threats (direct or indirect).**
- **Harassment**: in the form of targeted abuse or harassment of others. The factors considered include:
  o whether a primary purpose of the reported account is to harass or send abusive messages to others;
  o whether the reported behaviour is one-sided or includes threats;
  o whether the reported account is inciting others to harass another account; and
  o whether the reported account is sending harassing messages to an account from multiple accounts.
- **Private information:** the publication without consent of other people's private and confidential information, such as credit card numbers, street address, or Social Security/National Identity numbers or intimate photos or videos that were taken or distributed without the subject's consent.
- **Impersonation:** the impersonation of others through the Twitter service in a manner that is intended to or does mislead, confuse, or deceive others.

YouTube

1.87   YouTube provides a page for reporting[9]:

- Abuse/harassment;
- Privacy (if a featured individual is uniquely identifiable by image, voice, full name, National Insurance number, bank account number or contact information (e.g. home address, email address));
- Defamation.

---

[9] https://www.youtube.com/reportabuse.

Instagram

1.88 Instagram provides forms for Notice requiring removal of

- Harassment or bullying;
- Nudity or pornography;

Wikipedia

1.89 While any user can edit, add or amend content on Wikipedia, the site has strict guidelines in terms of what content is appropriate and its editors will often reject changes that fall outside its guidelines. In relation to the categories of content discussed in this book, its guidelines provide for the removal (by a user) of:

- Unsourced information;
- Inaccurate information;
- Inappropriate content for Wikipedia (the guidelines including specifically content that is attacking in its nature).

NOTICE AND TAKE DOWN PROCEDURES

Introduction

1.90 Notice and Take Down is a process where a person makes an application or demand for the removal from a website or sites of specific content alleged to be illegal and the resultant removal by the recipient of the Notice of the content specified there.

1.91 Notice and Take Down usually applies to content that might be actionable by the applicant as a result of libel, privacy, harassment or other such claims. For the most part their systemisation by operators aims to mitigate liability in line with the provisions of either the US Digital Millennium Copyright Act 1998 or the E-Commerce Directive[10]. Both instruments provide for limits to liability subject to the expeditious removal of (or removal of the source of access to) content following proper notification of alleged illegality (see para 7.42ff).

1.92 US legislation in this context is more prescriptive – and thus clearer in its implications – than its European counterpart. Art 14 of the E-Commerce Directive absolves online hosts of liability for "illegal activity or information" carried out on its sites where the host has no "actual knowledge" of the

---

[10] Directive 2000/31/EC of 8 June 2000 on certain legal aspects of information society services, in particular electronic commerce, in the Internal Market (E-Commerce Directive).

activity or information and subject to the host acting expeditiously following Notice to remove the information (where it is hosted by the host) or to restrict access to the information (where the host provides access to the information). The Directive does not specify but certainly envisages the creation of processes and systems to provide for notice and takedown.

1.93   As a result, most major operators now provide online forms to facilitate the submission of a Notice. Search engines and social media platforms may also have forms to assist in notification of other types of content that may contravene their own terms of usage and/or be illegal. These include but are not limited to child sexual exploitation, nudity, sexually suggestive content, hate speech, self-harm, violence, spam and fake news, all of which fall outside the scope of this book except insofar as they may trigger civil claims for libel, privacy, harassment, or data protection.

1.94   This section focuses on the Notice and Take Down provisions that apply to major search engines and social media operators in relation to unlawful content. The "right to be forgotten" is dealt with in Chapter 2. We will focus on the applicable partly-automated procedures that have been created by the most prominent operators and on the practical and technical implications of an application.

1.95   Each of the major technology platforms listed below provides a list of the types of content that it will consider removing subject to receipt of a Notice in its specified form via its website. Some such notices are rejected and there are complex situations that will fall outside of the respective specified lists but it is often expedient in the first instance, to the extent that content falls within one of the categories listed by a platform, to issue a Notice in the format specified by the operator.

Google search

1.96   Google has a webpage for those who are seeking to remove content from any of its services under applicable laws. It provides a short video[11] explaining the process. If the content that is the target of takedown exists on the websites of different Google products, a separate application is required for each product. In this section we consider only Google Search. As already indicated, applications under the "right to be forgotten" procedure are considered in the next Chapter.

---

[11] https://support.google.com/legal/answer/3110420.

1.97   A report can be made in relation to Google search covering a number of other areas including:

- For removal of personal information, such as a bank account number, an image of a handwritten signature, or a nude or sexually explicit image or video by completing the "Remove information from Google"[12] form. Google explains that it evaluates requests for the removal of Personal Information on the following basis:

    "To decide if a piece of personal information creates significant risks of identity theft, financial fraud, or other specific harms, we as:

    - Is it a government-issued identification number?

    - Is it confidential, or is it publicly available information?

    - Can it be used for common financial transactions?

    - Can it be used to obtain more information about an individual that would result in financial harm or identity theft?

    - Is it a personally identifiable nude or sexually explicit photo or video shared without consent?"

- For the removal of defamatory content (reached via the "I would like to remove my personal information from Google's search results" or "I have a legal issue that is not mentioned above" options). It is necessary to complete the form entitled "Report other legal removal issue"[13].

1.98   An application can be made by the individual whose privacy is infringed or by an agent on their behalf but in either case a copy passport or similar government-issued form of identification must be submitted with the application. It is advisable to obscure all information other than the information required to confirm the applicant's identity. Photographs can be obscured except in applications to remove pages including photographs of the applicant.

1.99   The Notice requires completion of two key sections: Reason for Removal and a list of URLs.

---

[12] https://support.google.com/websearch/troubleshooter/3111061#ts=2889054.

[13] https://support.google.com/legal/contact/lr_legalother?product=websearch&uraw=.

- Under Reason for Removal, the Notice must explain (1) how the page relates to the subject of the request and (2) why the content in question is unlawful, inaccurate or outdated.
- The list of offending URLs must be in the correct and full form.

1.100   In order for a Take Down Notice to have maximum impact, it is important to consider the territories where the offending results may appear (note that the results by territory are different and an application for removal in one territory will not see the results removed in another) and the search phrases for which they appear (note that an application to remove results for a search of "John Smith" will not remove the results returned for a search for "John and Jane Smith").

1.101   Google and other search engines provide through their paid advertising platforms data on how many searches are performed monthly in a given jurisdiction for a specific word or phrase. It can thus be prudent to seek this data through a technology provider in order to inform the target name variations and/or territories where damage may be caused.

1.102   It should be noted that the results for most phrases on Google and other search engines will be materially different territory-by-territory, even where a common language is shared, and it is not possible without the use of proxies to evaluate the results in a foreign territory from a domestic computer.

1.103   Except in situations where successful Take Down Notices relate to Google services other than the Google search engine, takedown by Google results in the relevant listings no longer featuring in the results for searches on the Google search engine for (a) the complained of phrases when entered in their exact form as the search phrase and that (b) originate in an EU territory that was the subject of the Notice. Users of the Google search engine performing searches either outside the EU or outside of the territories specified in the Notice may still see the results complained of. The the content complained of will of course remain on the site that was linked to by Google. In practice this means consideration (concurrently) of a direct application to or action against the publisher of the offending content may also be prudent.

Yahoo!

1.104   Yahoo! provides a form for Notice and Take Down[14]. The information required and process for submission is very similar to that requested by Google (above).

---

[14] A shortened version of the link is goo.gl/8Y4yM9.

Bing

1.105   There is a form for Notice and Take Down[15] on Bing. The process is largely similar to that of Google (above) but its form provides additionally for:

- Explanation where the name for which the content complained of may rank does not match the legal name of the complainant (for example where a maiden name is used) and
- Questions related to the complainant and any public role they may undertake.

Instagram

1.106   The categories of content listed by Instagram that involve the types of content that might give rise to civil claims are:

- Hacked accounts;
- Impersonation accounts;
- Hate accounts (an account established with the intent of bullying or harassing another);
- Exposed private information; and
- Abuse.

1.107   Notice can be submitted via the forms provided[16] and requires:

- A contact email address;
- A link to (URL) and description of the offending content; and
- The country from which the complaint is being made.

Twitter

1.108   The categories of content listed by Twitter that involve the types of content that might give rise to civil claims are:

- Impersonation;
- Privacy infringement; and
- Abusive behaviour and violent threats.
- There is a "How to Report Violations"[17] page.

---

[15] https://www.microsoft.com/en-gb/concern.

[16] https://help.instagram.com/372161259539444.

[17] https://support.twitter.com/articles/15789#report-from-tweet.

1.109   Reports on "exposed private information"[18], "abusive or harassing behaviour"[19] require notification of

- The offending username;
- URL of the offending Tweet;
- Contact email address.

YouTube

1.110   YouTube is a Google service that provides two relevant web-based forms for an application to remove content:

- The "YouTube Flagging Process", which is designed to provide notification of content which is illegal or offensive (or which otherwise contravenes the company's own user guidelines) which is available via the menu options provided on any of its pages and which requires logging into a user account; and
- The "Privacy Complaint Process" being its Notice and Takedown function for privacy violations[20].

1.111   As to the YouTube Flagging Process" the categories of content for which YouTube provides forms for applications for removal, the following are relevant to matters which might give rise to civil claims, being those that:

- Contain sexual, violent, repulsive, hateful or abusive content;
- Contain misleading content; or
- Infringe the rights of a third party (applicant).

1.112   Having logged into an active YouTube account, users are able to access the form by clicking "More" above the video page in question, then selecting "Report". The form requires the selection of the category of content complained of and complainants can additionally flag the timestamp of the point in the video at which the content complained of appears and provide up to 500 characters explaining the complaint.

1.113   As to the Privacy Complaint Process, this provides for notice and takedown of content which may be a breach of an individual's privacy rights.

1.114   The company encourages the complainant first to contact the person responsible for having uploaded the offending video. It also encourages use of its Flagging Process (detailed above) to the extent that the offending

---

[18] https://support.twitter.com/forms/private_information.

[19] https://support.twitter.com/forms/abusiveuser.

[20] https://support.google.com/youtube/answer/142443.

content violates the company's Community Guidelines (also available via the same web page). It can often be expeditious in removal of offending content to notify a company that the content in question breaches their own terms of usage and this method should be considered in advance of, or in conjunction with, notice and takedown.

1.115   The Complaint Process requires a full name, address and email address of the complainant and the specific URL (or URLs) being complained of. The nature of the private information, location of that information (whether in title, description, the video itself or within a channel background image) and whether the content has been copied from the complainant's own YouTube channel are also required in completing the form.

Facebook

1.116   Facebook provides through its user accounts a reporting mechanism for content which violates its "Community Standards". In addition to the categories of content which are analogous to those listed above as potentially giving rise to a civil claim in the YouTube Flagging Process, Facebook also provides a specific category of Fake News.

1.117   Facebook provides a submission form[21] for Notice of a privacy rights violation. The form requires only the Notice giver's name, URL of the offending content (or a description of where it might be found), identification of the individual whose privacy rights are allegedly violated and their country of residence.

---

[21] https://www.facebook.com/help/contact/144059062408922.

CHAPTER 2: THE RIGHT TO BE FORGOTTEN

CHAPTER SYNOPSIS

- Looks at the "right to be forgotten" – the ability to have search results delisted by search engines, established in EU data protection law by the CJEU judgment in *Google Spain*.
- Summarises the *Google Spain* decision and outlines the Article 29 Working Party Guidelines on the practical implementation of the decision.
- Discusses using online removal procedures, looking specifically at Google's approach, the public interest test, and the scope of delisting. Notes that where a search engine refuses a request, individuals may either make a complaint to the UK's data protection regulator the ICO, or bring civil proceedings challenging the refusal.
- Outlines the new regime in the GDPR – the article 17 "right to erasure" and the notification requirement in article 19.

INTRODUCTION

2.1   Search engines such as Google and Bing are the go-to resource for members of the public seeking to find information on the internet. As their use has become ubiquitous, with trillions of searches each year, search results have become a major focus of individuals' attempts to assert their privacy rights online. If a search engine can be persuaded to delist certain search results, then in practice this information is likely to receive a very much reduced readership. The right to require search engines to delist search results under European data protection law in certain specific cases was created by the Court of Justice of the European Union ("CJEU") in its May 2015 judgment in *Google Spain SL & Anor v Agencia Española de Protección de Datos & Anor*[1] (*"Google Spain"*).

2.2   This case established, for the first time, that living individuals have a right, under the Data Protection Directive, to require search engines to remove search results generated by searches including a person's name, where those search results are "inadequate, inaccurate, no longer relevant, or excessive". This is generally known as "the right to be forgotten" but is more properly called "the right to delist". This Chapter looks at the legal principles underpinning the right and the practical issues that arise when the right is exercised.

---

[1] [2014] QB 1022.

2.3   This Chapter deals with the "right to delist" under the Data Protection Directive, as interpreted by *Google Spain*: how the right is balanced against the public's right to have access to information on issues of public interest, how the right has been implemented in practice and some a number of legal issues concerning its scope, where the law is still evolving.

2.4   From May 2018 the legal framework will change as a result of the inclusion of a new "right to erasure" in the General Data Protection Regulation ("GDPR"). This will continue to form part of English law after Brexit. The "right to erasure" builds on and significantly broadens the "right to delist" and is the focus of the second half of this Chapter.

THE JUDGMENT IN *GOOGLE SPAIN*

2.5   The *Google Spain* case arose from a complaint brought by a Spanish national, Mario Costeja Gonzalez, who wanted to remove two links on Google Search to an auction notice of his repossessed home on a Spanish newspaper's website. He complained that the auction notice following his bankruptcy was many years out of date and was no longer relevant. When the newspaper and Google declined to remove the links to the notice, he brought a complaint to the Spanish data protection authority against the newspaper, Google Inc., the operator of Google Search, and Google Spain SL, its Spanish subsidiary.

2.6   Google Inc is the American company domiciled in the United States that is the operator of Google Search, while Google Spain SL is its Spanish subsidiary, whose main responsibility is marketing advertising for the Spanish market. The CJEU reasoned that Google Inc. was bound by the Directive because it had set up a subsidiary in an EU Member State that was intended to promote and sell advertising space offered by Google Search and that orientated its activity towards the inhabitants of that state. Google Inc. was therefore a data controller of personal data being processed by Google Search and was required to comply with the Data Protection Directive.

2.7   The CJEU made the following key findings in its judgment:

- The activity of a search engine in finding, indexing, storing and making information available to the public in ranked search results produced in response to searches on a person's name amounts to the processing of personal data and the operator of a search engine is the data controller in relation to that processing ([28], [33], [41]). As such, the operator of a search engine is under an obligation to comply with the Data Protection Directive and to ensure that the privacy rights of data subjects are protected.

- The processing of personal data by a search engine can be distinguished from, and is additional to, that of the original publisher of information on the internet [35].

- Search engines play a central role in disseminating personal data, by making it accessible to any internet user who carries out a search on the basis of the subject's name, including people who wouldn't otherwise have found the web page of the original publisher ([36]).

- Search results enable internet users carrying out such searches to get a structured overview of the information relating to that individual and to establish a detailed profile of that person ([37]). Search engines therefore have a significant additional impact on the privacy rights of individuals over and above that of website publishers.

- Individuals have the right to request search engines to remove name-based search results linking to webpages containing information about them published by third parties, even where the information continues to be published by the original publisher and even though publication by the original publisher may be lawful. The fact that a Spanish newspaper continued lawfully to publish the information on its website did not therefore absolve Google Inc. from its responsibility to comply with the Directive as the data controller. The CJEU held that the search engine's action, in making access to the information so much easier, was liable to constitute a more significant interference with the data subject's right to privacy than the publication by the original publisher.

- Where a person requests removal of name-based search results and the data controller refuses to comply with that request, the national authority can require the search engine to remove those search results in order to protect the data subject's rights to privacy and to data protection. Although the ruling does not refer to a "right to be forgotten", this right was initially referred to by that term and more recently has become known as the "right to erasure".

- It was not necessary for a data subject to show that the search result caused him prejudice in order for him to be able to invoke the "right to erasure";

- Where a national authority has to decide whether to order the removal of search results following a request from the data subject, it has to strike a fair balance between the data subject's privacy rights and the legitimate interest of internet users potentially interested in having access to that information. In other words, the CJEU held that a national court has to balance the right to privacy with the right to freedom of expression. However, the CJEU stated that, "as a general rule", the data subject's rights override the interests of internet users in having access to information.

- Important factors that a national authority should take into account when striking the balance between privacy and free expression included the nature of the information in question, in particular the sensitivity for the data subject's private life, versus the interest of the public in having access to the information, in particular the role played by the data subject in public life.

2.8 There are three important points to note about the scope of the judgment:

2.9 First, it only applies to name-based search results, i.e. search results displayed following a search using the data subject's name. Searches using different search terms are not affected by the ruling, even if they lead to retrieval of information which would be, or has been, removed on a name-based search. For example, a search using "Barack Obama" would be caught by the Ruling, but not a search using "first black President of the United States". This has subsequently been confirmed by the Article 29 Working Party (see below).

2.10 Second, the ruling did not address the relationship between the EU data protection regime and the E-Commerce Directive, which provides safe harbours for internet intermediaries who act expediously to remove unlawful content following notification (see para 7.54). The reason for this is that although it was notified of the unlawful content and asked to remove it, Google Inc. did not remove the search result prior to judgment. In the circumstances it had not complied with the Notice and Take Down provisions of the E-Commerce Directive and so the availability of safe harbours was not in issue.

2.11 Third, the ruling does not address the scope of the removal of information that is required to give effect to the CJEU's judgment. There are a range of legal issues that arise in this context, some of which are the subject of guidance from the Article 29 Working Party, or that have arisen in cases before national data protection authorities in Europe, which sometimes adopt different approaches (see further below).

THE ARTICLE 29 WORKING PARTY GUIDELINES

2.12 Following the judgment in *Google Spain,* the Article 29 Working Party – a body established under the Data Protection Directive composed of representatives of the national data protection authorities in Europe – initiated a process of consultation with search engine providers to discuss their practical implementation of the judgment. In November 2014, the Article 29 Working

Party adopted Guidelines for the implementation of the *Google Spain* judgment.

2.13   The Article 29 Working Party Guidelines gave the following general guidance concerning the application of the *Google Spain* decision:

(a) It only applied to search results produced in response to searches on a person's name and did not require the deletion of links to search results from the indexes of the search engine altogether.

(b) De-listing limited to EU domains was insufficient and that "de-listing should also be effective on all relevant domains, including .com."

(c) Search engines were entitled to make general statements to the public about the fact that removals had taken place following successful removal requests, but only if they did not identify the requester.

(d) Search engines should not, as a general practice, inform webmasters of the fact that certain URLs had been de-listed from their search results but it was legitimate for a search engine to contact the original publisher when assessing a request to de-list.

(e) In order to enable search engines to make their assessments, data subjects should provide the reasons why they require de-listing, identify the specific URLs and indicate whether they fulfil a role in public life, or not.

(f) When a search engine refused a de-listing request, it should provide sufficient explanation to the data subject about the reasons for the refusal.

(g) The right to de-listing does not apply to internal search engines within websites.

(h) While the right to data protection applies to "everyone" under the Charter of Fundamental Rights of the European Union, art 8, European Data Protection Authorities ("DPAs") would in practice focus on claims where there is a clear link between the data subject and the EU.

2.14   The Article 29 Working Party also set out in Part II of the Guidelines the criteria that DPAs (including the Information Commissioner's Office (ICO)) should use when deciding whether to order the de-listing of search results. The Working Party said the list of criteria is intended as a "flexible working tool", that it is non-exhaustive and that no one factor is determinative. The list of criteria is as follows:

(1)   **Does the search result relate to a natural person and come up against a search on that person's name?** DPAs should also consider pseudonyms and nicknames when an individual can show that they were linked to his real identity.

(2)   **Does the data subject play a role in public life, or is the data subject a public figure?** The Working Party said that this exception concerns anyone who plays a role in public life, such as politicians, senior public officials, business-people and professional people. This exception also covers public figures – individuals who, due to their functions/commitments, have a high degree of media exposure. This would include individuals in the economy, the arts and sport, as well as politics.

(3)   **Is the data subject a minor?** In general, if the data subject is a minor, this is a factor that favours de-listing.

(4)   **Is the data accurate?** In general, if data is factually inaccurate and presents an inaccurate, inadequate or misleading impression of an individual, delisting is more likely to be required. Where a dispute about the accuracy of information is ongoing, DPAs may choose not to intervene until the process is complete, e.g. a court case or a criminal investigation.

(5)   **Is the data relevant and not excessive?** Under this heading, DPAs should assess relevance by reference to whether:

- The data relates to the working life of the subject, or to his or her private life. The former is likely to be much more relevant than the latter.

- The search result links to information that is excessive or allegedly constitutes hate speech/slander/libel or similar offences of expression against the person. While DPAs cannot rule on these matters, they are competent to assess whether data protection laws have been complied with.

- It is clear that the data reflects an individual's personal opinion, or whether the data appears to be verified fact. The former is less likely to require de-listing than the latter.

(6)   **Is the information sensitive?** Sensitive information, such as information about a person's health, sexuality or religious beliefs, has a greater impact on a person's private life than ordinary personal data and is more likely to require protection.

(7)   **Is the data up to date?** Data that is out-of-date when judged by the purpose of the original processing should be removed more readily.

(8)   **Is the data processing causing prejudice to a data subject?** Although a data subject does not need to establish prejudice to invoke the right to erasure, evidence of prejudice is a strong factor in favour of de-listing.

(9)   **Does the search result link to information that puts the data subject at risk?** If the information leaves the data subject at risk of identity theft or stalking, for example, this is a factor favouring de-listing.

(10) **In what context was the information published?** Where an individual originally gave consent to information being published, but has subsequently revoked that consent, this is a factor that favours de-listing.

(11) **Was the original content published in the context of journalistic purposes?** The fact that information is published by a journalist whose job is to inform the public is a factor to weigh in the balance.

(12) **Does the publisher of the data have a legal power, or a legal obligation, to make the personal data publicly available?** This may be a factor that counts against a de-listing request.

(13) **Does the data relate to a criminal offence?** De-listing is more likely to be appropriate for minor offences committed a long time ago, than for serious offences that happened more recently.

ONLINE REMOVAL PROCEDURES AND POLICIES

Introduction

2.15   Google's search engine (Google Search) dominates the UK search engine market with about 85% market share, followed by Microsoft's Bing with about 10% and Yahoo with about 3%. Following *Google Spain*, each of these search engines introduced online forms to enable individuals to request the de-listing of search results. The online forms are available at these links:

- Google: Request removal of content indexed on Google Search based on data protection law in Europe
- Bing: Request to Block Bing Search Results in Europe
- Yahoo Search: Requests to Block search results in Yahoo Search: Resources for European Residents

2.16   The forms adopt a broadly similar format and require applicants to identify each URL whose removal is sought.

2.17   Where a search engine refuses to remove a search result following such a request, individuals may either make a complaint to the UK's data protection regulator, the ICO, or bring civil proceedings challenging the refusal.

Google's approach

2.18   Google provides further information about its procedures and policies on its Frequently Asked Questions. Google explains that it evaluates removal requests in accordance with the Article 29 Working Party's Guidelines (see paras 2.12, 2.13) and that after a request has been submitted via the webform it undergoes a "manual review" and that "there are no categories of request that are automatically rejected by humans or machines".

2.19   Google describes its evaluation process as consisting of four steps:

(1)   Does the request contain all the necessary information for us to be able to make a decision?

(2)   Does the person making the request have a connection to a European country, such as residency or citizenship?

(3)   Do the pages appear in search results for the requester's name and does the requester's name appear on the page(s) requested for delisting?

(4)   Does the page requested for removal include information that is inadequate, irrelevant, no longer relevant, or excessive, based on the information that the requester provides? Is there a public interest in that information remaining available in search results generated by a search for the requester's name?

2.20   In terms of the information required, Google requires requesters to inform it of the specific Uniform Resource Locator (URL) or web address of the search result in question.

2.21   Google explains that when it removes a search result that this applies only to a search in which the search term is the name of the individual concerned, and does not apply when other search terms are used that may also produce the same search result.

2.22   Where Google acceded to a removal request, Google will remove name-based search results from the European versions of its search engines i.e. country domains targeting EU and EFTA countries, but not from its non-European versions of search such as google.com. This was subsequently questioned by the Article 29 Working Party, leading to a change of policy (see para 2.36).

2.23   Google has the same removal process for all its search engine facilities, namely Google Search, Image Search, Video Search and Google News.

2.24   Google also discloses some common scenarios for de-listing pages:

(1)   **Clear absence of public interest**: For example, aggregator sites with pages that contain personal contact or address information, instances where the requester's name no longer appears on the page, and pages that are no longer online.

(2)   **Sensitive information:** Pages with content that relates solely to information about someone's health, sexual orientation, race, ethnicity, religion, political affiliation and trade-union status.

(3)   **Content relating to minors:** Content that relates to minors or to minor crimes that occurred when the requester was a minor.

(4)   **Spent convictions/exonerations/acquittals for crimes:** Consistent with local law governing the rehabilitation of offenders, we tend to weigh in favor of delisting content relating to a conviction that is spent, accusations that are proven false in a court of law, or content relating to a criminal charge of which the requester was acquitted. We also consider the age of this content and the nature of the crime in our analysis.

2.25   Some common scenarios where Google does not delist pages are:

(1)   **Alternative solutions:** There's another avenue for the requestor to delist that page from our search results. For example, a requester may have published the content to a site that allows users to prevent the content from appearing in search results. It points requesters to information about these tools when it can.

(2)   **Technical reasons:** An incomplete or broken URL is a common technical error. Requesters also sometimes ask to delist pages for a query that doesn't match his/her name or the name of the person the requester claims to represent.

(3)   **Duplicate URL by same individual:** A requester submits multiple requests to delist the same page for the same name.

(4)   **Strong public interest:** Google may decline to delist if it determines that the page contains information that is strongly in the public interest. Determining whether content is in the public interest is complex and may mean considering many diverse factors, including – but not limited to –whether the content relates to the requester's professional life, a past crime, political office, position in public life, or whether the content itself is self-authored content, government documents, or journalistic in nature.

2.26   In its Transparency Report, Google details the total number of requests for removal that it has received from the United Kingdom (about 71,000, relating to 273,000 URLs at the time of publication) and the total number of URLs that it has removed (about 107,000 at the time of publication). Google also provides information about the top ten sites for removal requests, which include Facebook, Profilengine, Google Groups, Annuaire, YouTube, Twitter, Google Plus, Badoo, and Wherevent.

Steps to be taken if a request is refused

2.27   If a search engine refuses a request to delist, an individual has two options. First, they can make an application to the ICO seeking an enforcement notice, under the Data Protection Act 1998, s 40, against the search engine. The ICO provides an online form for making a request to challenge a decision of a search provider not to delist a link. The ICO asks applicants for details of the search term and search engine, to provide the URLs of the search results whose removal is sought, to explain the basis of their concerns and provide the response of the ISSP. The ICO then reviews the complaint against the data protection principles, balancing the applicant's privacy against the public interest in publication.

2.28   Secondly, legal action can be brought against the search engine in the English Courts seeking an order under the Data Protection Act 1998, s 10 requiring the "delisting" of the URL(s) (see para 6.55ff).

GENERAL ISSUES CONCERNING DELISTING

The public interest test

2.29   The CJEU in *Google Spain* referred to the need to balance the "right to delist" against the principle of freedom of expression and the public's right of access to information online, but gave very little guidance on what public interest factors would favour refusal of a delisting request, save for a passing reference to the "role played by the data subject in public life".[2] The Article 29 Working Party Guidelines, which seek to put flesh on the bones of the decision, suggest that this principle does not only concern politicians, but applies to anyone who plays a prominent role in any aspect of public life.

2.30   Whether a particular individual who is the subject of e.g. a newspaper article is a "public figure" is one potentially relevant public interest factor. It is not however, the sole or even the most important criterion. An article may contribute to a public interest debate when it does not concern a public figure;

---

[2] *Google Spain*, at [81].

conversely, many articles about public figures rank relatively low in the scale of public interest e.g. tittle-tattle about the lives of celebrities.[3]

2.31   The touchstone for whether an article is on matter of public interest is, according to the European Court of Human Rights' well-established case law, the "contribution that it makes to a debate of public interest". In appropriate cases whether information is capable of contributing to such a debate will constitute "*the decisive factor*" in the balancing exercise between the right of freedom of expression and any countervailing interests.[4]

2.32   The test of whether a publication contributes to a debate of general interest is a broad one. In *Couderc & Anor v France*[5], the Grand Chamber of the European Court of Human Rights held that the public interest relates to matters that affect the public to such an extent that it may legitimately take an interest in them, which attract its attention, or which concern it to a significant degree, especially insofar as they affect the well-being of citizens or the life of the community. The Court also held that the public interest is engaged with regard to matters that are capable of giving rise to considerable controversy, or that concern an important social issue, or that involve a problem that the public would have an interest in being informed about.

2.33   The right to delist under the Data Protection Directive seeks to give practical effect to the rights to privacy and protection of personal data under the Charter of Fundamental Rights of the European Union, arts 7, 8 and the right to privacy under the European Convention for the Protection of Human Rights and Fundamental Freedoms, art 8 and is to be balanced against the right to freedom of expression under art 11 of the Charter and ECHR, art 10. As a result, in principle the same public interest test should apply as in other contexts where this balancing exercise is required. It seems likely therefore that the European Court of Human Rights' jurisprudence on public interest will be regarded as relevant by national courts tasked with deciding whether a refusal to delist links to a given publication is justified in the public interest. To date there have been few cases on the public interest balancing exercise under the right to delist.

---

[3] *Jameel (Mohammed) & Anor v Wall Street Journal Europe Sprl* [2007] 1 AC 359 at [147]; *Campbell v Mirror Group Newspapers Ltd* [2004] 2 AC 457 at [149].

[4] *Von Hannover v Germany* (2005) 40 EHRR 1 at [76]; *ETK v News Group Newspapers Ltd* [2011] 1 WLR 1827 at [10(5)]; *Couderc & Anor v France* (2015) 40 BHRC 436 at [110].

[5] (2015) 40 BHRC 436.

Scope of delisting

2.34   As the world's largest search engine and the defendant in *Google Spain*, Google has been the main focus of the debate around the scope of delisting required to give effect to that ruling. Initially Google's policy was that when it acceded to a delisting request the relevant search results would only be delisted on European versions of Google e.g. Google UK, Google France, Google Germany etc, but not on its global search engine google.com, or country versions of Google outside Europe, e.g. Google Australia, Google Japan. This approach was criticised on the basis that it was ineffective in preventing access to delisted material, as the same information could readily be found by using non-European versions of the search engine.

2.35   The Article 29 Working Party guidance emphasised that delisting should be implemented to achieve "effective and complete" protection and that delisting should be effective across all domains, including .com.

2.36   In March 2016 Google announced a change of policy, the effect of which is that where Google accedes to a delisting request it will block access to the restricted URL on all Google Search domains, when such searches are undertaken from any European country. This is achieved using geolocation signals like IP addresses to establish the likely country from which the search is taking place. So if a person is searching from a European country (EU or EFTA), delisted search results will now no longer appear on non-European versions of Google e.g. google.com and Google Australia. This makes it much harder for Europe-based searchers to circumvent de-listing by switching to different versions of the search engine. Determined individuals can nonetheless get access to delisted search results using both technical and non-technical strategies.

2.37   It appears that a number of European data protection authorities have accepted that Google's current approach based on geolocation amounts to a satisfactory implementation of *Google Spain* and the Article 29 Working Group's guidance. This appears to be the position of the ICO in the UK, as following the Article 29 Working Party's guidance its enforcement notices have required Google to prevent links to articles from being visible "to anyone directly accessing any Google search services from within the UK". Likewise, the Spanish data protection authority has accepted delisting based on geolocation.

2.38   The French data protection regulator CNIL has however gone further by ordering Google to delist search results across all domains accessible not only from Europe but from anywhere in the world. Google strongly objects to this approach, pointing out that it has the effect of imposing French interpretations of data protection laws on non-European countries, as information that may be unlawful in France may not be unlawful e.g. in the US, where the First Amendment of the Constitution provides strong protection for free speech. Google has refused to accept the decision of CNIL, resulting in ongoing fines and has appealed to France's highest court, the Conseil d'Etat, which in a decision of 19 July 2017, referred the issue to the CJEU.

Notice to webmasters

2.39   The Article 29 Working Party's position is that search engines should not, as a general practice, inform webmasters of the fact that certain URLs have been de-listed from their search results. However, the Working Party did accept that it would be legitimate for a search engine to contact the original publisher when assessing a request to de-list.

2.40   Google's policy is to notify webmasters when it has removed links to certain pages on a webmaster's site following a request to de-list. Google does this "in the interest of transparency" and also to provide the webmaster with an opportunity to request Google to re-consider its decision. It could be argued that Google's policy of notification is logical and provides an important safeguard for freedom of expression. The original author of an article e.g. a journalist will usually know a lot more about the background to the article and the evidence in support of its central factual allegations than will be apparent to any third party such as Google. The journalist and the original publisher are also likely to be better informed about recent developments that may be relevant to the public interest considerations in favour of Google continuing to make the link available in search results.

2.41   The e-commerce safe harbours (considered in detail in Chapter 7) create a strong incentive for internet intermediaries such as Google to remove potentially unlawful content swiftly following notification, as significant delays can deprive such intermediaries of safe harbour protection, rendering them vulnerable to claims in damages. In the circumstances it is logical that Google removes links before notifying webmasters and seeking their comments, rather than continuing to make search results available in the hope of a response from a webmaster that many not be forthcoming.

2.42   Google provides the webmaster with the affected URLs but does not provide the webmaster with the name of the person who has requested the removal or any other details, in order to respect the privacy of the individuals concerned. However, in cases where a publication is focussed on one individual, the identity of the likely requester will be obvious to the webmaster, although the position may be different in respect of an article that makes allegations against several individuals.

2.43   The kinds of considerations Google takes into account in evaluating requests to reinstate links in search results are evident from some of the questions put to webmasters on the webform:

> "(a) Are there facts or context that Google may not have been aware of at the time the removal was performed, which bear on the interest in the public in seeing this page appear in Google's search results?
>
> (a) Have circumstances changed since the removal was performed, such that a stronger public interest exists than before? (For example, is a person mentioned on the page now running for political office?)
>
> (b) Is there some other reason, not clear on the face of the page, why the inclusion of this URL in Google's search results is in the public interest?"

Reporting on earlier removals

2.44   There is a legitimate public debate about the delisting of search results and whether the right balance is being struck between privacy and freedom of expression. However, insofar as any reporting about these issues identifies individuals, it risks exacerbating the very harm the applicant sought to avoid by requesting delisting in the first place.

2.45   That this is a highly fact-sensitive issue is illustrated by the following cases. After the *Google Spain* judgment was handed down, Mr Costeja sought to invoke the "right to delist" to force search engines to remove links to articles relating to the case. This attempt was rejected by the Spanish data protection authority on the basis that his case had become part of a broader public debate about the "right to delist", while Mr Costeja had himself publicised the case by giving media interviews.

2.46   The UK's data protection authority, the ICO, took a different view in one case when requiring Google to remove links to recent news articles concerning a minor crime where the claimant had successfully invoked the "right to delist" to remove articles concerning the original story. The effect of the recent articles was to revive the original story, so on 18 August 2015 the Information Commissioner issued an enforcement notice against Google requiring the removal of "nine links to current news stories about older reports which themselves were removed from search results under the 'right to be forgotten' ruling."

Extension to web archives

2.47   In *Google Spain* the CJEU held that Google was required to delist the search results that linked to the article the claimant sought to have delisted, although the original publisher could continue to publish the article in its archives. The CJEU reasoned that different considerations applied to search engines and news publishers, as the latter may have journalistic defences not available to the former, while the impact of a search engine on an individual's privacy was liable to be greater.[6] The European Court of Human Rights reached a similar conclusion in the pre-*Google Spain* case of *Węgrzynowski & Anor v Poland*.

2.48   Notwithstanding this reasoning, a number of individuals have brought cases seeking to extend the "right to delist" to news archives, with mixed results. There is no English case law on this issue, but there have been some cases in other EU jurisdictions.

2.49   Thus, in *A & Anor v Ediciones El Pais SL*[7] the Spanish Supreme Court refused to order the removal of the articles from the newspaper archive itself, or their de-indexing from the website's internal search engine. However, the Court did require the newspaper to take steps to ensure that archived articles reporting the applicants' 1980s drug convictions were not indexed by search engines.[8]

2.50   In contrast, in the case of *Olivier G v Le Soir*[9] the Belgian Court of Cassation upheld an order that a newspaper should anonymise an article in its online archive that referred to a fatal road traffic accident. This decision referred to *Google Spain* in passing, but relied on a general "Article 8 right" to be forgotten.[10] The publisher criticised the ruling, which it said "opens the door to a rewriting of history".[11]

---

[6] *Google Spain*, at [83]–[87].

[7] Tribunal Supremo. Sala de lo Civil. Judgment of 15 October 2015.

[8] See https://inforrm.wordpress.com/2015/11/19/case-law-spain-a-and-b-v-ediciones-el-pais-newspaper-archive-to-be-hidden-from-internet-searches-but-no-re-writing-of-history-hugh-tomlinson-qc/#more-32376

[9] Judgment of 29 April 2016.

[10] See https://inforrm.wordpress.com/2016/07/19/case-law-belgium-olivier-g-v-le-soir-right-to-be-forgotten-requires-anonymisation-of-online-newspaper-archive-hugh-tomlinson-qc/#more-34745

[11] http://www.flanderstoday.eu/business/right-be-forgotten-extends-newspaper-archives

2.51   This is a controversial area and it is not clear what direction the English case law will take.

Sensitive personal data

2.52   France's highest court, the Conseil d'Etat, has requested a preliminary ruling from the CJEU concerning the right to be delisted and the obligations of search engines in relation to the processing of sensitive personal data.[12]

2.53   Under the Data Protection Directive, "sensitive personal data" is data relating to a data subject's racial or ethnic origin, political opinions, religious beliefs, trade union activities, physical or mental health and sexual life. The French cases arise from complaints about a video about the nature of the relationship between a person and another person holding public office, an article about the suicide of a member of the Church of Scientology, various articles relating to criminal proceedings concerning an applicant and articles relating to the conviction of another applicant for sexual offences against children. The French data protection regulator, CNIL, rejected the complaints and the applicants appealed to the Conseil d'Etat.

2.54   Few details are available in English about the specific issues on which the CJEU has been asked to rule. However, it is noteworthy that the grounds for justifying the processing of sensitive personal data under art 8 of the Data Protection Directive are very limited and none of the grounds is of obvious application to search engines.

THE GENERAL DATA PROTECTION REGULATION

Introduction

2.55   The EU's GDPR, which will establish a new data protection framework across the EU, was finally adopted in April 2016. There is a two year transitional period and the Regulation will come into effect on 24 May 2018. Art 17 contains the "right to erasure" – a new right of general application that significantly develops and will supersede the right established by *Google Spain*, and a new notification requirement in art 19 where such erasure has taken place.

---

[12] http://english.conseil-etat.fr/Activities/Press-releases/Right-to-be-delisted

The right to erasure

2.56 Art 17 of the GDPR is entitled "Right to erasure ('right to be forgotten')" and provides as follows:

"1. The data subject shall have the right to obtain from the controller the erasure of personal data concerning him or her without undue delay and the controller shall have the obligation to erase personal data without undue delay where one of the following grounds applies:

(a) the personal data are no longer necessary in relation to the purposes for which they were collected or otherwise processed;

(b) the data subject withdraws consent on which the processing is based according to point (a) of Article 6(1), or point (a) of Article 9(2), and where there is no other legal ground for the processing;

(c) the data subject objects to the processing pursuant to Article 21(1) and there are no overriding legitimate grounds for the processing, or the data subject objects to the processing pursuant to Article 21(2);

(d) the personal data have been unlawfully processed;

(e) the personal data have to be erased for compliance with a legal obligation in Union or Member State law to which the controller is subject;

(f) the personal data have been collected in relation to the offer of information society services referred to in Article 8(1).

2. Where the controller has made the personal data public and is obliged pursuant to paragraph 1 to erase the personal data, the controller, taking account of available technology and the cost of implementation, shall take reasonable steps, including technical measures, to inform controllers which are processing the personal data that the data subject has requested the erasure by such controllers of any links to, or copy or replication of, those personal data.

3. Paragraphs 1 and 2 shall not apply to the extent that processing is necessary:

(a) for exercising the right of freedom of expression and information;

(b) for compliance with a legal obligation which requires processing by Union or Member State law to which the controller is subject or for the performance of a task carried out in the public interest or in the exercise of official authority vested in the controller;

(c) for reasons of public interest in the area of public health in accordance with points (h) and (i) of Article 9(2) as well as Article 9(3);

(d) for archiving purposes in the public interest, scientific or historical research purposes or statistical purposes in accordance with Article 89(1) in so far as the right referred to in paragraph 1 is likely to render impossible or seriously impair the achievement of the objectives of that processing; or

(e) for the establishment, exercise or defence of legal claims".

2.57   There are three key differences between the scope of the right established by *Google Spain* and the "right to erasure" in the GDPR.

2.58   First, the "right to be forgotten" in *Google Spain* was established in relation to search engines and its application in other contexts was unclear. There is no equivalent limitation in the Regulation; the "right to erasure" is of general application and may be invoked against any data controller that processes personal data. So, a claimant can use the right to erasure not only to seek removal of search results from a search engine but also to seek removal of a posting on a social networking site such as Facebook, or a photograph posted or Instagram, or an article published on a newspaper's website, or film footage published on a broadcaster's website, or a blog published by a citizen blogger.

2.59   Secondly, in *Google Spain* the CJEU's focus was on the removal of search results that were linked to content that was "inadequate, inaccurate, no longer relevant, or excessive". The Court's focus was on the lack of accuracy or relevance of the information in question, based on data protection principles in the Data Protection Directive. Art 17 of the Regulation, however, contains a much wider range of situations where the "right to erasure" can be invoked. These mirror a number of the data protection principles that apply to all personal data in art 6 of the Regulation, as well as principles that apply to the "special categories" of personal data in art 9 thereof.

2.60   Thirdly, the "right to erasure" under art 17 of the Regulation refers only to personal data and makes no distinction between personal data and sensitive personal data (which are called "special categories of personal data" under the Regulation). It follows that while under the "right to delist" a search engine's potential defences will be different according to whether the information concerns personal data or sensitive personal data, under the Regulation the same defences apply to all personal data, of which the most relevant will be a general defence of freedom of expression.

2.61   As a result of the greatly widened scope of the "right to erasure", it will apply in a much wider range of situations than the "right to delist". Thus both the grounds for erasure and the potential objections to an erasure request (or defences) concern a whole range of different situations (which in most cases are not relevant in the context of delisting of search results by search engines). Accordingly, the remainder of this Chapter addresses this wider range of erasure scenarios. At the time of writing the GDPR is not yet in force, therefore there is currently no case law on these provisions.

Grounds for erasure

Personal data no longer necessary

2.62   The first ground for erasure under art 17(1)(a) is that the personal data are no longer necessary having regard to the purpose for which they were collected or otherwise processed.

2.63   Necessity is a touchstone for the processing of personal data under art 6 of the Regulation (see art 6(1)(b)–(f)) and the processing of special categories of personal data under art 9 (see art 9(2)(b)–(d), (f)–(j). Unless a data controller can demonstrate that continued processing of personal data is necessary under those provisions, or that it has a defence to continued processing under art 17(3), it would have to accede to a request for erasure.

2.64   If the police published photographs of suspects alleged to be involved in violent disorder who they were seeking to identify and arrest, for example, the likely justification for the processing of that personal data would be that it was necessary for the performance of a task carried out in the public interest or in the exercise of official authority vested in the controller (art 6(1)(d)). However, if a given suspect had later been ruled out of the police's investigation he could argue that continued publication of his photograph was no longer necessary – having regard to the original purpose for which the data was processed – and should be erased.

Data subject withdraws consent

2.65   The second ground under art 17(1)(b) of the GDPR is that the data subject withdraws consent to the processing of his personal data/special categories of personal data, having previously given his consent to such processing under art 6 or 9.

2.66   However, the data subject's withdrawal of consent is not on its own determinative of whether the data controller is obliged to erase the data; art 17(1)(b) is qualified so that withdrawal of consent only creates an obligation to erase data "where there is no other legal ground for the processing".

2.67   If an individual consented to provide financial information in order to secure a loan, for example, and later withdrew his consent to any processing of that data, the data controller would be obliged to erase that information unless there was another legal ground for the processing. Such other legal ground might be, for example, that for regulatory purposes it was obliged to retain records about the financial information provided by people who had obtained loans for a certain period of time.

The data subject objects to the processing

2.68   Art 17(1)(c) concerns the right to object to the processing of personal data. This is governed by art 21 of the GDPR, which creates a right to object to the processing of personal data in two specific circumstances.

2.69   The first situation is based on art 6(1)(e), where the processing is necessary for the performance of a task in the public interest or in the exercise of official authority vested in the controller. This is most likely to be relevant to the processing of personal data by public authorities, such as central government, government departments and services like the police or social services.

2.70   The second situation where a data subject can object is based on art 6(1)(f), where the processing is necessary for the legitimate interests pursued by the data controller or a third party. This is the ground that is most likely to be relevant to, and relied on, by publishers, including news publishers and social media.

2.71   The difference between the withdrawal of consent and the right to object is that in the case of the latter the data subject will not have consented to the processing of his personal data in the first place. However, in common with the right to withdraw consent, the right to object is not itself determinative of whether the data controller must erase the data. The data controller may be able to demonstrate, under art 21(1), "compelling legitimate grounds for the processing that override the interests, rights and freedoms of the data subject", or that continued processing is required for the establishment, exercise or defence of legal claims.

2.72   In the case of processing for the purposes of direct marketing under art 21(2) the right to object is unqualified, so if a data subject objects to continued processing the data controller is unable to override his wishes and "the personal data shall no longer be processed for those purposes" (art 21(3)). This right to object could be invoked against marketing that processes personal data for the purpose of sending text messages, making phone calls or sending unwanted flyers to a home address.

The personal data have been unlawfully processed

2.73   Art 17(1)(d) creates a right to erasure where there has been "unlawful processing", a catch-all provision that encompasses both EU law provisions and the national law of the Member State concerned.

2.74   This ground for erasure includes any form of unlawfulness under the GDPR itself, such as processing in breach of art 6 (personal data) or art 9 (special categories of personal data), as well as unlawfulness under other relevant EU law, or national legal provisions, whether civil or criminal. Typical examples of relevant national laws would be breach of contract, defamation, misuse of private information, infringement of copyright and harassment.

The personal data have to be erased for compliance with a legal obligation

2.75   Art 17(1)(e) provides a ground for erasure where personal data have to be erased in order to comply with a legal obligation under EU or Member States' law.

2.76   Art 23 of the GDPR permits the EU or Member States to impose restrictions on certain rights under the Regulation including the right of erasure under art 17, where such a restriction "respects the essence of the fundamental rights or freedoms and is a necessary and proportionate measure in a democratic society" to safeguard a number of specific interests, such as national security, defence and the protection of the data subject or the rights and freedoms of others.

2.77   This provision enables a data controller lawfully to take steps to erase personal data in order to comply with its legal obligations and to defend itself in the event that the data subject or subjects seek to challenge the data controller's actions. For example, social network providers typically have terms of service that prevent certain kinds of offensive content or content that infringes intellectual property rights from being posted. If such offensive or copyright-infringing content is posted, this ground of erasure enables the data controller to remove it.

Personal data collected for information society services offered to a child

2.78   Art 17(1)(f) provides a ground for erasure where the personal data have been collected in relation to the offer of information society services referred to in art 8(1).

2.79   Art 8(1) concerns information society services offered directly to a child, which is lawful where the child is at least 16 years of age, or where there has been parental consent in the case of a child under 16. This ground of erasure could be invoked, for example, if personal data had been collected in the context of offering information society services directly to a child under 16 but without parental consent.

Informing other data controllers

2.80   Art 17(2) obliges data controllers who have made personal data public and who are obliged to erase personal data under art 17(1) to take reasonable steps to inform other data controllers that the data subject has requested that they should also erase the data. This obligation is limited to "reasonable steps", taking into account technical measures and that what is reasonable will be judged by reference to the available technology and the cost of its implementation.

2.81   Art 17(2) only applies where a data controller is obliged to erase personal data, having no available defence under art 17(3). If the data controller has such a defence, there is no requirement to inform other data controllers.

2.82   Art 17 does not address the situation where a data controller such as a social media platform or a search engine contacts another data controller such as a news publisher for the purpose of obtaining additional information to inform its decision on a request for erasure. As noted above, it is Google's policy to notify webmasters of requests to remove search results and to give them the opportunity to comment. This is a valuable safeguard for freedom of expression as the original publisher will usually be much better informed about the underlying facts and other relevant circumstances than any subsequent publisher. Although the Article 29 Working Party has questioned the practice of inviting comment, there appears to be nothing in the GDPR that prevents such consultation and it is suggested that it would normally be justifiable under art 6(1)(f) or 9(2)(g).

OBJECTIONS TO AN ERASURE REQUEST

Introduction

2.83   Where a data subject has a ground for erasure under art 17(1), the data controller may rely on one of the five grounds for objection set out in art 17(3).

Freedom of expression

2.84   Art 17(3)(a) provides that art 17(1), (2) shall not apply to the extent that processing is necessary for exercising the right to freedom of expression and information.

2.85   This is a very important provision that is broad in scope and likely to be relied upon in a very wide variety of circumstances by all kinds of publishers including search engines. What art 17 requires is a balancing of the data subject's right to erasure under art 17(1) and the data controller's right to freedom of expression and information under art 17(3)(a).

2.86   Art 17 gives equal weight to the two competing rights, neither of which has precedence over the other, consistent with the European Court of Human Rights' jurisprudence on balancing arts 8 (right to respect for private and family life) and 10 (freedom of expression) of the Convention. This is reinforced by recital 65 to the GDPR, which sets out the right to be forgotten and then qualifies it by reference to freedom of expression.

2.87   The *Google Spain* judgment was criticised for failing to refer to the right to freedom of expression in the EU Charter and for stating that the rights of data subjects should generally override those of internet users, suggesting that the balance was weighted in favour of protecting personal data.[13] Art 17 restores a balanced approach to the two competing rights, indicating that any statements to the contrary in *Google Spain* are not to be followed. Whether *Google Spain* involved a serious error of approach or was merely misunderstood by commentators is now of largely academic interest.

2.88   The European Commission, responsible for promoting the right to erasure while the GDPR was being negotiated, had indicated that the Regulation would give equal priority to the data subject's rights and freedom of expression. In a factsheet about *Google Spain,*[14] the Commission defended the

---

[13] See https://inforrm.wordpress.com/2014/05/21/google-spain-whatever-happened-to-freedom-of-expression-guy-vassall-adams/.

[14] European Commission, Factsheet on the "Right to be Forgotten" ruling (C-131/12).

judgment on the basis that it "did not elevate the right to be forgotten to a 'super right' trumping other fundamental rights, such as freedom of expression or freedom of the media". The Commission pointed out that:

> "Neither the right to the protection of personal data nor freedom of expression are absolute rights. A fair balance should be sought between the legitimate interest of internet users and the person's fundamental rights."

Compliance with legal obligations/performance of official tasks

2.89   Art 17(3)(b) includes two discrete grounds. The first is where the processing is necessary for compliance with a legal obligation under EU or national law. In some circumstances, a data subject may want his personal data to be erased but a data controller will be required by law to retain that information for a set period of time, or while certain specific conditions are fulfilled.

2.90   The second ground is where processing is necessary for the performance of a task in the public interest or in the exercise of official authority by the data controller. This defence is most relevant to the work of public authorities such as government departments and public services like the police. The law governing the retention by the police of previous criminal convictions is an example of personal data the processing of which is regulated by national law.

Public health

2.91   Art 17(3)(c) protects processing that is necessary for reasons of public interest in the area of public health. The relevant provisions are: art 9(2)(h), which includes processing that is necessary for the purposes of preventative and occupational medicine, for the assessment of the medical capacity of an employee, for medical diagnosis and other public health purposes; and art 9(2)(i), where the processing is necessary for reasons of public interest in the field of public health, such as protecting against serious cross-border threats to public health. These provisions are likely to be relied on by government departments concerned with issues of public health and social care, health institutions, companies engaged in medical research and medical professionals.

Archiving and other purposes

2.92   Art 17(3)(d) provides a specific ground where processing is necessary for archiving in the public interest, scientific or historical research purposes or statistical purposes, which is governed by art 89 of the GDPR. This defence prevails only in so far as the right of erasure is "likely to render impossible or seriously impair the achievement of the objectives of that processing". In other words, the fact that personal data has been retained for archiving purposes will not be sufficient; it is necessary to show that allowing erasure of personal data will make impossible or seriously impair the objective of the archive.

Defending legal claims

2.93 Art 17(3)(e) establishes a ground for refusal where processing is necessary for the establishment, exercise or defence of legal claims. This defence protects information collected for the purpose of a future legal claim, information required for bringing a claim and information required for defending a claim.

The notification requirement

2.94 Art 19 requires a data controller to communicate any erasure of personal data under art 17 to each recipient to whom the personal data have been disclosed, unless this proves impossible or involves disproportionate effort. The controller is also required to inform the data subject about those recipients if the data subject requests it. This notification requirement also applies to rectification of personal data under art 16 or restriction of processing under art 18.

2.95 This is not a new provision as art 12(c) of the Data Protection Directive contained a similar requirement. Where information has been conveyed to a limited class of people whose identities and contact details are known by the data controller, the notification requirement appears workable. But it is difficult to see how it will apply in practice in the context of different kinds of publications online that may be communicated to very large numbers of people, where their identities and contact details may not be known to the data controller. It seems likely that there will be extensive reliance on the impossibility and disproportionate effort exemptions.

CHAPTER 3: IDENTIFYING THE DEFENDANT

CHAPTER SYNOPSIS

- Deals with issues surrounding the identification of the defendant. Looks at who the author or publisher of online material is, and who is responsible at law for the publication of the material online.
- Considers the use of *Norwich Pharmacal* orders and their effectiveness in identifying anonymous publishers. Also examines how "unmasking orders" can be used in conjunction with *Norwich Pharmacal* orders to compel the anonymous publisher to reveal their identity. Further, outlines practical steps when seeking information from online service providers that, if taken, are likely to make the process of obtaining the order from the court easier.
- Examines case law and legislation on the question of who bears legal responsibility for online content. Looks at the position of such internet intermediaries as hosts, website operators, internet service providers and search engines.
- Focuses on the principles by which the law attaches responsibility to particular parties in claims in defamation, breach of confidence, misuse of private information, harassment and breach of the Data Protection Act 1998 (and copyright).

INTRODUCTION

3.1   When objectionable material is published online a potential claimant will know what the content is, the URL at which it is published and whether a search engine lists that URL. There are, however, three questions that then arise:

(1)   Who is the author or publisher of the material?

(2)   Who is responsible, in law, for the publication of the material online?

(3)   What steps can be taken to remove the objectionable material and obtain compensation?

The first two questions are dealt with in this Chapter.

WHO IS THE AUTHOR OR PUBLISHER?

Introduction

3.2   In many cases of online publication the identity of the author or publisher will be obvious: a publication may be in a mainstream media publication and bear the name of the journalist, it may be on a blog that identifies the authors of the posts. It may be a social media publication by an identified individual. In such cases, the first and most obvious person to bring a claim against is the identified author.

3.3   Problems may, of course, arise where that author is unreachable for some reason or where s/he is a "person of straw" – someone which no resources to pay damages and who may ignore court orders because, for example, they are resident abroad. In that situation, it is necessary to consider the liability of others who "participate" in the publication of the online material: hosts, internet service providers and search engine operators. The liability of such "secondary publishers" is dealt with in the next section of this Chapter (see para 3.48ff).

3.4   In some cases, however, the author or publisher may be anonymous. It is now easier than ever to have an online presence while shielded by a cloak of anonymity. A user can sign up to use social media services such as Twitter and Facebook without using a real name. There has been a greatly increased use of proxy registrant services. Individuals can defame, harass, or otherwise make life difficult for others without ever having to reveal their true identity. This can make legal action very difficult.

3.5   There are, however, steps that can be taken to compel disclosure of the identities of those who publish anonymously. The efficacy of such steps depends in large part on the enforceability of court orders. Particular difficulties can arise in circumstances where the company that holds identifying information is based out of the jurisdiction. For example, Twitter, Google Inc., and WordPress are all headquartered in California and therefore subject to Californian law. The English courts must also be satisfied that they have the jurisdiction to make the orders sought.

3.6   This section will consider the use of *Norwich Pharmacal* orders and their effectiveness in identifying anonymous publishers. It will also examine how "unmasking orders" can be used in conjunction with *Norwich Pharmacal* orders to compel the anonymous publisher to reveal their identity.

Norwich Pharmacal orders: introduction

3.7   *Norwich Pharmacal* orders may be made against individuals or companies who are not actually guilty of any wrongdoing but who are somehow involved in that wrongdoing and can provide relevant information to someone who is considering bring a claim against the perpetrator of the wrongdoing.

3.8   The orders get their name from the case of *Norwich Pharmacal Co & Ors v Commissioners of Customs and Excise.*[1] The applicant held a patent for a chemical compound. In breach of the patent, unknown others were importing the "pirate" compound into the UK. After various unsuccessful attempts to find out by other means, applicant sought an order against Her Majesty's Customs and Excise that it disclose the names and addresses of the importers, which was information collected by it in the exercise of its statutory function. The House of Lords ultimately upheld the order made by the judge. In holding that the respondent was under an equitable duty to "co-operate" and to "assist" the applicant, the respondent was ordered to provide "full information and disclos[e] the identity of the wrongdoers".

3.9   Lord Reid summarized the principle underlining the making of such orders against otherwise "innocent" third parties at as follows:

> "[The cases] point to a very reasonable principle that if through no fault of his own a person gets mixed up in the tortious acts of others so as to facilitate their wrong-doing he may incur no personal liability but he comes under a duty to assist the person who has been wronged by giving him full information and disclosing the identity of the wrongdoers. I do not think it matters whether he became so mixed up by voluntary action on his part or because it was his duty to do what he did. It may be that if it causes him expense the person seeking the information ought to reimburse him. But justice requires that he should co-operate in righting the wrong if he unwittingly facilitated its perpetration."[2]

3.10   *Norwich Pharmacal* orders are not limited to cases where the identity of the wrongdoer is unknown but where, for example, the third party holds "crucial information" to enable a claimant to sue.[3] Furthermore, the information sought does not need to be from an "innocent" wrongdoer but may also be

---

[1] [1974] AC 133.

[2] Ibid, 175B–D.

[3] *Mitsui & Co Ltd v Nexen Petroleum UK Ltd* [2005] 3 All ER 511, per Lightman J, at [19].

obtained where the third party is also guilty of wrongdoing.[4] The latter may arise where, for example, an Information Society Service Provider (ISSP) has been given notice of a defamatory post on its website but has failed to take any action to remove it.

3.11   *Norwich Pharmacal* orders are now commonly sought against ISSPs in order to compel disclosure of information held by them about their users. They will not disclose such information without a court order. For example, Twitter will not disclose information about the identity of the operators of "anonymous" accounts without a court order. However, as discussed below (see para 3.36), it often makes practical sense to approach the ISSP prior to making the application to see if agreement can be reached as to the terms of such an order.

Norwich Pharmacal: the three-stage test

Introduction

3.12   There are three conditions that must be satisfied before a court will make a *Norwich Pharmacal* order:

(1)   that a wrong has been carried out or arguably carried out by an ultimate wrongdoer;

(2)   that there is a need for an order to enable action to be brought against the ultimate wrongdoer; and

(3)   that the person against whom the order is sought be mixed up in it so as to have facilitated the wrongdoing and is able or is likely to be able to provide the information necessary to enable the ultimate wrongdoer to be sued.[5]

3.13   These criteria are designed to prevent claimants from using the *Norwich Pharmacal* jurisdiction to embark upon a fishing expedition. For example, it would be inappropriate to seek to obtain a *Norwich Pharmacal* order in response to online posts that, while unpleasant, could not reasonably be said to give rise to a cause of action in, for example, libel or harassment.

Wrong by ultimate wrongdoer

3.14   The first limb was described in *Mitsui & Co Ltd v Nexen Petroleum UK Ltd* as requiring a claimant to show that they have a "real prospect" of establishing a cause of action against the wrongdoer. The claimant must show a "good

---

[4] *CHC Software Care v Hopkins and Wood* [1993] FSR 241.

[5] For example, *Mitsui & Co v Nexen Petroleum UK Ltd* [2005] 3 All ER 511, at 21.

arguable case".[6] However, other cases have said that the *Norwich Pharmacal* jurisdiction extends to cases

> "where there is a good indication of wrongdoing, but not every piece of what the claimant needs to plead a case is fully in position."[7]

Norwich Pharmacal orders have even been granted in circumstances where the claimant is not sure whether they have a viable cause of action, although such cases are likely to be rare.[8]

3.15 While it is not necessary for a claimant to show that their claim *would* succeed, consideration must be given to any obvious defences that might arise or any other obvious difficulties with the claim. Jurisdiction is one such difficulty that is considered in greater detail below. In reality it will often be very difficult for prospective claimants to particularise their claim(s) in any detail when making an application for a *Norwich Pharmacal* order and the courts are unlikely to take an overly prescriptive approach to the first limb.

Necessary to enable action to be brought

3.16 The second limb is that the court must be satisfied that the order is necessary to enable an action to be brought against the ultimate wrongdoer. In this regard, it is sometimes said that a *Norwich Pharmacal* order is one of "last resort".[9] The courts will consider whether the information required is reasonably available from alternative sources. Thus, the claimant must be able to satisfy the court that it would not be able to obtain the required information via pre-action disclosure from the defendant. In *Mitsui & Co Ltd v Nexen Petroleum UK Ltd,* the application for disclosure via a *Norwich Pharmacal* order was refused on this basis.[10] However, *Norwich Pharmacal* orders are no longer regarded as an "exceptional remedy" but can be granted whenever it is "just and convenient in the interests of justice to grant it".[11]

3.17 It is likely to be easy to establish this condition in the majority of cases involving online publication by anonymous individuals. In such cases, there is no known defendant and as such there is no means by which pre-action

---

[6] *Ramilos Trading Ltd v Buyanovsky* [2016] EWHC 3175 (Comm) [12]–[23].

[7] *Carlton Film Distributors v VCI* [2003] FSR 47 at [11].

[8] *P v T Ltd* [1997] 1 WLR 1309.

[9] *Mitsui & Co Ltd v Nexen Petroleum UK Ltd* [2005] 3 All ER 511 at [24].

[10] Ibid, [28].

[11] *President of State of Equatorial Guinea v Bank of Scotland* [2006] UKPC 7 [16].

disclosure could be obtained. The position may be different where the ISSP is said to also be a wrongdoer.

Mixed up in the wrongdoing

3.18   The third limb is that the respondent must be "mixed up in it so as to have facilitated the wrongdoing". It is often said that disclosure cannot be ordered against a "mere witness" or bystander.[12] The limits of this requirement were considered in *Various Claimants v News Group Newspapers Ltd & Anor (No 2)*.[13] In that case the claimants sought a *Norwich Pharmacal* order against the police for disclosure of information gathered in the course of a criminal investigation into phone hacking. Mann J held that the Court had jurisdiction to make a *Norwich Pharmacal* order against a third party who, although not having participated in or facilitated the defendant's wrongdoing, had an engagement with it such as to make the third party more than a mere witness or bystander. In that case, since the police had been under a duty to acquire information about the offending act, and had provided information to the applicants pursuant to a perceived obligation to do so, they had sufficient engagement for the court to have jurisdiction to make the order.

Discretion

3.19   Even where the three conditions set out above are satisfied, the jurisdiction is discretionary and will be exercised taking into account what would be reasonable and proportionate in the circumstances. Accordingly, the court may, in the exercise of that discretion, determine whether to grant relief and if so in what form.

3.20   The leading case on the exercise of the discretion is the decision of the Supreme Court in *Rugby Football Union v Consolidated Information Services Ltd*.[14] Lord Kerr, giving the judgment of the Supreme Court, observed that: "The essential purpose of the remedy is to do justice. This involves the exercise of the discretion by a careful and fair weighing of all relevant factors".[15] Lord Kerr went on to identify these factors as follows:

---

12 *Norwich Pharmacal* [974] AC 133, at 173–174 (per Lord Reid); at 188 (per Viscount Dilhorne).

13 [2014] 1 Ch 400.

14 [2012] 1 WLR 3333.

15 Ibid [17].

(i)   The strength of the possible cause of action contemplated by the applicant for the order.[16]

(ii)   The strong public interest in allowing an applicant to vindicate his legal rights.

(iii)   Whether the making of the order will deter similar wrongdoing in the future.

(iv)   Whether the information could be obtained from another source.

(v)   Whether the respondent to the application knew or ought to have known that he was facilitating arguable wrongdoing.

(vi)   Whether the order might reveal the names of innocent persons as well as wrongdoers, and if so whether such innocent persons will suffer any harm as a result.

(vii)   The degree of confidentiality of the information sought.

(viii) The privacy rights under EHCR, art 8 of the individuals whose identity is to be disclosed.

(ix)   The rights and freedoms under the EU data protection regime of the individuals whose identity is to be disclosed.

(x)   The public interest in maintaining the confidentiality of journalistic sources, as recognised in the Contempt of Court Act 1981, s 10 and ECHR, art 10 ([17]).

3.21   In an online publication case, where a website has a "privacy policy" to the effect that a user's personal information would not be disclosed to third parties without their consent, this is factor that may be taken into account when deciding not to exercise discretion in favour of making an order.[17]

3.22   The list of factors to be taken into account in the exercise of discretion does not include consideration of whether the applicant intends to commence legal proceedings as a relevant factor in the exercise of discretion. It is not necessary for an applicant to demonstrate an intention to commence proceedings.[18]

Norwich Pharmacal jurisdictional issues

3.23   A number of jurisdictional issues arise in the context of anonymous wrongdoing online. Firstly, where the person who is the "ultimate wrongdoer" is unknown it will often be very difficult to know whether they are present within the jurisdiction. Secondly, the party against whom the order

---

[16] For example, *Sheffield Wednesday Football Club & Ors v Hargreaves* [2007] EWHC 2375 (QB) [17] (disproportionate to order disclosure when posts were "barely defamatory").

[17] *Clift v Clarke* [2011] EWHC 1164 (QB) [40]–[41], [2011] Info TLR 13.

[18] *Golden Eye (International) Ltd & Ors v Telefónica UK Ltd* [2013] Bus LR 414.

is sought is likely to also be based out of the jurisdiction; most likely within the United States in the case of Twitter, Google, Apple or Microsoft.

3.24   When claimants first started using *Norwich Pharmacal* orders against internet corporations, the courts were generally unconcerned with matters of jurisdiction. This was the case, for example, in *Applause Store Productions & Anor v Raphael*,[19] one of the first reported cases in which a *Norwich Pharmacal* order was granted against Facebook. The order required the disclosure of registration details, including the email addresses and the IP addresses for all computers used by the owner of those email addresses that had accessed Facebook. The court took a similar approach in the case of *G & G v Wikimedia Foundation Inc*,[20] where an order was made to identify an anonymous editor of a Wikipedia page who had uploaded private information about the claimants.

3.25   This approach has been subject to closer scrutiny in more recent cases. In *Lockton Companies International & Ors v Persons Unknown & Anor*[21] the court questioned whether it had jurisdiction to make an order against a company based in the United States without a place of business in England. The claimant was seeking to identify the sender of anonymous emails, which it claimed were defamatory and contained private and confidential information. The claimant faced two difficulties:

(1)   The general rule is that it is vexatious to join a defendant solely for the purposes of obtaining disclosure.[22]

(2)   In order for the court to have such jurisdiction the claimant must bring the claim within one of the "gateways" in CPR PD 6D, para 3.1 (see para 4.20ff).

3.26   In *Lockton,* the applicants contended that the court could draw an inference that the anonymous sender of the emails was in the jurisdiction and that, once identified, service could be effected domestically. In relation to the two issues identified in the previous paragraph it was argued that *Norwich Pharmacal* relief was "substantive relief" and did not, therefore, offend against the rule that a party could not be joined solely for the purposes of disclosure. Further, it was said that Google Inc. was a "necessary and proper party" for disclosure of the information needed to identify the defendant and that service out of the jurisdiction could be ordered under CPR PD 6B, para 3.1(3) (see para 4.23).

---

[19] [2008] Info TLR 318.

[20] [2010] EMLR 14.

[21] [2009] EWHC 3423 (QB).

[22] *Unilever Plc v Chefaro Proprietaries Ltd & Anor* [1994] FSR 135.

Eady J accepted these submissions, granted permission to serve out and made the *Norwich Pharmacal* order.

3.27 Until recently, *Lockton* was authority for those seeking *Norwich Pharmacal* orders against ISSP based outside of the jurisdiction. Many such orders were obtained and were usually not opposed by companies such as Twitter and Google that agreed to comply with their terms as when they were made.

3.28 However, Teare J took a different approach in the case of *AB Bank Ltd v Abu Dhabi Commercial Bank PJSC*.[23] In that case, the applicant was a Bangladeshi bank and the respondent a bank based in Dubai. The claimant had been defrauded out of several million dollars by a third party and sought a *Norwich Pharmacal* order on the basis that the respondent had knowledge of where the money had gone. Proceedings were to be issued in England. A *Norwich Pharmacal* order was made without notice and the respondent applied to set it aside.

3.29 The applicant had relied on three jurisdictional gateways:

(a) where a claim is for an interim remedy under the Civil Jurisdiction and Judgments Act 1982, s 25(1) (CPR PD 6B, para. 3.1(5));

(b) where a claim is made for an injunction ordering the defendant to do or refrain from doing an act within the jurisdiction (CPR PD 6B, para. 3.1(2)); and

(c) where the claimant wishes to serve the claim form on another person who is a necessary or proper party to that claim (CPR PD 6B, para. 3.1(3)).

The court rejected the application under all three gateways.

3.30 As to the first gateway, the judge held that *Norwich Pharmacal* relief was a self-standing claim rather than a form of interim relief. This is consistent with the decision in *Lockton*.

3.31 As to the second gateway, it was held that the order did not require the respondent to take any steps within the jurisdiction – as it could obtain the information in the UAE and provide it to the applicant in the UAE or Bangladesh. The position would have been different if the order had required the provision of the information to the applicant's solicitors in England.

3.32 As to the third gateway, the judge held that as no allegation of fraud was being made against the respondent who was not alleged to be a "necessary and proper party" to the action alleging fraud ([19]). The judge refused to follow *Lockton*.

---

[23] [2017] 1 WLR 810.

3.33   The judge's reasoning on this point is difficult to follow as it is not a requirement of CPR PD 6B, para 3.1(3) that the claim against the person to be served is a "necessary and proper party" to a claim based on the same cause of action.[24] Furthermore, CPR 7.3 provides that a claimant may use a single claim for "to start all claims which can be conveniently disposed of in the same proceedings". Such claims may be tried separately.[25] This provision does not seem to have been considered by Teare J.

3.34   As a general rule, where there are two conflicting decisions of the High Court, the later one should be followed if it was reached after full consideration of the earlier decision – unless the third judge is convinced that the second was wrong in not following the first.[26] It is arguable that *AB Bank* is wrong on the "necessary or proper party" point and should not be followed.

3.35   In any event, the *AB Bank* case should not present difficulties for claimants seeking *Norwich Pharmacal* orders against providers such as Google or Twitter because the applicant can satisfy the requirements of CPR PD 6A, para 3.1(2) ("claim for injunction ordering the defendant to do an act within the jurisdiction") by seeking an order that the information be delivered to solicitors in England and Wales.

Practical steps and procedure

General issues

3.36   There are a number of practical steps when seeking information from online service providers that, if taken, are likely to make the process of obtaining the order from the court easier. In particular:

- A court order is generally necessary when seeking information from the major online companies. However, consideration should always be given as to whether there are alternative means by which the information sought can be obtained.

- Contact with the intended respondent should be made at the outset. Although Twitter, Google and Facebook, for example, will only release information about their users with a court order, obtaining their confirmation that they will not oppose the application and

---

[24] The judge also relied on *Unilever Plc v Chefaro Proprietaries Ltd & Anor* [1994] FSR 135 – but in that case the Court recognised that although joining a party solely for the purposes of disclosure was not permitted, it was open to the claimant to apply for a *Norwich Pharmacal* order.

[25] S Bushell, "Should *Norwich Pharmacal* have extra-territorial reach?" (2017) 133 LQR 188–191.

[26] *Colchester Estates (Cardiff) v Carlton Industries* [1986] Ch 80, at 85.

their agreement to the form of order in advance makes it far more likely that a judge will grant the order sought and may reduce costs as there is little risk of having to return to court to resist an application to set aside the order.

- The application can be made in an existing action against "Persons Unknown", by way of a fresh "Part 8" claim or simply by issuing an application under CPR Part 23.
- Unless there is genuine urgency, the usual 3 clear days' notice should be given for the application. This also affords the respondent greater opportunity to agree the terms of the order.

Terms of the order

3.37   When it comes to the terms of the order itself, there does not seem to be any restriction on the form in which disclosure under *Norwich Pharmacal* orders can be provided. The required disclosure may take any appropriate form. Usually it takes form of production of documents, but it may also include providing witness statements, answering interrogatories or attending court to give oral evidence.[27] Applicants may therefore seek disclosure by, for example, providing IP addresses or email account user details. The information may be provided in documentary form or in a witness statement.[28]

3.38   A *Norwich Pharmacal* order should be endorsed with a "penal notice".[29] This means that the order can be enforced by way of committal proceedings against a non-complying respondent. Because such an order is a "final order" it can be enforced by way of committal proceedings against foreign respondents, with the need for permission to "serve out" (see para 9.126). Such respondents, although they may not have offices in the United Kingdom, may have personnel or assets against which, in theory, there could be enforcement.

3.39   One important question concerning the terms of the order is whether it should contain a provision preventing the respondent from informing the intended defendant that the order has been made. An applicant will often wish to include such a term to prevent the intended defendant being "tipped off" and thus, being able to evade service (by for example, deleting an email

[27] *Mitsui & Co Ltd v Nexen Petroleum UK Ltd*, [2005] 3 All ER 511 at [18].

[28] For example, *Patel v Unite* [2012] EWHC 92 (QB) at [5]–[6]; *Football Association Premier League v Wells & Anor* [2016] Bus LR 350 at [4]. See also, *Brady v PKF* [2011] EWHC 3178 (QB) at [19]–[22] (disclosure of information contained in telephone records in addition to delivering up copies of telephone records).

[29] CPR 81.9 and CPR PD 81, para 1.

account used to open an anonymous Twitter account). On the other hand, many ISSPs will oppose the inclusion of such a term as they will wish to inform their customers and give them an opportunity to object to the order being made. Such a provision may not be enforceable in the US (see para 3.45).

3.40   The applicant should consider the means by which service will be effected on the anonymous publisher/intended defendant, assuming that their identity is revealed. The information provided by the online platform is likely to be an email address or a telephone number. It may therefore be necessary to seek permission to serve by a range of electronic means, such as by email to any email address or by text or multimedia message to any phone number, or even by private Twitter or Facebook message (see para 9.83).

Costs

3.41   In a normal case, the applicant for a *Norwich Pharmacal* order should be ordered to pay the costs of the respondent. These will include the costs of making the disclosure. Although there may be cases where the circumstances require a different order these do not include cases where:

> "(a) the party required to make the disclosure had a genuine doubt that the person seeking the disclosure was entitled to it; (b) the party was under an appropriate legal obligation not to reveal the information, or where the legal position was not clear, or the party had a reasonable doubt as to the obligations; or (c) the party could be subject to proceedings if disclosure was voluntary; or (d) the party would or might suffer damage by voluntarily giving the disclosure; or (e) the disclosure would or might infringe a legitimate interest of another".[30]

Enforcing *Norwich Pharmacal* orders in the United States

3.42   As already mentioned, US-based ISSPs have in general cooperated with English court orders and have responded to them without requiring US enforcement proceedings. However, in recent years, the position has changed with some ISSPs requiring the applicant to obtain a US court order before they will comply with a *Norwich Pharmacal* order. In those circumstances an applicant could, potentially, bring committal proceedings (see para 3.38) but may wish to use the relevant US procedures.

---

[30] *Totalise Plc v Motley Fool Ltd & Anor* [2002] 1 WLR 1233 at [30].

3.43   By 28 U.S. Code §1782 it is provided that

"The district court of the district in which a person resides or is found may order him to give his testimony or statement or to produce a document or other thing for use in a proceeding in a foreign or international tribunal, including criminal investigations conducted before formal accusation".

An application under this provision may be made by any interested person.

3.44   The Court has a discretion as to whether to make such an order. The US Supreme Court has identified the following factors to consider in exercising such discretion:

(1)   whether the person from whom discovery is sought is a participant in the foreign proceeding; if he is, the need for a §1782 order is not readily apparent;

(2)   the nature of the foreign tribunal and its proceedings and its receptivity to U.S. federal court assistance;

(3)   whether the request for assistance under §1782 conceals an attempt to circumvent foreign discovery restrictions; and

(4)   whether the request is unduly intrusive or burdensome.[31]

3.45   §1782 is limited by the cable privacy provision of the Communications Act, 47 US Code § 551(c). S 551(c) provides, in relevant part, that a cable operator cannot disclose personal identifying information regarding a subscriber unless the subscriber consents or the cable operator acts pursuant to a court order with notice to the subscriber. If an application under §1782 is made in relation to a "cable operator" it must to provide formal notice of the subpoena within 7 days to the user whose identity was sought and the court gave the user 21 days after receiving notice to file any objection to the subpoena. For example, an order under §1782 was made in the case of *Comcast Cable v Hourani*[32] but, after notice was given to the subscriber, there was a further hearing and the order was set aside.[33]

---

[31] *Intel Corp v Advanced Micro Devices, Inc.* 542 US 241, 260 (2004). Id. at 264–65.

[32] US District Court for District of Columbia, 23 February 2016.

[33] US District Court for District of Columbia, 23 May 2016 (this was on the basis of an error in the English order), see Letters Blogatory, Case of the Day: Comcast v. Hourani, 1 June 2016.

"Unmasking Orders" against anonymous publishers

3.46   The High Court has a general jurisdiction under the Senior Courts Act 1981, s 37(1) to grant injunctive relief "in all cases in which it appears to be just and convenient to do so". This jurisdiction has been held to be a very wide one and is not limited to legal wrongdoers.[34] This provides a useful tool for those seeking to identify anonymous publishers online and can be used in conjunction with an application for a *Norwich Pharmacal* order against an online intermediary to require the anonymous wrongdoer to identify or "unmask" themselves.

3.47   The information sought from online platforms may not in fact provide a real name or a means of establishing where or who the anonymous publisher is for the purposes of issuing proceedings. In many cases, anonymous publishers will provide fake names when setting up their accounts. However, it is more likely that there will be a genuine means of communicating with the wrongdoer, for example an email address or telephone number. It provides a possible means of identifying the defendant in the event that, for example, a social media platform is unable to ascertain the true identities of the wrongdoers from the information provided to them via their accounts. It is a mandatory injunction, requiring the wrongdoers to reveal their true identity to the claimant.[35]

LEGAL RESPONSIBILITY FOR ONLINE MATERIAL

Introduction

3.48   The question of who bears legal responsibility for online content has given rise to considerable discussion in the case law and has also been addressed in legislation. Particular attention has been directed to the position of such internet intermediaries as hosts, website operators, ISPs and search engines.

3.49   This focuses on the principles by which the law attaches responsibility for online material to particular parties in claims in defamation, breach of confidence, misuse of private information, harassment and breach of the Data Protection Act 1998. It does not address the elements of those causes of action (which is discussed in Chapters 5 and 6) or the defences available under the E-Commerce Directive (see Chapter 7).

---

[34] *Cartier International AG & Ors v British Sky Broadcasting Ltd & Ors* [2017] 1 All ER 700.

[35] Such orders will most likely need to be served by alternative means (see para 9.82–9.83).

Defamation

Introduction

3.50   Liability for defamatory material extends to any person who participates in or authorises its publication.[36] This will, of course, include persons such as authors and editors but may also apply to those who, although not having originated the content, were involved in disseminating it.

3.51   In a traditional claim brought against the "author" of a defamatory statement and/or the person who has published it, the question of responsibility for publication will usually be uncontentious. Where such material is published on the internet, however, it may not be viable or practical to sue the person who posted the content because s/he is not identifiable[37] or may be thought to lack the funds to meet any order for damages and costs. Consideration may therefore need to be given to the issue of proceedings against other parties involved in the online publication. While it is well-established that publication of such material takes place when it is accessed by the user, the question of whether parties engaged in the intermediate process of facilitating such access should be held responsible in law is a more nuanced one.

3.52   This issue breaks down into two questions:

- Is the potential defendant a publisher at common law? and
- Is so, can the potential defendant defeat the claim by relying on one or more of the defences applicable to certain types of publisher who take a subordinate role in the process of publication?

These questions are discussed in turn below.

Is the potential defendant a publisher at common law?

Introduction

3.53   The "author" of an online publication will be liable for it as will the "editor" or "publisher" of a website – that is, a person who responsible for commissioning and editing the content and the person responsible for maintaining the site. These are equivalent to the "author", "editor" and "publisher" of a newspaper or magazine. No special issues arise in relation to their liability for such publication.

---

[36] *Watts v Times Newspapers Ltd* [1997] QB 650, 670.

[37] See above para 3.7ff for steps that may be taken in order to identify those responsible for posting material online.

3.54   The difficult issues arise when it is suggested that other kinds of "participants" in online publication are liable for the publication of defamatory content. There are, three relevant types of participants:

(1)   hosts of platforms on which users post material,

(2)   other internet service providers, and

(3)   search engines.

Since, as the case law has developed, distinct approaches have been taken to each of these types of internet intermediary, that classification is adopted in the discussion below.

Platform hosts

3.55   The leading English case on the principles applicable to determining whether a host of an internet platform is responsible for publication is the decision of the Court of Appeal in *Tamiz v Google Inc*.[38] This concerned a claim relating to blog comments posted on the Blogger platform operated by Google Inc (which is incorporated under the laws of Delaware and based in California). Following the grant of permission to serve the claim form out of the jurisdiction, Google Inc applied to it set aside service on the basis that (among other things) it was not a publisher of the material at common law. At first instance Eady J held that Google Inc was not a publisher, either before or after it had been notified by the claimant of the comments (although the claim itself was based only on the period after notification).

3.56   The Court of Appeal agreed that Google Inc was not a publisher during the pre-notification period, applying the

> "long established line of authority that a person involved only in dissemination is not to be treated as a publisher unless he knew or ought by the exercise of reasonable care to have known that the publication was likely to be defamatory" [26].

Since Google Inc had neither this actual nor constructive knowledge before notification it was not a publisher at this stage.

3.57   This analysis (albeit *obiter*) appears to depart from the approach taken in the earlier case of *Godfrey v Demon Internet Ltd*,[39] in which Morland J held that the defendant ISP was a publisher at common law of any material posted on to its Usenet news server that was transmitted to another user (whether or not the ISP had been notified of the material).

---

[38] [2013] 1 WLR 2151.

[39] [2001] QB 201.

Similarly, in *Oriental Press Group v Fevaworks Solutions*[40] the Hong Kong Court of Final Appeal departed from this aspect of *Tamiz*, holding that a website host that had not been notified of the defamatory statement was responsible for publication, although able to rely on a defence of innocent dissemination (see para 3.67).

3.58   As to the position after notification, the Court of Appeal in *Tamiz* drew on the authority of *Byrne v Deane*[41] in which the proprietors of a golf club were held to be publishers of an allegedly defamatory verse affixed to the wall of their club on the basis that, although they had not posted it themselves, they were aware of its presence and were able to, but did not, remove it. Applying that reasoning Richards LJ considered that it could arguably be inferred that, after notification of the presence of the material on the blog, Google Inc had made itself responsible for the continued publication by refraining from removing it. In support of this inference the court placed particular weight on the facts that Google Inc made Blogger available on terms of its own choice and was able readily to remove or block access to any content that did not comply with those terms.[42] The inference of responsibility did not arguably arise until Google Inc had had a "reasonable time within which to act to remove the defamatory comments".[43] On the facts, Eady J had held that a period of about five weeks between notification and removal of the material had been sufficient, a conclusion upheld in the Court of Appeal.

3.59   As was made clear in the judgment, *Tamiz* goes no further than to decide the circumstances in which it was arguable that Google Inc was a publisher after notification of particular material. Whether an inference should in fact be drawn that a particular host has made itself responsible for material on its platform will ultimately turn on the circumstances of the case, including the manner in which the host operates the platform. Nonetheless the reasoning in *Tamiz* provides generally applicable guidance as to the circumstances in which a host qualifies as a publisher in English law, and to the factual considerations relevant to determining this question.[44]

---

[40] [2013] HKFCA 47.

[41] [1937] 1 KB 818.

[42] *Tamiz*, at [33]–[34].

[43] *Tamiz*, at [35].

[44] See also, to similar effect, *Davison v Habeeb & Ors* [2012] 3 CMLR 6 at [28]–[48].

ISPs

3.60 The issue of whether an ISP is legally responsible for publishing online material that it does not host was considered in *Bunt v Tilley & Ors.*[45] This was an application by three ISPs for orders striking out, or for summary judgment in, a claim brought in defamation based on words allegedly transmitted by means of the services provided by the ISPs. Eady J held that:

> "to impose legal responsibility upon anyone under the common law for the publication of words it is essential to demonstrate a degree of awareness or at least an assumption of general responsibility, such as has long been recognised in the context of editorial responsibility".[46]

In other words, in order to establish liability "there must be knowing involvement in the process of publication of *the relevant words*": it is insufficient "that a person merely plays a passive instrumental role in the process".[47]

3.61 Having observed that there was no basis for considering that any of the ISPs had been asked to remove the material complained of prior to the service of proceedings, Eady J held that there was no realistic prospect of the claimant establishing that the ISPs had knowingly participated in the relevant publications and therefore qualified as publishers.[48] He went on to express the broader view that

> "as a matter of law… an ISP which performs no more than a passive role in facilitating postings on the Internet cannot be deemed to be a publisher at common law".[49]

Eady J's approach was endorsed by the Court of Appeal in *Tamiz*, although the Court took the view that Google Inc's role in respect of Blogger blogs was not purely a passive one.[50]

Search engines

3.62 The position of search engines was considered in *Metropolitan International Schools Ltd v Designtechnica Corp & Ors.*[51] In that case a provider of adult distance

---

[45] [2007] 1 WLR 1243.

[46] Ibid, at [22].

[47] Ibid, at [23] (emphasis in the original).

[48] Ibid, at [25]–[36].

[49] Ibid, at [36].

[50] *Tamiz*, at [23].

[51] [2011] 1 WLR 1743.

learning courses brought proceedings against the host of an online bulletin board for allegedly defamatory comments posted on the bulletin board. Google UK Ltd and Google Inc were also sued on the basis that they had published search results that contained allegedly defamatory "snippets" taken from those comments. Google Inc applied to set aside service of the claim form out of the jurisdiction on the ground that, among other things, it was not a publisher of the material complained of (Google UK's case was that it did not operate the Google search engine at all, a proposition accepted by Eady J[52]).

3.63   Eady J noted that the Google search engine displays search results (including snippets taken from the webpages) by the use of webpage indices and rankings all of which have been automatically generated.[53] He considered that the absence of human agency in this process precluded any knowing involvement by Google Inc in the publication of snippets on its webpages. Therefore, following the principles applied in *Bunt* (see para 3.60–3.61), Google Inc could not be considered a publisher at common law of such material, at least prior to its having been notified of the defamatory content.[54]

3.64   As to the position after notification, Eady J accepted the general proposition (subsequently applied in *Tamiz*)[55] that an internet intermediary can become liable for publication of defamatory material on a webpage that it hosts by acquiescing in its continued publication after having been informed of its presence.[56] However the judge observed that a search engine was "a different kind of internet intermediary".[57] In particular, although Google operated a "takedown" policy for specific URLs (that had in the instant case been used to block URLs complained of by claimant), the automated processes by which its search results were generated meant that it could not generally prevent defamatory material from appearing in snippets, or at least not without blocking a huge amount of other material which, though containing some of the words in the offending snippet, would in themselves be unobjectionable. For those reasons, Google Inc could not, while it was taking steps to block URLs that the claimant had made complaint of, properly be fixed with

---

[52] Ibid, at [6], [8] and [28].

[53] Ibid, at [10]–[13].

[54] Ibid at [48]–[53].

[55] See para 3.61.

[56] *Metropolitan International Schools*, at [54].

[57] Ibid, at [55].

responsibility for publication after notification on the basis of authorisation, approval or acquiescence.[58]

3.65   The reasoning in *Metropolitan International Schools* has met with a mixed reception in other common law jurisdictions, having been endorsed by the Supreme Court of New South Wales[59] and Supreme Court of British Columbia[60] but not followed by the Hong Kong Court of First Instance,[61] High Court of New Zealand[62] and Supreme Court of Appeal of Victoria.[63] Nonetheless it remains good law in England: it was approved by Sharp J (as she then was) in *Budu v BBC*[64] and implicitly endorsed by the Court of Appeal in *Tamiz*.[65]

Defences for secondary publishers

Introduction

3.66   Various defences applicable to persons who are involved in the publication of defamatory material as secondary or subordinate publishers may be relevant to proceedings brought in respect of internet material. Three such defences are discussed below: the common law defence and the statutory defences under the Defamation Act 1996, s 1 and 5 of the Defamation Act 2013, s 5. The related defence provided for by the E-Commerce Directive is considered in Chapter 7.

Common law defence

3.67   At common law a person who is not the author, editor or printer of defamatory material but has otherwise published the material may avoid liability on the basis that s/he was an innocent disseminator. In order to rely on the defence such a publisher must establish that s/he did not know that the publication contained defamatory matter and had no reason to believe

---

[58] *Metropolitan International Schools*, at [56]–[64].

[59] *Bleyer v Google Inc* [2014] NSWSC 897.

[60] *Niemela v Google Inc*, 2015 BCSC 1024.

[61] *Yeung v Google Inc* [2014] HKCFI 1404.

[62] *A v Google New Zealand Ltd* [2012] NZHC 2352.

[63] *Google v Trkulja* [2016] VSCA 333.

[64] [2010] EWHC 616 (QB) at [74]–[76].

[65] *Tamiz*, at [23].

that it was likely to contain defamatory matter.[66] This defence has largely been superseded by the statutory protection afforded by s 1 of the 1996 Act (discussed below). In *Metropolitan International Schools*, Eady J suggested that, although the common law defence had not been abolished by s 1, there was no significant difference between the two.[67]

Defamation Act 1996, s 1

3.68   By s 1(1) of the 1996 Act a person has a defence to a defamation claim if s/he shows that:

"(a) he was not the author, editor or publisher of the statement complained of,

(b) he took reasonable care in relation to its publication, and

(c) he did not know, and had no reason to believe that what he did caused or contributed to the publication of a defamatory statement".

3.69   For these purposes "author" means the originator of the statement, but does not include a person who did not intend that his statement be published at all; "editor" means a person having editorial or equivalent responsibility for the content of the statement or the decision to publish it; and "publisher" means a commercial publisher, that is, a person whose business is issuing material to the public, or a section of the public, and who issues material containing the statement in the course of that business.[68] Several types of publisher are defined as falling outside the definition of "author, editor or publisher" for the purposes of s 1(1)(a), including (of relevance for present purposes) persons who are involved only (a) in operating or providing any equipment, system or service by means of which the statement is retrieved, copied, distributed or made available in electronic form; or (b) as the operator of or provider of access to a communications system by means of which the statement is transmitted, or made available, by a person over whom he has no effective control.[69]

3.70   The issue of whether an internet intermediary falls within s 1(1)(a) of the 1996 Act will depend on the function played by the intermediary in the process of

---

[66] *Sun Life Assurance Co of Canada v WH Smith & Son Ltd* (1934) 150 LT 211, 212. See also *Emmens v Pottle* (1885) 16 QBD 354; *Vizetelly v Mudie's Select Library Ltd* [1900] 2 QB 170; *Goldsmith v Sperrings Ltd & Ors* [1977] 1 WLR 478.

[67] *Metropolitan International Schools*, at [70].

[68] S 1(2) of the 1996 Act.

[69] S 1(3) of the 1996 Act.

dissemination. In *McGrath & Anor v Dawkins & Ors*[70] it was held that Amazon was not an editor or publisher (within the meaning of s 1(1)(a)) of material posted on its website, and could therefore in principle rely on the statutory defence. Amazon took no steps in relation to the content of the statements posted on its website and its primary business was than of an online bookseller rather than commercial publisher.[71]

3.71 Similarly in *Tamiz* the Court of Appeal held that Google Inc, in hosting the Blogger platform, was not a publisher under s 1(1)(a) since it did not, in that capacity, "issue" the defamatory statements to the public.[72] By contrast in an *obiter* passage in *Metropolitan International Schools*, Eady J considered that if Google Inc (in its capacity as operator of the Google search engine) were a publisher at common law of snippets displayed on its search engine it would be difficult to see how it could escape a finding that it was also a publisher under s 1(1)(a), and on that basis the defence under s 1 would not have been available.[73]

3.72 In determining, for the purposes of s 1(1)(b) and (c) of the 1996 Act, whether a person who falls within s 1(1)(a) took reasonable care, and/or had reason to believe that what s/he did caused or contributed to the publication of a defamatory statement, regard shall be had to:

(a) the extent of his/her responsibility for the content of the statement or the decision to publish it,

(b) the nature or circumstances of the publication, and

(c) the previous conduct or character of the author, editor or publisher.[74]

3.73 Where an internet intermediary disseminates information by the use of purely automated processes it may be difficult for a defendant to satisfy the reasonable care criterion, although in an individual case there may be counter-arguments that such processes are sufficient, particularly in relation to large websites.[75] In *Tamiz*, the forwarding by Google Inc of the claimant's complaint to the blogger who had posted allegedly defamatory material on Google Inc's Blogger platform was sufficient to satisfy s 1(1)(b), albeit that

---

[70] [2012] Info TLR 72.

[71] Ibid at [40]–[41].

[72] *Tamiz*, at [40].

[73] *Metropolitan International Schools*, at [80].

[74] S 1(5) of the 1996 Act.

[75] *Metropolitan International Schools*, at [75]; *McGrath*, at [44].

the Court of Appeal recognised that such a conclusion "may have been a generous view".[76]

3.74 As to the condition in s 1(1)(c), in *Tamiz* the Court of Appeal held that, following notification of the complaint, Google Inc could not establish, on a summary basis, that it did not know, and had no reason to believe that what it did caused or contributed to the publication of a defamatory statement.[77] By contrast in *Bunt* the s 1(1)(c) test was met in circumstances where the ISPs had not received proper notification of the claimant's complaint.[78]

Defamation Act 2013, s 5

3.75 S 5 of the 2013 Act confers a defence on the operator of a website in respect of a statement posted on the website by a person other than the operator.[79] In such cases the claim will fail unless the claimant shows that:

(a) it was not possible for the claimant to identify the person who posted the statement,

(b) the claimant gave the operator a notice of complaint in relation to the statement,

(c) the operator failed to respond to the notice of complaint in accordance with any provision contained in regulations or

(d) the operator of the website has acted with malice in relation to the posting of the statement.[80]

For these purposes it is possible for a claimant to "identify" a person only if the claimant has sufficient information to bring proceedings against the person.[81] The defence under this s is not defeated by reason only of the fact that the website operator moderates the statements posted on it by others.[82]

3.76 Certain of the information that must be contained in a notice of complaint is set out at s 5(6) of the 2013 Act.[83] A detailed regime governing further aspects of the notice that must be given, and the action that must be taken by the

---

[76] *Tamiz*, at [43].

[77] *Tamiz*, at [44]–[46].

[78] *Bunt*, at [66]–[67].

[79] s 5(1) and (2) of the 2013 Act,.

[80] s 5(3) and (11) of the 2013 Act.

[81] s 5(4) of the 2013 Act.

[82] s 5(12) of the 2013 Act.

[83] s 5(6) of the 2013 Act.

website operator, for the purposes of s 5 of the 2013 Act, has been prescribed by the Defamation (Operators of Websites) Regulations 2013.

3.77 In summary, on receipt of a valid notice, the website operator must notify the poster of the complaint unless the operator has no means of contacting the poster, in which case it must remove the statement complained of from the relevant locations of the website (a course of action that must also be taken if the poster, having been notified, does not respond). If the poster does respond and wishes the statement to be removed, then the operator must remove it. If, on the other hand, the poster does not wish it to be removed, the poster must provide his/her name and address to the operator, which must inform the complainant that the statement has remained online and provide him/her with the poster's name and address (if the poster is willing for that information to be supplied). This regime is more demanding for a claimant than the requirements of the E-Commerce Directive (this is dealt with in Chapter 7).

Defamation Act 2013, s 10

3.78 By s 10 of the 2013 Act the court lacks jurisdiction to hear and determine an action for defamation brought against a person who was not the "author, editor or publisher" (as those terms are defined in s 1 of the 1996 Act) (see para 3.69) of the statement complained of, unless the court is satisfied that it is not reasonably practicable for an action to be brought against the author, editor or publisher. In *Brett Wilson v Persons Unknown*[84] it was held that, based on the description of the defendants in the Particulars of Claim, they could not be classified as "publishers" for the purpose of s 10, but were "editors" under that provision, and there was therefore jurisdiction to hear the claim.[85] The circumstances in which it is not reasonably practicable for an action to be brought against an author, editor or publisher have not yet been the subject of judicial decision.

Misuse of private information

3.79 Given the speed and ease with which information can be disseminated via the internet, it is unsurprising that there are numerous examples of claims in misuse of private information brought against the authors or editors of online material. However the English courts have not yet considered the principles by which responsibility for publication of internet material is to be determined in the context of a claim for misuse of private information brought against an

[84] [2016] 4 WLR 69.
[85] Ibid, at [22]–[23].

internet intermediary. In general, however, the court's approach to the question of responsibility for publication in a claim for misuse of private information is similar that adopted in defamation proceedings.[86] The considerations set out above relating to the position of internet intermediaries in defamation proceedings are therefore also likely to apply by analogy to this cause of action.

3.80   In a series of claims in misuse of private information brought against Facebook Ireland Ltd in Northern Ireland, the court appears to have proceeded on the basis that Facebook's responsibility for posts added by its users is to be determined by reference to principles developed in defamation claims, and in particular that such responsibility has arisen following Facebook's receipt of notification of the material complained of.[87] While this issue has arisen mainly in the context of the reliance by Facebook on the defence under the E-Commerce Directive (see Chapter 7), the court has also held that the defamation case law is relevant to the prior question of responsibility for publication.[88]

Harassment

3.81   It is a precondition of liability under the Protection from Harassment Act 1997, s 1(1) that a person has pursued a harassing course of conduct that he knows or ought to know amounts to harassment of the other (see para 5.84ff). A person who establishes a website for the purpose of harassing particular individuals or a particular class of individuals by disseminating material authored by others may meet this test.[89]

3.82   Whether legal responsibility for publication under the 1997 Act will be attributed to an entity which, lacking such a purpose, merely hosts material posted by others is likely to turn on that entity's knowledge about the material in issue. In the Northern Ireland case of *J20 v Facebook Ireland Ltd*, Colton J, having held that the posts in issue were insufficiently oppressive to be actionable in harassment, concluded that Facebook avoided liability on the additional ground that there was no basis for considering that, once notified of the complaint, it ought to have known that refusing to remove the posts

---

[86] *Douglas & Ors v Hello! Ltd & Ors (No 2)* [2003] EMLR 28, at [36].

[87] *XY v Facebook Ireland Ltd* [2012] NIQB 96, at [16]; *CG v Facebook Ireland Ltd* [2015] NIQB 11 (reversed in part in *CG v Facebook Ireland Ltd* [2016] NICA 54); *J20 v Facebook Ireland Ltd* [2016] NIQB 98.

[88] *J20*, at [48].

[89] *Law Society v Kordowski* [2014] EMLR 2.

amounted to harassment.[90] While the two conclusions reached by Colton J plainly overlap, they nonetheless indicate that the issue of notification will be central to claims against website hosts in harassment, as in defamation and misuse of private information.

Data Protection Act 1998

Introduction

3.83   Remedies for breach of the Data Protection Act 1998 in respect of personal data[91] are available against the data controller of those data. Whether a person is a suitable defendant to a claim under the 1998 Act therefore depends on whether s/he meets the definition of a data controller. If so a further question may arise as to whether the data controller falls within the territorial scope of the 1998 Act. Those two issues are discussed in turn below. This requires consideration of the terms of, and case law under, both the 1998 Act and Directive 95/46/EC ("the Data Protection Directive") to which the 1998 Act gives effect.

Who is a data controller?

3.84   A data controller is a person who (either alone or jointly or in common with other persons) determines the purposes for which and the manner in which any personal data are, or are to be, processed.[92] This is subject to the exception that where personal data are processed only for purposes for which they are required by any enactment to be processed, the person on whom the obligation to process the data is imposed by that enactment is, for the purposes of the 1998 Act, the data controller.[93]

3.85   A person who determines the purposes for which data is processed as the agent for a data controller is not him/herself a data controller in respect of

---

[90] *J20*, at [17]. In that passage Colton J noted that the Protection from Harassment (Northern Ireland) Order 1997, the legislation that provides for the tort of harassment in that jurisdiction, does not have a similar provision to s 7(3A) of the 1997 Act in England and Wales which extends "conduct" to aiding, abetting, counselling or procuring another's conduct.

[91] For the definition of "personal data", see para 6.39–6.40.

[92] S 1(1) of the 1998 Act. See also art 2(d) of the Data Protection Directive: "'controller' shall mean the natural or legal person, public authority, agency or any other body that alone or jointly with others determines the purposes and means of the processing of personal data; where the purposes and means of processing are determined by national or Community laws or regulations, the controller or the specific criteria for his nomination may be designated by national or Community law."

[93] S 1(4) of the 1998 Act.

those data. Therefore where decisions about data are taken by an individual, s/he will not be a data controller if the decisions are made as an agent of a company of which s/he is a director. On the other hand, if a person makes decisions about personal data on his/her own behalf s/he will be a data controller as regards those data.[94]

3.86   In *Google Spain SL & Anor v Agencia Espanola de Proteccion de Datos & Anor* ("*Google Spain*"),[95] the Court of Justice of the European Union ("CJEU") held that the operator of a search engine determines the purpose and means of the activity conducted by the engine in respect of personal data processed by it and is therefore a data controller of that data. Informing this conclusion was the court's view that a broad meaning should be given to the term "controller" and its observation that the activities of search engines play a decisive role in the accessibility to users of data held on the internet.[96]

Does the data controller fall within the territorial scope of the 1998 Act?

3.87   The obligations imposed by the 1998 Act apply to a data controller in respect of any data only if (a) the data controller is established in the UK and the data are processed in the context of that establishment, or (b) the data controller is established neither in the UK nor in any other European Economic Area State but uses equipment in the UK for processing the data otherwise than for the purposes of transit through the UK.[97] Various forms of association with the UK are specified as amounting to establishment in the UK for these purposes.[98]

3.88   The meaning of "establishment" in the context of the Data Protection Directive was also considered in *Google Spain*. By art 4(a) of the Directive, a Member State's national data protection measures apply to processing by a data controller where (among other things) "the processing of personal data is carried out in the context of the activities of an establishment of the controller on the territory of a member state". The CJEU held that this test was satisfied in respect of processing by a search engine where the operator of the search engine, Google Inc (although not itself based in the Member State) had set up a subsidiary, Google Spain SL, which was intended to

---

[94] *Ittihadieh v 5-11 Cheyne Gardens RTM Company Ltd & Ors* [2017] EWCA Civ 121, at [70]–[71].

[95] [2014] QB 1022.

[96] Ibid, at [32]–[41].

[97] s 5(1) of the 1998 Act. This provision gives effect to art 4 of the Data Protection Directive which governs the territorial scope of the Directive.

[98] s 5(3) of the 1998 Act.

promote and sell advertising space offered by the search engine and that orientated its activity towards that Member State.[99] As with the court's interpretation of the term data controller, this was based on a broad approach to the application of the Data Protection Directive which turned on the contribution made by Google Inc's processing operations to the profitability of Google Spain's commercial activities.

3.89   The territorial application of the Directive and the 1998 Act have been the subject of further discussion in *Weltimmo v Nemzeti Adatvedelmi ("Weltimmo")*[100] and *CG v Facebook Ireland Ltd*.[101] In *Weltimmo* the issue was whether a data controller registered in Slovakia, which operated a website dealing with Hungarian properties, was established in Hungary. The CJEU answered the question in the affirmative on the basis that the website operator pursued a real and effective activity, which was exercised through various stable arrangements (such as a representative, a bank account and a management address) in Hungary, through its website.[102] The same conclusion was reached in *CG*, in which Facebook Ireland was held to fall within s 5 of the 1998 Act since Facebook (UK) Ltd was established in the UK and Facebook Ireland Ltd processed data in the context of that establishment.[103]

3.90   The consequence of this case law is that an internet intermediary based outside the UK will normally fall within the scope of the 1998 Act where a subsidiary, located within the UK, undertakes commercial activities in that jurisdiction, the profitability of which are supported by the processing operations of the intermediary. This is a significantly broader test than one based solely on territorial presence of the data processing entity.

[99] *Google Spain*, at [42]–[60].

[100] [2016] 1 WLR 863.

[101] [2017] 2 CMLR 29.

[102] *Weltimmo*, at [24]–[41].

[103] *CG*, at [76]–[91].

CHAPTER 4: JURISDICTION AND CHOICE OF LAW

CHAPTER SYNOPSIS

- Examines issues around jurisdiction (in this Chapter, meaning whether domestic courts can hear a dispute which has a connection with another country, or countries) and choice of law.
- Explains the law and procedure relating to questions of jurisdiction in England and Wales and under the Recast Brussels Regulation. It also deals with the jurisdiction of data protection regulators in light of recent CJEU case law.
- Where a domestic court has jurisdiction, it does not necessarily follow that domestic law applies to the claim. Looks at common law, statutory and EU law rules around the choice of law, including in the special case of data protection. Outlines the role of domestic rules in such claims – and the substance/procedure distinction.

JURISDICTION: INTRODUCTION

4.1   Issues about jurisdiction (meaning, for the purposes of this Chapter, whether English courts can hear a dispute which has a connection with another country, or countries) arise frequently in the context of claims about online publication. Statements published online are, as a general rule, available worldwide as soon as they are uploaded. When can claimants with reputations or other interests in England and Wales sue here for damage done to those interests as a result of an internet publication?

4.2   The first part of this Chapter explains the law and procedure relating to questions of jurisdiction in England and Wales. It also deals with the jurisdiction of data protection regulators in light of recent case law of the Court of Justice of the European Union ("CJEU") on that subject.

4.3   The jurisdiction of English courts over "civil and commercial matters" is governed by the Recast Brussels Regulation ("the Regulation").[1] However, where a defendant is not domiciled in an EU Member State, jurisdiction in England and Wales will be determined by applying a set of domestic rules which are now codified in the Civil Procedure Rules 1998 ("CPR"). We will begin by considering those rules before turning to the Regulation itself.

---

[1] Regulation (EU) No 1215/2012 (12 December 2012). The Regulation replaces the earlier Brussels I Regulation (EC) No 44/2001 with effect from 10 January 2015: see art 8.

4.4   The UK may well agree to continue to be bound by the General Data Protection Regulation ("GDPR), or by an arrangement very similar to it, notwithstanding the "Brexit" vote in the recent referendum on UK membership of the EU. This part of the EU regulatory regime is generally considered a success and there is little political pressure on government to break from it.

JURISDICTION: DOMESTIC LAW

Introduction

4.5   In domestic law, the basis for jurisdiction is service of the claim form: if a claim form has been properly served, the court has jurisdiction. In broad terms, if a defendant is present in the jurisdiction, the claim form can be served on the defendant and the court will have jurisdiction, though it may subsequently stay proceedings on *forum non conveniens* grounds.

4.6   If the defendant is out of the jurisdiction, a claimant must apply for permission to serve the claim form out of the jurisdiction, which is only granted if a number of criteria are satisfied and may subsequently be set aside. Both of these situations will be explored in turn.

Service within the jurisdiction

Introduction

4.7   The basic domestic rule of jurisdiction is that defendants can be served within the jurisdiction if they are present within the jurisdiction; or if they otherwise submit to its jurisdiction.

Presence

4.8   For individuals, "presence" has a literal meaning. Defendants who are present in the jurisdiction can be served with proceedings, even if their visit is fleeting and has nothing to do with the subject of the litigation.[2] There is probably an exception where a defendant is fraudulently "lured" to the jurisdiction and is then served.

4.9   Corporate defendants who are registered or incorporated in England or Wales are certainly "present" for jurisdictional purposes. Other corporate defendants will be present if they have a "fixed place of business" in the jurisdiction. The activity of the business must be carried on at that place for a

---

[2] *Maharanee Seethadevi Gaekwar of Baroda v Wildenstein* [1972] 2 QB 283.

certain amount of time before it will be deemed "fixed", but this threshold has been satisfied, for example, by the presence of a stand at a temporary trade fair.[3]

4.10 In certain circumstances the place of business of a representative or agent of the company that carries on the company's business can constitute the company's *own* place of business for jurisdictional purposes, even if the agent also works for other businesses.[4]

Submission

4.11 Defendants may preclude themselves from objecting to the court's jurisdiction by their conduct prior to or after the service of the claim form. Submission can take many forms, incorporating any conduct which evinces an intention not to pursue a jurisdictional objection.

4.12 Defendants may contest the jurisdiction of the court without being taken to have submitted by making an application in accordance with CPR 11. The defendant should first file an acknowledgment of service and then make an application disputing jurisdiction. This application must be made within 14 days of filing the acknowledgment of service and be supported by evidence (CPR 11(4)). If a defendant files an acknowledgement of service but does not then apply for an order under CPR 11, s/he will be taken to have submitted (CPR 11(5)).

Methods of service

4.13 CPR 6.3–6.52 sets out the methods by which the claim form may be served. These rules take effect subject to the authorities on presence or submission being pre-requisites to jurisdiction (and indeed many of the permitted methods only make sense for defendants who are present or have submitted).

4.14 The effect of CPR 6.3(2) is that companies may be served by any method permitted under the CPR or under the Companies Act 2006.[5] Specific provision is made for methods of service on partnerships in CPR 6.3(3), 6.5(3)(c) and 6.9(2).

---

[3] *Dunlop Pneumatic Tyre Co Ltd v Actien-Gesellschaft für Motor und Motorfahrzeugbau Vorm Cudell & Co* [1902] 1 KB 342.

[4] See *Adams v Cape Industries Plc* [1990] Ch 433.

[5] See especially, the Companies Act 2006, s 1139(2).

Forum non conveniens

4.15   Even where a defendant is present within the jurisdiction and is served with process, it can, in limited circumstances, apply to the court for a stay on *forum non conveniens* grounds. This can be done when the defendant is "present" in the jurisdiction but not "domiciled" for the purposes of the Regulation (see para 4.64). The applicable principles are the same as those which govern the question of *forum conveniens* where permission to serve out of jurisdiction is sought. Those principles are discussed below.

Service out of the jurisdiction

Introduction

4.16   Permission is required to serve the claim form abroad. A claimant has six months from the date of issue of the claim form to serve it out of the jurisdiction, which allows ample time to make the application for permission. The application will typically be dealt with on the papers without notice to the other side. It needs to be supported with evidence and the applicant is under a strict duty to make full and fair disclosure of all relevant facts, but it is relatively common for permission to be granted at this stage. It is then open for the defendant to apply to set aside permission and at that stage, the tests for permission to serve out will be much more closely scrutinised.

4.17   To obtain permission to serve out the claimant must satisfy the court that:

(1)   there is a serious issue to be tried on the merits;

(2)   the claim falls within one of the "gateways" to jurisdiction in CPR PD 6B, para 3.1; and

(3)   England is the proper place to bring the claim.

Each of these requirements will be discussed in turn. Even if all of these conditions are satisfied, the court still at least technically has a discretion about whether or not to grant permission.[6]

Serious issue to be tried

4.18   This merits test has been equated with the general test for summary judgment, namely whether a claim has a real and not fanciful prospect of success.[7] CPR 6.37(1)(b) refers to a "reasonable prospect of success". Where the claim is

---

[6] *Vidal-Hall & Ors v Google Inc* [2016] QB 1003 at [7].

[7] *AK Investment CJSC v Kyrgyz Mobil Tel Ltd* [2012] 1 WLR 1804 at [71].

governed by a foreign law the test will have to be satisfied by reference to that law.

4.19   In internet cases applications to set aside service have often been made on the basis that there is no real prospect of showing that a defendant internet service provider or search engine operator was a "publisher" for the purposes of a defamation claim.[8]

The CPR PD 6B gateways

4.20   The claimant must show a "good arguable case" that their claim falls within one of the gateways, which has been equated with showing they have "*much the better of the argument*".[9] However, pure legal questions about whether a claim (involving undisputed facts) falls within one of the gateways must be decided on the merits.[10]

4.21   There are more than twenty gateways in CPR PD 6B, para 3.1. What follows is a consideration of those which are most commonly relied on in claims based on internet publications.

4.22   Para 3.1(2): "*A claim is made for an injunction ordering the defendant to do or refrain from doing an act within the jurisdiction*": The injunction need not be the only relief sought; but it should be a substantial[11] and genuine[12] part of the ultimate relief sought and should have a reasonable prospect of being granted. This gateway only applies to claims for injunctions *which are only to have effect in this jurisdiction*.[13]

4.23   Para 3.1(3): "*Necessary and proper party*": This "piggybacking" gateway allows a second defendant ("D2") to be sued if (i) the claimant has or is also going to serve another defendant ("D1") (with a proper jurisdictional basis) (ii) there is a real issue to be tried between the claimant and D1 and (iii) D2 is a necessary or proper party to that claim. The basis on which the court has jurisdiction over D1 is immaterial. As to point (iii), the court will ask whether D1 and D2 would have been proper parties if both had been domiciled in England. That condition will be satisfied where the claims involve one

---

[8] *Metropolitan International Schools Ltd v Designtechnica Corp & Ors* [2011] 1 WLR 1743. See now also the Defamation Act 2013, s 5.

[9] *AK Investment*, at [71].

[10] *VTB Capital Plc v Nutritek International Corp & Ors* [2012] 2 Lloyd's Rep 313 at [99].

[11] *GAF Corp v Amchem Products Inc* [1975] 1 Lloyd's Rep 601 at 605–606.

[12] *Watson & Sons v Daily Record Ltd* [1907] 1 KB 853.

[13] *Conductive Inkjet Technology Ltd v Uni-Pixel Displays Inc* [2014] 1 All ER (Comm) 654 at [61]; see also discussion between [53]–[62].

investigation or are "*closely bound up*".[14] However, if, in defamation proceedings, jurisdiction over D1 is established via the Regulation and D2 is added under para 3.1(3) , it will be open to D2 (but *not* D1) to rely on the Defamation Act 2013, s 9 (see para 4.46).

4.24   Para 3.1(4A): *Closely connected facts:* This new ground effectively ensures that where one claim can be brought against the defendant through almost any of the other "gateways", further claims arising out of the same or closely connected facts can be brought at the same time. Authority on its proper interpretation is awaited.

4.25   Para 3.1(5): *Interim relief:* The court has jurisdiction over claims for interim relief under the Civil Jurisdiction and Judgments Act 1982, s 25. This allows a claimant to bring a claim seeking interim relief in support of litigation taking place elsewhere, such as in other parts of the UK or in other Regulation/Lugano Convention states, even where the claimant does not seek to bring any substantive action in this jurisdiction.

4.26   Para 3.1(9): *Claims in tort:* This is the most important gateway for present purposes. Courts have jurisdiction where:

"A claim is made in tort where –

(a) damage was sustained, or will be sustained, within the jurisdiction; or

(b) damage which has been or will be sustained results from an act committed, or likely to be committed, within the jurisdiction".

4.27   Claims made in tort include actions in defamation,[15] misuse of private information[16] and claims brought under the Data Protection Act 1998.[17] It also covers claims for infringement of IP rights.[18] Claims in "traditional" breach of confidence were excluded,[19] but these are now covered by the new CPR PD 6B, 3.1(21) (see para 4.30 below). In relation to para 3.1(9)(a), it is enough that the damage sustained in this jurisdiction is "*significant*" even if

---

[14] *AK Investment*, at [87].

[15] *Berezovsky v Michaels & Ors* [2000] 1 WLR 1004.

[16] *Vidal-Hall*, at [43].

[17] For example, *Hegglin v Person(s) Unknown & Anor* [2014] EWHC 2808 (QB) at [20]. This contention was not disputed by the defendant at first-instance in *Vidal-Hall* [2014] 1 WLR 4155 at [50].

[18] *Magnesium Elektron Ltd v Molycorp Chemicals & Oxides (Europe) Ltd* [2016] RPC 18 at [44].

[19] *Kitechnology BV & Ors v Unicor GmbH Plastmaschinen & Ors* [1995] FSR 765 at 777.

damage has also occurred elsewhere.[20] It appears that consequential loss does not count as "damage" for the purposes of the jurisdictional gateway.[21]

4.28   As to para 3.1(9)(b), there is no requirement that the act was committed exclusively within the jurisdiction, but the damage must result from *"substantial and efficacious acts"* committed within the jurisdiction.[22] Where there are multiple defendants, the act of one will be sufficient to bring them all within the range of the gateway.[23]

4.29   Where the contents of an internet publication are relied on, the act of publication occurs at the place where it is downloaded or viewed.[24] Courts have tended to ask whether the publications complained of in England constitute a *"real and substantial tort"*. This test is effectively part of the *forum (non) conveniens* analysis.[25]

4.30   Para 3.1(21): *Claims in breach of confidence:* This new gateway covers claims for breach of confidence or misuse of private information. It is formulated in identical terms to para 3.1(9) save that it refers to *"detriment"* being *"suffered"* rather than damage being sustained. The change was motivated by continuing uncertainty about whether any other gateway could accommodate a breach of confidence claim.

England is the proper place to bring the claim

4.31   The court must decide whether England is the proper place – i.e. the *forum conveniens* – for the dispute.

4.32   The ultimate question is whether the English courts or those of another jurisdiction, is the place where the dispute can most suitably be tried in the interests of all the parties and of justice. Following *The Spiliada Maritime Corporation v Cansulex (Ltd), "The Spiliada",*[26] this is typically broken down into two stages.

4.33   *At the first stage,* the court determines whether England, or instead another place, is the "clearly or distinctly more appropriate" forum for the dispute –

---

[20] *Metall und Rohstoff AG v Donaldson Lufkin & Jenrette Inc & Anor* [1990] 1 QB 391 at 437.

[21] *Erste Group Bank v JSC "VMZ Red October" & Ors* [2015] 1 CLC 706 at [104]–[105].

[22] *Metall und Rohstoff* above, at 437.

[23] *Puchsner v Palmer Ltd & Anor* [1989] RPC 430.

[24] *Jameel (Yousef) v Dow Jones & Co Inc* [2005] QB 946 at [48].

[25] This is how it is explained in a number of cases, such as *Jameel* above, at [48]–[50].

[26] [1987] AC 460.

in other words, which is the place which has the most real and substantial connection with the dispute?[27]

4.34   There are a multitude of "connecting factors" which the court can take into account in making this determination. They include the place where the events giving rise to the dispute took place; the location of witnesses, experts and other evidence; and the existence of parallel proceedings abroad. The law governing the dispute will also be taken into account, especially where the legal issues are complex or where there are significant differences between English law and the applicable foreign law.[28]

4.35   The court will also have to be satisfied that the foreign forum is *available* – i.e. that it would take jurisdiction over the dispute.

4.36   There is very extensive case law on the principles governing the issue of *forum (non) conveniens*.[29] What follows is a discussion of the cases which have most relevance to claims relating to internet publications. In the context of defamation claims, these authorities must be understood as now subject to the Defamation Act 2013, s 9 (see para 4.46).

4.37   At stage 1 of *The Spiliada* analysis, the starting point is that the most appropriate forum is the place where, in substance, the tort was committed.[30] However, the Supreme Court has discouraged the view that this amounts to a presumption.[31]

4.38   In claims relating to internet publications, where each publication constitutes a separate tort, the place of the tort in relation to publication in England will by definition be England.[32]

4.39   In internet cases there will almost always be worldwide publication. In *Berezovsky v Michaels,* the House of Lords' majority rejected the "global tort" theory whereby, for the purposes of establishing the natural forum to hear the complaint, the court would assess all of the publications in England and abroad as part of a single cause of action.[33]

---

[27] *The Spiliada*, at 478.

[28] *Owners of Cargo Lately Laden on Board the Ship or Vessel Eleftheria v The Eleftheria, "The Eleftheria"* [1970] P 94 at [105]. See para 4.92ff, on applicable law.

[29] For a full discussion, see Dicey, Morris & Collins, *The Conflict of Laws* (15th edition, Sweet and Maxwell 2012) at para 12-007–12-054.

[30] This principle was established in *Cordoba Shipping Co v National State Bank, Elizabeth, New Jersey, "The Albaforth"* [1984] 2 Lloyd's Rep 91 and affirmed in *Berezovsky v Michaels* above, at 1014.

[31] *VTB Capital v Nutritek International Corp & Ors* [2013] 2 AC 337 at [51].

[32] *King v Lewis* [2005] EMLR 4 at [27].

[33] *Berezovsky v Michaels* [2000] 1 WLR 1004 at 1011–1013, per Lord Steyn.

4.40 However, the extent of publication here and abroad remains relevant to the stage 1 *Spiliada* analysis. First, the English court needs to be satisfied that there has been a "real and substantial tort" committed in England; accordingly, if publication in England has been trivial, the court will not hear the dispute.[34]

4.41 Second, and more generally, the court will still consider if there is a more appropriate forum notwithstanding the starting point. In this respect:

- The more tenuous the claimant's connection with England and the more substantial any publication abroad, the weaker the case that England is the natural forum notwithstanding that it is the place of the tort;[35]

- Claimants are in a stronger position in relation to internet publications compared to, for example, newspapers published in multiple jurisdictions. That is on the basis that having published something on the internet (which is in principle available everywhere), defendants should not be too fastidious about where they are then sued.[36]

4.42 Cases such as *Berezovsky* and *Jameel* provide some guidance about how the exercise of establishing the most appropriate forum should be conducted in these kinds of cases. The relative importance of the claimant's reputations in the competing forums is plainly relevant. In *Jameel*, the Court of Appeal suggested that it was not a good enough reason for suing in England that it would vindicate a claimant's reputation abroad ([66]). However, at stage 2 of the *Spiliada* analysis, it may be relevant that corruption or bias associated with a foreign judicial system means that a good outcome abroad would not repair the damage to reputation.[37] For a recent case in which the *Albaforth* "starting point" was displaced in a claim for misuse of private information, see *Ahuja v Politika Novine I Magazini DOO & Ors.*[38]

4.43 *At the second stage,* if the dispute is more closely connected with another forum, the English court will ask whether the interests of justice nevertheless require that the claim is heard in England. At this stage, the burden will be on the claimant. The fact that a personal / juridical advantage (such as a more

---

[34] *Jameel* at [48]–[50]; see also *Sloutsker v Romanova* [2015] Costs LR 321 at [41].

[35] *King v Lewis* above at [27].

[36] *King v Lewis* above at [31].

[37] *Berezovsky v Michaels* [2000] 1 WLR 1004 at 1014 and 1024.

[38] [2016] 1 WLR 1414 at [76]–[78].

favourable disclosure or costs regime in England) will not be available abroad will not normally be sufficient.

4.44   The claimant may satisfy the second stage by demonstrating that justice would not be obtained in the foreign forum, whether because the foreign system is demonstrably corrupt, incompetent, beset by delays,[39] or indeed not operating at all.[40] However, to succeed with this kind of allegation, the claimant must produce *"cogent evidence"* demonstrating a real risk that justice will not be obtained in the foreign court.[41]

4.45   There are various other circumstances in which the court may refuse a stay at stage two, including in exceptional cases where the claimant has access to financial support in England that would not be available abroad with the effect that s/he will be unable to sue abroad at all.[42]

Section 9 of the Defamation Act 2013

4.46   The Defamation Act 2013, s 9 is a response to perceived "libel tourism" by foreign claimants in the English courts. In relevant part it provides that:

"(1) This section applies to an action for defamation against a person who is not domiciled –

(a) in the United Kingdom;

(b) in another Member State; or

(c) in a state which is for the time being a contracting party to the Lugano Convention.

(2) A court does not have jurisdiction to hear and determine an action to which this section applies unless the court is satisfied that, of all the places in which the statement complained of has been published, England and Wales is clearly the most appropriate place in which to bring an action in respect of the statement.

(3) The references in subsection (2) to the statement complained of include references to any statement which conveys the same,

---

[39] *AK Investment,* above at [95].

[40] *Alberta Inc v Katanga Mining Ltd* [2009] 1 BCLC 189.

[41] *AK Investment,* above at [95]–[97].

[42] *Lubbe & Ors v Cape Plc* [2000] 1 WLR 1545; *Connelly v RTZ Corporation Plc & Ors* [1998] AC 854.

or substantially the same, imputation as the statement complained of."

4.47   This new jurisdictional rule applies equally whether the claimant has served the defendant in or out of the jurisdiction. The section does not apply to claims where jurisdiction has been taken under the Regulation or the Lugano Convention, as in those cases the defendant can be sued "as of right" under the rule in *Owusu v Jackson & Ors*[43] (see para 4.83). It only applies to actions for defamation.

4.48   This new provision seems effectively to adopt the "global tort" approach rejected by the House of Lords in *Berezovsky*. The Explanatory Notes to the Defamation Act 2013 state (at para 66) that:

> "It is intended that (the Defamation Act 2013, s 9) will overcome the problem of courts readily accepting jurisdiction simply because a claimant frames their claim so as to focus on damage which has occurred in this jurisdiction only. This would mean that, for example, if a statement was published 100,000 times in Australia and only 5,000 times in England that would be a good basis on which to conclude that the most appropriate jurisdiction in which to bring an action in respect of the statement was Australia rather than England. There will however be a range of factors which the court may wish to take into account including, for example, the amount of damage to the claimant's reputation in this jurisdiction compared to elsewhere, the extent to which the publication was targeted at a readership in this jurisdiction compared to elsewhere, and whether there is reason to think that the claimant would not receive a fair hearing elsewhere."

4.49   This passage suggests that the analysis envisaged is very similar to a *forum non conveniens* analysis, including the "stage 2" question of whether justice can be done abroad.

4.50   In the *Ahuja* case the court accepted that questions such as the convenience of witnesses and the relative expense of suing in different jurisdictions would be relevant ([70]).

4.51   *Ahuja* suggests that the claimant has to produce the fullest reasonably available evidence as to publication in all places in which the words complained of have been published ([29]). The burden on claimants will be heavy. They will presumably be expected to produce worldwide statistics on

---

[43] [2005] QB 801.

publication, not only of the particular article / statement in question, but of ones like it (in light of s 9(3) of the 2013 Act).

4.52   The question of how exactly s 9 of the 2013 Act differs from the typical *forum non conveniens* test was not explicitly addressed in *Ahuja*. One difference seems to be that the burden of proof will now always be on the claimant (unlike where a defendant seeks a stay on the basis of *forum non conveniens*). It is plainly no longer appropriate to think or talk in terms of a "starting point" in favour of England for defamation claims.

Subject matter jurisdiction / justiciability

4.53   There is a long-established principle of English law that English courts would not take jurisdiction over claims which depended on establishing title to foreign land.[44] For some time English courts extended this principle to claims relating to foreign intellectual property rights,[45] refusing jurisdiction over them too. However, the Supreme Court in *Lucasfilm Ltd & Ors v Ainsworth & Anor*[46] has now established that there is nothing to prevent the English court hearing claims alleging infringement of foreign copyrights. The position in relation to other intellectual property rights is less clear, but the tenor of the *Lucasfilm* judgment would suggest that so long as an action for infringement is brought and no question of validity or registration of the right is raised, English courts will take jurisdiction over them too. That would reflect the distinction drawn in art 24(4) of the Regulation (see para 4.66).

Applications to set aside service / disputing jurisdiction

4.54   CPR 11 sets out the procedure to be followed by defendants who wish to apply either for the court to set aside service of the claim form (on the basis that it lacks jurisdiction); or not to exercise its jurisdiction. In both cases, the defendant:

- Must first file an acknowledgement of service;
- Must then apply for the order sought within 14 days or such other period as the court may direct. The application should be made under the CPR 23 procedure.

---

[44] *British South Africa Co v Campanhia de Mocambique & Ors* [1893] AC 602.

[45] English courts had repeatedly applied the decision of the High Court of Australia in *Potter v Broken Hill Pty Ltd* (1906) 3 CLR 479.

[46] [2012] 1 AC 208.

4.55   If the defendant files an acknowledgement of service but makes no such further application, it is treated as having submitted to the court's jurisdiction (CPR 11(5)).**Error! Bookmark not defined.**

4.56   Applications made in accordance with CPR 11 will often result in a hearing involving both parties. Despite constant emphasis on the need for proportionality in the determination of these matters,[47] the reality is that hearings about appropriate forum are often long, complex and costly, requiring expert evidence and extensive legal submissions.

JURISDICTION: THE RECAST BRUSSELS REGULATION

Introduction

4.57   The Regulation is the successor to the Brussels I Regulation and, before it, the Brussels Convention, concluded on 27 September 1968. The similarities between the successive instruments far outweigh their differences and case law on the interpretation of the earlier instruments will continue to be authoritative when interpreting the equivalent provisions of the Regulation.

4.58   Alongside the Regulation, the EU agreed the revised Lugano Convention of 30 October 2007 with Iceland, Norway and Switzerland. The jurisdictional regime it creates is effectively identical to that set out in the earlier Brussels I Regulation. These rules apply in the situations which are parallel to those covered by the Regulation, e.g. when an English court is faced with a claim brought against an Icelandic, Norwegian or Swiss-domiciled defendant.

4.59   Finally, the Regulation does not itself regulate how courts should divide up jurisdiction *within the different legal systems of the UK* (which is a single Member State for the purposes of EU law). Where the Regulation confers jurisdiction on the "UK courts", the division of jurisdiction between them is in turn determined by the rules in the Civil Jurisdiction and Judgments Act 1982, Sch 4. The rules for dividing jurisdiction between the UK courts in this Schedule are similar, but not identical, to those for dividing jurisdiction between Member States in the earlier Brussels I Regulation.

4.60   This Chapter analyses the parts of the Regulation most relevant to claims relating to internet publications; specialist textbooks should be consulted for a detailed explanation of the differences between the Regulation and the Lugano Convention / the rules in the Civil Jurisdiction and Judgments Act 1982, Sch 4.[48]

---

[47] *VTB Capital* above at [82].

[48] For example, Briggs, *Civil Jurisdiction and Judgments* (6th edn OUP 2015).

Scope of the Regulation

4.61   The Regulation applies to any claims which raise "*civil and commercial matters*" save for a number of listed exclusions which are in general not relevant in claims arising from internet publications (see art 1 of the Regulation).

4.62   In addition, the Regulation does not prejudice the application of rules of jurisdiction on specific matters contained in other Union instruments (such as the adapted rules for claims regulated by Regulations (EC) No 6/2002 (on Community designs) and (EC) No 207/2009 (on Community trade marks) (see art 67)).

4.63   The outline of the regime which applies to the claims covered by the Regulation is as follows.

4.64   **First**, a defendant domiciled in England may be sued here unless another court has exclusive jurisdiction by virtue of arts 24 or 25 of the Regulation (art 4(1)). A defendant can have more than one place of domicile. Art 63(1) of the Regulation defines domicile in the case of corporate defendants. UK courts must apply their own rules to determine if an *individual* defendant is domiciled in the UK[49] and the law of another Member State to determine if that defendant is domiciled in *that* Member State (art 62 of the Regulation). "Member States" for the purposes of the Regulation includes all EU Member States.

4.65   **Second**, art 7 of the Regulation sets down a wide range of circumstances in which defendants domiciled in any Member State can also be sued in a different Member State ("the Special Jurisdiction Rules"). It is these rules which raise the most difficult issues in the context of claims for internet publications. These are discussed in the next section.

4.66   **Third**, in certain circumstances, defendants who are not domiciled in the EU may (or even must) nevertheless be sued in a Member State. In brief the specific circumstances are as follows:

• In the five very specific situations set out in art 24 of the Regulation the court identified in that article has exclusive jurisdiction and the court of the defendant's domicile (if different) may not take jurisdiction. The only of the five situations that may arise in the context of claims about internet publications is art 24(4) of the Regulation, which provides that in proceedings concerned with the registration or validity of intellectual property rights which need to be deposited or registered (i.e. not including copyright), exclusive

---

[49] As set out in the Civil Jurisdiction and Judgments Order 2001, Sch 1, para 9.

jurisdiction rests with the courts of the Member State where the deposit or registration for the right has been applied for, has taken place or is deemed to have taken place. In other words the issue of validity or registration of the right has to arise in the proceedings, even if it does so by way of a defence (e.g. to an action for infringement). However, a pure action for damages for infringement of those rights is not caught by art 24;[50]

- Except in the cases covered by art 24, the court can take jurisdiction over any defendant who submits to its jurisdiction (art 26(1));
- If the parties have agreed that a particular Member State court is to have jurisdiction to settle their dispute/s, and the agreement satisfies the conditions in art 25 of the Regulation then that court will have jurisdiction. Unless the parties have agreed otherwise, the chosen court will have exclusive jurisdiction such that the court of the defendant's domicile (if different) should decline jurisdiction.

4.67   **Fourth**, subject to the exceptions in the **third** point above, jurisdiction over defendants domiciled outside the EU is generally determined by the (domestic) law of the court faced with the dispute (the art 6(1) of the Regulation). Accordingly, where these claims come before the English courts, English domestic rules on service and jurisdiction apply. These rules are explained above.

The Special Jurisdiction Rules – art 7(1) and (2) of the Regulation

4.68   The Special Jurisdiction Rules are to be interpreted restrictively since they derogate from the *general rule* that defendants should be sued in the place of their domicile.[51]

4.69   The key Special Jurisdiction Rules for claims relating to internet publications is art 7(2) of the Regulation. Art 7 provides that:

> "A person domiciled in a Member State may be sued in another Member State:
>
> (1) (a) in matters relating to a contract, in the courts for the place of performance of the obligation in question; . . . .
>
> (2) In matters relating to tort, delict or quasi-delict, in the courts for the place where the harmful event occurred or may occur . . . ."

---

[50] *Land Oberoesterreich v CEZ AS* [2006] ECR I-4557 at [26].

[51] *Shevill & Ors v Presse Alliance SA* [1995] 2 AC 18 at [18].

4.70   Art 7(2) is most relevant here as it covers claims in defamation and misuse of private information. It would also include claims in equitable breach of confidence, insofar as those claims do not "relate to" a contract (in which case they would fall within art 7(1) instead).

4.71   There is extensive case law on the interpretation of art 7(1) of the Regulation which will not be discussed here.[52] It suffices for present purposes to note that the art 7(1) is limited to claims based on obligations freely undertaken vis-à-vis another person.[53]

4.72   In *Handelskwekerij G J Bier B & Anor v Mines de Potasse d'Alsace SA* [54] the CJEU established that the "place where the harmful event occurred" is in fact two places: the place where the event *giving rise to the damage* occurred; and the place where *the damage itself* occurred. Where those two places are different, art 5(3) of the Regulation allows a claimant to bring the claim in either jurisdiction.

4.73   However, a claim brought in the place where damage occurred can only relate to the damage *suffered in that jurisdiction* (unless that is also the place of the defendant's domicile or the place where the event giving rise to damage occurred). As such where a claimant has suffered damage in multiple jurisdictions s/he may bring claims in each jurisdiction but only in respect of the damage which occurred there:

> "The place where the damage occurred" means the place where the tort "directly produced its harmful effects on the person who is the immediate victim of that event".[55]

It does not include indirect damage.

4.74   In *Shevill & Ors v Presse Alliance SA*,[56] the CJEU applied this to a claim for libel. A French defendant was sued in England over an article which it published in its French newspaper, which had a very low circulation in England and Wales. The *Bier* analysis was applied such that the claimant was entitled to sue in England for the damage to reputation caused by publication there. The place where *the publisher of the statement is established* was the place "where the event giving rise to damage occurred" [24].

---

[52] For a full discussion of this case law, see Briggs, *Private International Law in the English Courts* (1st ed OUP 2014), at 4.230–4.249.

[53] *Jacob Handte & Co GmbH v Societe Traitements Mecano-Chiniques des Surfaces (TMCS)* [1992] ECR I-3967 at [15].

[54] [1978] QB 708.

[55] *Dumez France SA & Anor v Hessische Landesbank & Ors* [1990] ECR I-49 at [20].

[56] [1995] 2 AC 18.

4.75   Nevertheless, this meant that claimants who suffered damage in multiple states (but not in the state of the defendant's domicile/place of establishment) would need to bring claims in each of those states in order to obtain full redress for that damage (see *ShevillError! Bookmark not defined.* at [32]). This was always likely to pose problems for claims brought in relation to internet publications.

4.76   The CJEU provided a solution in its decision in the joined cases of *eDate Advertising GmbH v X*.[57] Both cases related to internet publications which were alleged to have interfered with the private lives of the two claimants.

4.77   In its judgment, the CJEU noted that the availability of internet content *"is in principle universal"* and acknowledged that:

> "It is not always possible, on a technical level, to quantify that distribution with certainty and accuracy in relation to a particular member state or, therefore, to assess the damage caused exclusively within that member state". [46]

4.78   For that reason, the Court ruled that it should also be possible for a claimant to bring the whole claim for infringement of personality rights at the court where s/he has his/her *"centre of interests"* [48]. That would usually be the claimant's habitual residence but could be elsewhere if, for example, the claimant had extensive professional connections abroad [49].

4.79   The result of *eDate* is that claimants seeking to vindicate their reputation following an infringement of their personality rights may be able to sue in several different Member States.

4.80   However, the *eDate* line of case law has not been applied outside of claims for infringement of personality rights, e.g. to claims for infringement of copyright or other IP rights.[58] Where copyright is infringed by way of content placed online, the place where the harmful event occurred will be the place where the decision to upload was taken.[59] As to the "place where the damage occurred", claims can be brought in any Member State where the website was accessible and where the copyright was guaranteed, but only in respect of the damage suffered in that jurisdiction.[60]

---

[57] [2012] QB 654.

[58] *Pinckney v KDG Mediatech AG* [2014] Bus LR 1313 at [36].

[59] *Hejduk v Energie Agentur.NRW GmbH* [2015] Bus LR 560 at [25].

[60] *Hejduk*, at [38].

Other special jurisdiction rules

4.81   Arts 7 and 9 of the Regulation set out a number of other grounds on which one Member State court can take jurisdiction over a defendant domiciled in another Member State. A few are potentially relevant to claims about internet publications:

- In disputes arising out of the operations of a branch, agency or other establishment, a defendant domiciled in a Member State can be sued in the courts of the place where that branch/agency/establishment is situated (art 7(5));
- Where a claimant wishes to sue numerous defendants domiciled in Member States, s/he can sue them in the Member State in which any of them are domiciled, so long as the disputes are so closely connected that it is expedient to hear and determine them together to avoid the risk of irreconcilable judgments (art 8(1));
- A counterclaim based on the same facts as the claim may be brought in the court where the claim is brought (art 8(3)).

Can a court decline jurisdiction arising under the Regulation?

4.82   At common law, an English court with jurisdiction over the claim has an inherent power to stay proceedings on the grounds of *forum non conveniens* (i.e. that there is a more appropriate forum for the dispute).[61] Does it retain this power where the basis for its jurisdiction is the Regulation?

4.83   In *Owusu v Jackson*,[62] the CJEU answered "no". A personal injury claim had been brought in England relating to an accident in Jamaica, which was plainly the most closely connected forum. However, the defendant was domiciled in England and so the court had jurisdiction over the claim. In these circumstances the CJEU decided that the English court had no power to stay proceedings on grounds of *forum non conveniens*. The Court justified its decision by reference to the mandatory wording of the Regulation and the aim of legal certainty which underpins the Regulation.

4.84   The basic principle that defendants domiciled in England cannot plead *forum non conveniens* has been affirmed on multiple occasions by English courts[63]

---

[61] This power is discussed in more detail at para 4.15ff.

[62] [2005] QB 801.

[63] *A v A (Children: Habitual Residence)* [2014] AC 1 at [31].

despite inventive attempts by defendants to re-open the issue.[64] It applies equally where the more appropriate forum is another EU Member State; and where jurisdiction is taken on a basis other than the defendant's domicile (e.g. Special Jurisdiction Rules).[65]

4.85   The position is less clear where an EU court has jurisdiction under the Regulation but there is some direct connection between the dispute and a *non-Member State court* of the kind set out in arts 24 and 25 of the Regulation. The authorities seem to support the view that the English courts retain a discretion to stay in these circumstances. In a decision just prior to *Owusu* the CJEU suggested that Member State courts should determine the effect to be given to third-country jurisdiction agreements according to their own rules of law.[66] A number of English authorities support this view.[67] This would also allow the English courts to act consistently with common law rules that certain disputes about foreign land and IP rights are non-justiciable (discussed further below in the section on domestic rules of jurisdiction).

4.86   Further, defendants can still plead *forum non conveniens* where a defendant is not domiciled in the EU and the English court determines whether it has jurisdiction under its own rules.

4.87   Even where *Owusu* does apply, there are still two potential procedural routes open to defendants seeking to prevent a claim being heard in England.

- **First**, it can be argued that bringing the claim in England amounts to an abuse of EU law. However, the limited case law on this subject suggests that a very high threshold has to be met if this plea is to be made out: the sole object of claimant must be the ousting of the jurisdiction of the court where the defendant is domiciled.[68]
- **Second**, the English court's power to stay its own proceedings as an exercise of its case management powers is probably unaffected by the Regulation. However, it appears that the court will only exercise this

---

[64] See, most recently, the decision of Coulson J in *Lungowe & Ors v Vedanta Resources Plc & Anor* [2016] BCC 774, especially at [56]–[57] and [65]–[67].

[65] *Equitas Ltd v Allstate Insurance Co* [2009] 1 All ER (Comm) 1137 at [64]; *Gomez & Ors v Encarnacion Gomez-Monch Vives & Ors* [2008] 3 WLR 309 at [112] and [113].

[66] *Coreck Maritime GmbH v Handelsveem & Ors* [2000] ECR I-9337 at [19].

[67] *Ferrexpo AG v Gilson Investments Ltd & Ors* [2012] Lloyd's Rep 588 at [140]–[143]; *Catalyst Investments v Lewinsohn & Ors* [2010] Ch 218 at [94]–[95]

[68] *Freeport Plc v Arnoldsson* [2008] QB 634; *Lungowe & Ors v Vedanta Resources Plc & Anor Plc* [2016] BCC 774.

power in *"rare and compelling circumstances"*[69] and it should not be a *"back door"* through which the *Owusu* principle is undermined.[70]

Multiple sets of proceedings

4.88   What should a Member State court do where similar claims to the one before it have already been brought in a different court?

4.89   In brief, where the parallel proceedings are brought in a different Member State, the Regulation provides that:

- If the proceedings involve the same cause of action and the same parties, the second seised court must stay its proceedings until the first seised court determines whether it has jurisdiction (art 29(1) of the Regulation). If the first court takes jurisdiction the second seised court must then decline jurisdiction (the art 29(3)). The "same cause of action" means that the claim has the same object and relies on the same facts and rules of law.[71] This narrow definition should not cover e.g. libel claims brought in a different Member State in respect of a publication in that state;

- There is now an exception to that principle in the case of exclusive jurisdiction agreements (the art 31(2)). There is no *explicit* exception where the second seised court appears to have jurisdiction under art 24 of the Regulation but the Court of Appeal has concluded that such an exception is implied;[72]

- Where the actions in the other Member State court are merely *related*, the second seised court has a *discretion* to stay its proceedings (art 30(1)). Related means actions which *"are so closely connected that it is expedient to hear and determine them together to avoid the risk of irreconcilable judgments resulting from separate proceedings"*.

4.90   The Brussels I Regulation was silent about parallel proceedings in *non-Member States* and it was unclear, following *Owusu*, that Member States could stay their proceedings in light of third state proceedings. This is resolved by the enactment of arts 33 and 34 of the Regulation. These create a tightly

---

[69] *Pacific International Sports Club Ltd v Soccer Marketing & Ors* [2009] EWHC 1839 (Ch) at [114]; *Lungowe* at [85].

[70] *Skype Technologies SA v Kasesalu & Ors* [2011] I L Pr 8 at [22].

[71] *Owners of Cargo Lately Laden on Board the ship Tatry v Owners of the Ship Maciej Rataj, "The Tatry"* [1999] QB 515.

[72] *Speed Investments Ltd & Anor v Formula One Holdings Ltd & Ors (No 2)* [2005] 1 WLR 1936 at [36]–[39].

circumscribed discretion to stay proceedings where there are identical or related actions in a third State. The Member State court must be satisfied that the third State court will give a judgment it can recognise and enforce; and that a stay is necessary for the proper administration of justice.

Service under the Regulation

4.91   Where the claim can be founded on a ground of jurisdiction within the Regulation, the claimant has the right to serve the claim form out of the jurisdiction without first obtaining the court's permission – see CPR 6.32 (for serving "out" to other jurisdictions within the UK) and CPR 6.33 (for service out to other EU and Lugano states). In both cases, the claimant should also file and serve a statement of the grounds on which the claimant is entitled to serve the claim form out of the jurisdiction (CPR 6.34(1)).

CHOICE OF LAW: INTRODUCTION

4.92   In cases with international elements, where the English court *does* have jurisdiction to hear the dispute, it does not necessarily follow that English law (e.g. the English law of defamation) applies to the claim. The court must ask whether English law, or the law of another country, applies to the claim.

4.93   For tort claims this question is generally governed by Regulation (EC) No 864/2007 on the law applicable to non-contractual obligations ("the Rome II Regulation"). However, this does not apply to claims based on rights of privacy or personality or to claims in defamation (art 1(2)(g)). In practice this excludes most claims arising from internet publications.

4.94   For claims falling within art 1(2)(g) of the Rome II Regulation one must again look to domestic (statutory and common law) rules on applicable law. Where the Rome II Regulation does not apply the statutory regime enacted in the Private International Law (Miscellaneous Provisions) Act 1995 remains in effect, but this regime does not apply to defamation claims (s 13(1) of the 1995 Act). For defamation claims the common law rule of "double actionability" applies, requiring a claimant to demonstrate that their claim would succeed both in English law and in the law of the place where the claim arose "in substance".

4.95   This part of the Chapter deals with (i) the common law double actionability rule; (ii) Private International Law (Miscellaneous Provisions) Act 1995; (iii) the Rome II Regulation and (iv) the specific applicable law rules for data protection.

4.96   Even where the applicable law is not English law, English rules remain relevant in some respects. English law continues to govern matters of evidence and procedure. English courts will still apply English laws which are "mandatory" in nature (i.e. rules intended to apply regardless of the law otherwise applicable) and may refuse to apply foreign laws where this would conflict with English public policy. This part of the chapter concludes by considering these issues.

DOUBLE ACTIONABILITY – DEFAMATION

4.97   As explained above, defamation claims fall outside the scope of the Rome II Regulation and the Private International Law (Miscellaneous Provisions) Act 1995, so the common law rule of double actionability applies. As defined in s 13(2) of the 1995 Act "defamation" for these purposes include claims in malicious falsehood.

4.98   The first question is whether the cause of action arose "in substance" in England. If so, the claim will be governed by English law. If a claimant sues in respect of an internet article but only in relation to its publication in England, a court is likely to find that the cause of action arises in substance in England, even if the publisher of the statement uploaded it abroad.[73] In those circumstances English law only will apply (assuming that the English court has jurisdiction, which it may not in such cases, applying Defamation Act 2013, s 9) (see para 4.46).

4.99   Where however the claim arose "in substance" abroad, the law of both countries will need to be applied. English courts can easily have jurisdiction over such claims: for example, where the claimant sues someone domiciled in Scotland, Northern Ireland or a Member State (in which case s 9 of the 2013 Act has no application).

4.100   Where the claim arose "in substance" abroad, the English court must be satisfied (i) that the defamation claim would succeed in English law and (ii) there would also be civil liability for the act in question under the applicable foreign law (though the claim need not also be classified or "characterised" as a "tort" under the foreign law).[74] Question (ii) will require evidence as to the content and application of foreign law, which the court will use as the basis of its conclusions; this is discussed further below.

4.101   There is however a flexible exception which allows the English court to disapply the double actionability rule, in favour of applying either English law

---

[73] See references to *King v Lewis* in paras 4.38, 4.41.

[74] *Red Sea Insurance Co Ltd v Bouygues SA & Ors* [1995] 1 AC 190 at 199.

or foreign law only. It can do so in respect of a particular issue, or even in respect of the whole claim. The circumstances in which this exception might apply have been explained only in very general terms, for example:

> "The necessary flexibility can be obtained... through segregation of the relevant issue and consideration whether, in relation to that issue, the relevant foreign rule ought, as a matter of policy or as Westlake said of science, to be applied. For this purpose it is necessary to identify the policy of the rule, to inquire to what situations, with what contacts, it was intended to apply; whether not to apply it, in the circumstances of the instant case, would serve any interest which the rule was devised to meet... The general rule must apply unless clear and satisfying grounds are shown why it should be departed from and what solution, derived from what other rule, should be preferred";[75] and

> "A particular issue may be governed by the law of the country which, with respect to that issue, has the most significant relationship with the occurrence and with the parties ... although the cases may be rare where the exception should be applied to the whole case [ie the whole claim], their Lordships do not consider that to apply the exception to the whole case is in principle necessarily excluded".[76]

4.102   For example, the claim in *Red Sea Insurance Co Ltd v Bouygues SA & Ors*[77] was for an indemnity relating to a construction project to be carried out in Saudi Arabia. All of the relevant contracts were governed by Saudi law and the construction project was to be performed in Saudi Arabia; the alleged breaches and the alleged damage occurred in Saudi Arabia. In those circumstances the Privy Council concluded that the exception should apply so that the claims should be analysed only by reference to Saudi law and not by the law of the forum (in that case Hong Kong).

4.103   By analogy, it may be arguable in some defamation cases that only the law of the place where the statement is published (i.e. downloaded or viewed) should apply; though this argument will not be straightforward given that internet publications, by definition, are available everywhere.

---

[75] *Boys v Chaplin* [1971] AC 356 at 391.

[76] [1995] 1 AC 190, at 206–207.

[77] Ibid.

CHOICE OF LAW: THE 1995 ACT AND MISUSE OF PRIVATE INFORMATION

Introduction

4.104   The Private International Law (Miscellaenous Provisions) Act 1995 determines the law applicable to claims (other than defamation) relating to interference with privacy or personality rights. It replaces double actionability which no longer applies in relation to those claims (s 10 of the 1995 Act).

The general rule – section 11

4.105   The general rule is that the applicable law is the law of the country in which "the events constituting the tort or delict in question occur" (Private International Law (Miscellaneous Provisions) Act 1995, s 11(1)). Where those events occur in more than one country, s 11(2) of the 1995 Act provides that the applicable law is:

(a) For claims in respect of personal injuries, the law of the country where the individual was when s/he sustained the injury;

(b) For claims in respect of damage to property, the law of the country where the property was when it was damaged;

(c) In any other case, the law of the country in which "the most significant element or elements of those events occurred".

4.106   Claims relating to internet publications would most commonly fall into the third category. This requires the court to identify the "events constituting the tort", meaning for these purposes the tort as it is understood in English law.[78]

4.107   In the case of misuse of private information in the context of an internet publication, for example, the key events would be: (i) the publishing of information online in respect of which the claimant had a reasonable expectation of privacy; and (ii) the damage caused to the claimant, which can include financial loss, distress or the damage to their right to control the use of their own private information.[79] The court will also ask whether the claimant's interest in the "private information" must yield to some other interest – most likely the publisher's right to freedom of expression under European Convention for the Protection of Human Rights and Fundamental Freedoms, art 10 – but that is not an "event" constituting the tort and so would seem to be irrelevant for the purposes of s 11(2) of the 1995 Act.

---

[78] *VTB Capital v Nutritek International Corp & Ors* [2012] 2 Lloyd's Rep 313 at [148]. The Court of Appeal's guidance on the interpretation of the 1995 Act, ss 11 and 12 was affirmed by the Supreme Court, reported at [2013] 2 WLR 398, in particular at [149], [199] and [203].

[79] *Gulati & Ors v Mirror Group Newspapers Ltd* [2017] QB 149 at [45]–[48].

4.108   The court must then identify where those events occurred. By analogy with the context of issues as to jurisdiction (see above), the act of publication takes place at the place where the article is viewed or downloaded; whereas damage takes place where it is directly suffered. That might be more than one place: for example, the claimant may suffer damage in the form of a loss of control of information in the place where the information is read; but the claimant may suffer distress elsewhere, on learning that a statement has been read abroad.

4.109   After identifying those events the court must then identify "the most significant element" or elements among them. This will not always be easy. It involves a "value judgment" based on the facts of the case. "Significance" means the significance of the element in relation to the tort in question, and does not require a judgment as to which element requires the most elaborate factual investigation.[80] There is plenty of scope for argument as to how this test should apply in particular cases.

The exception – section 12

4.110   Once the applicable law has been (prima facie) ascertained applying the Private International Law (Miscellaneous Provisions) Act 1995, s 11, it remains to ask whether the exception in s 12 of the 1995 Act ought to apply. S 12 provides that:

> "If it appears, in all the circumstances, from a comparison of
>
> > (a) the significance of the factors which connect a tort or delict with the country whose law would be the applicable law under the general rule (i.e. s 11); and
> >
> > (b) the significance of any factors connecting the tort or delict with another country,
>
> that it is <u>substantially more appropriate</u> for the applicable law for determining the issues arising in the case, or any of those issues, to be the law of the other country, the general rule is displaced and the applicable law for determining those issues or that issue (as the case may be) is the law of that other country (emphasis added)."

4.111   In effect s 12 of the 1995 Act requires a comparison of the connections which the claims share with the competing jurisdictions. The court can consider a very broad range of factors, going well beyond consideration only of where

---

[80] *VTB Capital,* at [148].

the elements of the claim arose (which is the focus of s 11(1)(c) of the 1995 Act). This is clear from s 12(2) of the 1995 Act, which indicates that relevant factors include factors:

> "relating to the parties, to any of the events which constitute the tort or delict in question or to any of the circumstances or consequences of those events".

4.112   The Court of Appeal in *VTB Capital* provides further guidance, noting that the factors can include a pre-existing relationship between the parties (whether contractual or otherwise); any applicable law expressly or impliedly chosen by the parties to govern that relationship; and whether the pre-existing relationship is connected with the events giving rise to the claim.[81]

4.113   Despite the broad terms of s 12 of the 1995 Act courts must be cautious in applying it: the general rule in s 11 "is not to be dislodged easily".[82] It has also been suggested that s 12 of the 1995 Act is especially unlikely to apply where s 11(2)(c) of the 1995 is in issue, since that section itself requires a comparison of connections between the claim and the different jurisdictions.[83]

ROME II REGULATION: HARASSMENT, BREACH OF CONFIDENCE AND IP CLAIMS

Introduction

4.114   The Rome II Regulation applies to claims based on non-contractual obligations, but not those arising out of "violations of privacy and rights relating to personality, including defamation" (art 1(2)(g)). Plainly, this excludes defamation and misuse of private information claims, and for reasons elaborated below, it seems also to exclude "data protection" type claims. On the other hand, it would include other claims covered by this book, namely claims in breach of confidence,[84] and harassment.

4.115   The Rome II Regulation only applies to claims based on events giving rise to damage where those events occurred after 11 January 2009 (arts 31 and 32, as interpreted in *Homawoo v GMF Assurances SA*[85]). Where events giving rise to

---

[81] Ibid, at [149].

[82] *Belhaj & Anor v Jack Straw MP & Ors* [2015] 2 WLR 1105 at [146].

[83] *Fiona Trust & Holding Corp & Ors v Skarga & Ors* [2013] EWCA Civ 275 at [16].

[84] *Innovia Films Ltd v Frito-Lay North America Inc* [2012] RPC 24 at [109].

[85] [2011] ECR I-11603.

harm occurred before that date the relevant rules will still be those in the Private International Law (Miscellaneous Provisions) Act 1995, s 11.

4.116   When applying the Rome II Regulation each of the legal systems of the UK should be treated as a separate "country": art 25(1).

4.117   The general rule, under art 4(1) of the Rome II Regulation, is that the applicable law is the law of the country in which the damage occurs. This is different from both (i) the place where the harmful event giving rise to the damage occurs; and (ii) the place where the indirect consequences of that event occur. As such art 4(1) of the Rome II Regulation tracks the same distinctions as the art 7(2) of the Recast Brussels Regulation; the case law discussed above in relation to that provision would be equally applicable here.

4.118   For example, a claim for harassment arising out of internet publications will be governed by the law of the place where the harassment victim initially suffers harm (e.g. distress) as a result of the online campaign.

4.119   That general rule is subject to two exceptions:

- Where the claimant and the person being sued both have their habitual residence in the same country at the time the damage occurs, the law of that country (if different) applies instead (art 4(2) of the Rome II Regulation);
- Both art 4(1) of the Rome II Regulation *and* (where applicable) art 4(2) should be disapplied where, taking account of "all the circumstances of the case", the tort/delict is "manifestly more closely connected" with a different country (art 4(3)). There are plainly similarities with the Private International Law (Miscellaneous Provisions) Act 1995, s 12; in both cases, the necessary connection may arise from a pre-existing relationship between the parties. It has been suggested that art 4(3) of the Rome II Regulation will only apply in "*exceptional circumstances*" and that proving a manifestly closer connection is a "*high hurdle*" to overcome.[86] In *OPO v MLA & Anor*,[87] the Court of Appeal found that the threshold was overcome in the context of proceedings brought to restrain publication of a book in reliance on the tort of intentional infliction of emotional harm (commonly known as the tort in *Wilkinson v Downton*[88]). While accepting that art 4(1) of the Rome II Regulation "should not generally be disapplied", and certainly not to allow a party to gain a juridical advantage, the exception was made out on the facts

---

[86] *Pan Oceanic Chartering Inc v Unipek UK Co Ltd & Anor* [2017] 2 All ER (Comm) 196 at [206].

[87] [2015] EMLR 4 at [95]–[112].

[88] [1897] 2 QB 57.

because all of the necessary acts on the part of the tortfeasor had occurred in England, and it was impossible to know, in advance, where harm would be suffered by the claimant.

Intellectual Property disputes

4.120   The law applicable to claims for (non-contractual) infringement of IP rights is determined not by art 4 of the Rome II Regulation but by art 8. The applicable law is the law of the country for which protection is claimed (art 8(1)). In the case of non-contractual obligations arising from the infringement of a unitary Community IP right, the applicable law (in so far as the relevant Community instrument does not provide an answer to the question) is the law of the country in which the act of infringement was committed.

4.121   Unlike under art 4 of the Rome II Regulation, there is no exception where a different legal system otherwise has a closer connection with the claim. The parties also may not agree between them that a different law should apply (art 8(3)).

Parties' choice

4.122   Art 14 of the Rome II Regulation provides that the parties may *agree* the law which is applicable to a claim, but only if (i) they do so after the event giving rise to damage occurs; or (ii) all parties are pursuing a commercial activity and enter into a freely negotiated agreement. A choice can be implied from an agreement even if it is not expressly set out, so long as the agreement demonstrates the choice with "*reasonable certainty*".

4.123   Where a choice is made in accordance with the art 14 of the Rome II Regulation, but all the "elements relevant to the situation at the time when the event giving rise to the damage occurs" are located in a different country, provisions of that country's law which cannot be derogated from by agreement should still be applied (art 14(2)). Where the chosen law is not the law of a Member State, but all of the relevant elements are located in one or more Member States at the time of the harmful event, non-derogable provisions of Community law should still be applied (where appropriate as implemented in the Member State whose court is seised of the dispute) (art 14(3) of the Rome II Regulation).

DATA PROTECTION: A SPECIAL CASE

4.124   It is not immediately clear from the text of the Rome II Regulation whether the instrument is intended to apply to "data protection"-type claims.

Nevertheless the better view is that those claims fall outside its scope. Data protection claims were probably intended to fall within the exception for claims based on "rights relating to privacy or to personality" (art 1(2)(g) of the Rome II Regulation). This view is supported by the terms of art 30(2), which required the Commission to produce a report on applicable laws issues arising out of violations of privacy and rights relating to personality and then, separately, "conflict-of-law issues related to (the Data Protection Directive)". This strongly suggests that the legislator understood data protection issues to be outside the scope of Rome II.[89]

4.125   Furthermore, there is a special, albeit partial, choice of law in the Data Protection Directive 95/46/EC ("the Directive") itself.

4.126   Art 4(1) of the Directive provides that a Member State shall apply its data protection rules to processing of personal data where the processing is carried out *"in the context of the activities of an establishment of the (data) controller on the territory of the Member State"* (art 4(1)(a) of the Directive). Further, where the controller is not established on EU territory but, for the purposes of processing personal data makes use of equipment, automated or otherwise, situated on the territory of a Member State, the law of that Member State applies to the processing, unless such equipment is used only for purposes of transit through the territory of the Union (art 4(1)(c)). A final rule provides that a Member State's law will also apply to processing done by a controller not established on its territory where this is required by international public law (art 4(1)(b)); this is likely to be of limited application.

4.127   Art 4(1)(a) and (c) of the Data Protection Directive are implemented in the Data Protection Act 1998, s 5(1).

4.128   The effect of the art 4(1)(a) of the Directive is that the court must identify the processing to which the claim relates and then identify the "establishment" whose activities provide the context for that processing. Different acts of "processing" done by a single data controller can be governed by different laws, if they are done in the context of the activities of different "establishments". If on the other hand the controller only has an establishment in one place, the processing will be governed by the law of that place, irrespective of where the processing *actually takes place*.

4.129   However, art 4(1) only provides a *partial* choice of law rule. In a case where processing is done by an establishment outside of the EU, and which does not fall within art 4(1)(c), the Directive does not identify the law which would

---

[89] See further Brkan, "Data Protection and Conflict-of-laws: A Challenging Relationship" (2016) 3 *European Data Protection Law Review* 324, at 330-332:
http://www.lexxion.de/pdf/edpl/EDPL%20Reading%20Sample_Maja%20Brkan.pdf.

govern a claim for violation of data protection rights. It is submitted that in these cases the law applicable to the claim would still be determined applying the Private International Law (Miscellaneous Provisions) Act 1995. This is a rare but not completely hypothetical situation. Other (non-EU) legal systems do provide actionable data protection rights; as only one example, the Canadian Personal Information Protection and Electronic Documents Act (S.C.2000, c.5), gives complainants the right to complain to a designated Commissioner, and ultimately to a Court, in respect of misuse of their "personal information".

4.130   S 5(3) of the 1998 Act clarifies that among those "established" in the UK for these purposes are (a) individuals ordinarily resident in the UK; (b) a body incorporated under the law of, or of any part of, the UK; and (c) a partnership or other unincorporated association formed under the law of any part of the UK; and (d) a person who maintains in the UK (i) an office, branch or agency through which he carries on any activity; or (ii) a regular practice.

4.131   The proper interpretation of art 4 (1) of the Directive (and, by extension, of s 5(1) of the 1998 Act) was recently considered in *Weltimmo sro v Nemzeti Adatvédelmi és Információszabadság Hatóság*.[90] In that case a Slovakian registered company which ran a property-dealing website for Hungarian properties was fined by the Hungarian data protection regulator. The company's connections with Hungary were very strong: it had a representative, a bank account and a letter box in Hungary. The website was in the Hungarian language.

4.132   On the question of whether Hungarian or Slovakian law applied to the processing, the Court noted that art 4(1) of the Directive specifically governed this question [21]. The CJEU decided that a company will be "established" in a State for the purposes of the Directive if it carries out *"real and effective activity"* through *"stable arrangements"* ([31]).[91] The legal form of the establishment is not determinative [28]. Applying this test courts must take account of the nature of the economic activity of the company in question. A particularly flexible analysis is needed for data controllers which offer services exclusively through the internet ([29]). An establishment may exist in a State even where the activity in question is very small scale, and even if it constitutes the acts of a single representative ([30]), but the mere fact a company's website is accessible in a place is not enough.[92] The processing does not need to have been done

---

[90] [2016] 1 WLR 863.

[91] Such a test was previously proposed in *Google Spain SL & Anor v Agencia Española de Protección de Datos & Anor* [2014] QB 1022 at [49].

[92] *Verein für Konsumenteninformation v Amazon EU Sàrl* [2017] QB 252 at [76].

by the establishment, so long as it was done in the context of the activities of the establishment.

4.133   The decision in *Weltimmo* was followed by the Court of Appeal in Northern Ireland in the case of *CG v Facebook Ireland & Anor*[93] which held that Facebook Ireland was "established" in the United Kingdom for the purposes of the 1998 Act. Facebook (UK) Limited engaged in the effective and real exercise of activity through stable arrangements in the United Kingdom and the processing of data by this company was carried out in the context of the activities of Facebook Ireland.[94]

4.134   It is convenient to deal at this juncture with the related issue of the jurisdiction of national data protection regulators over data controllers. Each Member State must arrange for one or more public authorities to be responsible for monitoring the application of the domestic data protection laws (art 28(1) of the Directive). These organisations must have investigative powers, effective powers of intervention, and the power to engage in legal proceedings or to bring violations to the attention of judicial authorities (art 28(3)). In the UK this is the Information Commissioner.

4.135   In *Weltimmo*, the Court also considered the extent to which the domestic regulators have "jurisdiction" to investigate the acts of companies registered elsewhere but operating in some way in their state's territory. In essence, the regulator is competent to investigate processing which is governed by its own law (so e.g. the Information Commissioner can investigate processing governed by English law). Further, even if a company is *not* established in a Member State, that state's regulator can still investigate complaints made about the company, though it cannot itself impose penalties and should coordinate with the authorities of the State where the company *is* established ([57]).

4.136   The effect of *Weltimmo* is that foreign companies which sell to the UK via the internet and have any kind of ongoing infrastructure in the UK to support those activities (i) are subject to English law in respect of any data processing done which is related to those activities and (ii) are likely to be subject to the controls of the Information Commissioner.

4.137   The law in this area will change when the General Data Protection Regulation,[95] which replaces the Directive, enters into force on 25 May 2018. It extends the territorial scope of EU data protection law to cover data

---

[93] [2017] 2 CMLR 29.

[94] Ibid, at [91].

[95] Regulation (EU) 2016/679.

controllers which are not established in the Union but whose processing activities relate to offering goods or services to data subjects in the Union.[96]

THE ROLE OF ENGLISH RULES IN CLAIMS GOVERNED BY A DIFFERENT LAW

The substance/procedure distinction

4.138   In both domestic and European conflict of laws there is an established distinction between matters of "substance" – which are governed by the applicable law, whatever it may be – and matters of "procedure", which are *not* governed by the applicable law and continue to be determined by the law of the forum (i.e., for present purposes, the law of England and Wales). This is reflected in Private International Law (Miscellaneous Provisions) Act 1995, s 14(3)(b), which preserves the applicability of English "*rules of evidence, pleading or practice* (and) *questions of procedure*"; and art 1(3) of the Rome II Regulation, to similar effect.

4.139   The question arises as to which issues count as matters of "substance" and which are matters of "procedure/evidence"? A helpful guide is art 15 of the Rome II Regulation, which lists various issues which must be governed by the applicable law (and are thus, for these purposes, matters of "substance" and not "procedure"). Those include "the existence, the nature and the assessment of damage or the remedy claimed" (art 15(c) of the Rome II Regulation) and "the manner in which an obligation may be extinguished and rules of prescription and limitation, including rules relating to the commencement, interruption and suspension of a period of prescription or limitation"(art 15(h)). In addition, notwithstanding that "evidence" is a matter for the law of the forum, any presumptions of law or other rules determining the burden of proof in the foreign applicable law must be applied (art 22(1)).

4.140   The definition of "procedure" for the purposes of double actionability/the 1995 Act is similar, but not in every respect identical. For example, for those purposes, while the issue of recoverable *heads* of damage is governed by the applicable law, questions as to the *quantification* of damage are still to be determined applying English rules: they are considered procedural.[97]

4.141   Whether particular foreign rules count as substance or procedure is not always obvious; see e.g. *Cox v Ergo Versicherung AG*,[98] where the Supreme Court found that a foreign rule requiring damages to be reduced in fatal accident

---

[96] See in particular recitals 23 and 24 and art 3.

[97] *Harding v Wealands* [2007] 2 AC 1.

[98] [2014] AC 1379.

cases to reflect maintenance received from a subsequent partner was substantive. Nevertheless, the decision in *Harding v Wealands*[99] marks a clear difference with the Rome II Regulation, pursuant to which assessment of damage is governed by the applicable law (art 15(c)).

4.142   By contrast both the domestic and European regimes identify limitation periods as matters of substance. In domestic law it has been clear since the Foreign Limitation Periods Act 1984 that foreign limitation periods will be applied as part of the applicable foreign law, save where this would yield a result contrary to English public policy (Foreign Limitation Periods Act 1984, s 2(1)).

Proving foreign law

4.143   Among the issues left to the English court is the issue of whether and how foreign law is to be proved. The following rules of English law are important in practice:

- The parties are under no duty to plead, prove or even refer to foreign law. Thus even if the 1995 Act or the Rome II Regulation provide that a foreign law applies to the claim, it is always open to the parties simply to proceed on the basis that English law applies to their dispute. This step is taken fairly often in practice. It has the practical benefit of avoiding the significant costs and delays which can be incurred in the process of proving the contents of foreign law.

- If by contrast one or more parties wishes to rely on foreign law they must adduce evidence which is sufficient to satisfy the court as to its content. The content of foreign law is a question of fact to be determined on consideration of expert evidence.

- Even if it is accepted that a foreign law applies to the claim, in the absence of adequate evidence as to the content of the foreign law, an English court will presume that its content is the same as English law and, in effect, apply English law. This remains the case even where the foreign law is applicable pursuant to the Rome II Regulation.[100] Courts may however be willing to strike out claims in certain circumstances where a party has failed to prove foreign law relied on in support of their claim.[101]

---

[99] [2007] 2 AC 1.

[100] *Brownlie v Four Seasons Holdings Inc* [2016] 1 WLR 1814 at [88]–[89].

[101] *Global Multimedia International Ltd v Ara Media Services & Ors* [2007] 1 All ER (Comm) 1160 at [37]–[39], per Sir Andrew Morritt.

Mandatory rules of English law

4.144   Even where a foreign law is applicable the English court retains a power to apply English rules of law which are *mandatory* (in this context meaning applicable irrespective of the law which otherwise applies to the claim). This power is expressly protected in s 14(4) of the 1995 Act and in art 16 of the Rome II Regulation , though there is some doubt as to whether the latter provision allows the English court to apply all mandatory rules or only those which are "overriding".[102]

4.145   As to whether particular rules are "mandatory", legislative instruments occasionally say expressly that they will apply irrespective of the law which governs a claim; otherwise whether a statutory provision is "mandatory" is essentially a question of statutory interpretation. The Supreme Court's decision in *Ergo v Cox Versicherung* provides some guidance on how to determine if legislation is mandatory.[103] The Human Rights Act 1998 is one example of "mandatory" legislation, as is the Equality Act 2010.[104]

4.146   In the context of a harassment claim it may be arguable that the Protection from Harassment Act 1997 is mandatory, either in whole or in part. Such an argument may be supported, for example, by the fact that under that Act harassment meeting the same statutory definition gives rise to both criminal and civil liability.

Public policy

4.147   Finally, English courts can disapply a foreign law which would otherwise be applicable on grounds that it is incompatible with English public policy.

4.148   The 1995 Act provides that the English court will not apply a foreign rule which *"would conflict with principles of public policy"* or *"would give effect to such a penal, revenue or other public law as would not otherwise be enforceable under the law of the forum"* (s 14(3)(a)). An equivalent principle appears in the Rome II Regulation but the threshold may be higher; applying a provision of the foreign law may be refused *"only if (the) application is manifestly incompatible with the public policy (ordre public) of the forum"* (art 26). Recital 32 of the Rome II Regulation suggests art 26 may only apply in *"exceptional circumstances"*.

4.149   In this context it is important that clashes between foreign laws and local public policy are not resolved in the abstract; the question is whether applying

---

[102] *Syred v Powszecnny Zaklad Ubezpieczen (Pzu) SA & Ors* [2016] 1 WLR 3211 at [144]–[151].

[103] [2014] 1 AC 1379 at [27]–[29].

[104] *Simpson v Intralinks Ltd* [2012] ICR 1343.

a particular foreign law in the circumstances of a particular case conflicts with domestic public policy. Plainly for the application of a foreign law to do so it must not merely differ from its equivalent in English law, but differ so greatly as to conflict with domestic legal principles which are in some sense fundamental.

4.150 By way of example, arguments as to public policy may arise in respect of foreign laws allowing damages which are penal and excessive in nature (see Recital 32 of the Rome II Regulation), or by contrasts, foreign laws which limit damages to a fraction of the compensation which a claimant would receive in England. They may arise in all sorts of other contexts, but in light of the high threshold which has to be met, parties should think carefully before leading an argument based on incompatibility with English public policy

CHAPTER 5: LIABILITY FOR ONLINE PUBLICATION: DEFAMATION, MALICIOUS FALSEHOOD AND HARASSMENT

CHAPTER SYNOPSIS

- Considers liability for online publication in: defamation, malicious falsehood and harassment.
- The law of defamation protects a person's reputation against unjustified interference. In human rights terms, it gives effect to the ECHR, art 8 positive obligation to protect the human right to reputation.
- The tort of malicious falsehood applies to false statements published maliciously, and which cause damage. It is, therefore, concerned not with reputation but with protecting the economic interests of claimants.
- The Protection from Harassment Act 1997 prohibits a "course of conduct" which a person knows or ought to know amounts to harassment of another. A "course of conduct" must involve conduct on at least two occasions. Harassment is both a crime and a civil wrong.

INTRODUCTION

5.1 An internet publication may be objectionable in a number of different ways. This book deals only with those which infringe rights recognised by the English civil law.

5.2 Four general areas are considered. We deal with online publications which make false or abusive statements, those which disclose private or confidential information and those which misuse the personal data of individuals.

5.3 Such rights can be considered under six headings:

(a) Right to reputation – protected by the tort of defamation;

(b) Right not to be damaged by certain kinds of false statement – protected by the tort of malicious falsehood;

(c) Right to be free from repeated unreasonable interference with a person's life – protected by the tort of harassment;

(d) Right to confidential information – protection by the action for breach of confidence;

(e) Right to privacy – protected by the tort of misuse of private information;

(f) Right to the fair and lawful processing of personal data;

The first three are considered in this Chapter, the remainder are covered in the next.

DEFAMATION

Introduction

5.4 The common law tort of defamation protects a person's reputation against unjustified interference. In human rights terms, this tort gives effect to the European Convention for the Protection of Human Rights and Fundamental Freedoms, art 8 positive obligation to protect the human right to reputation – although the relationship between the two rights has not been fully worked out.

5.5 The law of defamation is not directly concerned with whether false factual statements are made against someone: the question is whether a false defamatory allegation has been made. The English law operates with a "legal fiction" to the effect that words have only one "true" defamatory meaning. This ignores the practical reality that different readers understand words in different ways and makes the determination of "true meaning" a difficult exercise.

5.6 Under the modern English law of defamation, in order to establish a claim the claimant must show that:

(1) The defendant has published words to someone other than the claimant;

(2) Which refer to the claimant;

(3) Which make a defamatory allegation about the claimant; and

(4) Which has caused or is it likely to cause serious harm to the claimant's reputation?

5.7 In relation to each of stages (2), (3) and (4), the test is an objective one: it does not matter who the defendant intended to refer to or what allegation s/he intended to make.

5.8 If a defamatory allegation was made then the question arises as to what defences, if any, are available to the publisher. Although "truth" is a complete defence, the law presumes that defamatory allegations are false. The burden therefore falls on the defendant to prove truth.

5.9 The claimant does not have to prove anything about the state of mind of the defendant. This common law approach to defamation claims remains the position in, for example, Australia, Canada and Ireland. It was, until 1964, the position in the United States. As a result of the decision in *New York Times v*

Sullivan,[1] US defamation law is now out of step with the rest of the common law world: a claimant needs to prove falsity, harm and at least negligence on the part of the publisher. Public figures must show that false defaming statements are made with "actual malice". This means that internet companies – who are almost all US based – find the operation of defamation law in other common law jurisdictions unusual and oppressive. These differences must be borne in mind when communicating claims to such companies.

5.10   In this section of the Chapter we will consider the four "elements" of a defamation claim in English law and we will then outline the most important defences.

First element: publication

5.11   Publication occurs when a person intentionally or negligently takes part in or authorises the publication of a statement.[2] Liability is not just confined to the "author" and the "publisher" (in the commercial sense of the word) but extends to anyone who participates in, secures or authorises the publication. This includes printers and distributors – although they may have a defence of "innocent dissemination". The question as to whether "hosts", "internet service providers" and "search engines" are publishers is a difficult one, which depends on careful analysis of the factual position in each case (see para 3.53ff above).

5.12   When material is placed on the internet there is no "presumption" that it has been published to any reader.[3] If information is available as to the number of "hits" on a particular online publication then a claimant can prove the actual number of people to whom the material has been published. Otherwise, publication can be established by inference. The claimant must establish facts from which it can properly be inferred that publication within the jurisdiction has taken place.[4]

5.13   When material is made available on the internet "publication" takes place every time the material is "downloaded" onto the computer of a person who has used a web browser to pull the material from the web server.[5]

---

[1] (1964) 376 US 254.

[2] *Collins on Defamation,* para 4.02ff.

[3] *Al Amoudi v Brisard & Anor* [2007] 1 WLR 113, at [35].

[4] *ZAM v CFW & Anor* [2013] EMLR 27 at [108]; generally, *Collins on Defamation,* para 4.09ff.

[5] *Dow Jones & Co v Gutnick* (2002) 210 CLR 575 at [44].

5.14   It is not clear whether a person who provides "hyperlinks" to material on the internet is to be treated as the "publisher" of the content of the website which is linked to. In *Crookes v Newton*[6] the Supreme Court of Canada took the view that hyperlinks are essentially a reference rather than something communicating content. However, doubts have been expressed about this decision[7] and the issue has not been decided by an English Court which may take a more flexible approach.[8]

Second element: reference to claimant

5.15   The publication complained of must refer to the claimant. This is often straightforward – often the claimant is mentioned by name. Sometimes, however, the reference is indirect and allusive. The question is whether reasonable people would understand the words to refer to the claimant.

> "This is an objective test. If the words would be so understood by such people it is not necessary for the claimant to prove that there were in fact such people, who read the offending words; so an individual defamed by name in Cornwall has a cause of action even if he was unknown in that county at the time of publication".[9]

Third element: defamatory meaning

Introduction

5.16   The first thing to determine in any proposed defamation claim is the defamatory allegation being made by the publication – what is called the "meaning" of the words complained of or the "sting" of the libel. This is a purely objective question. The law of libel requires the Court to carry out an artificial exercise of determining the "single meaning" of words complained of in an action. This is a fiction adopted by the law for practical reasons.[10] "Meanings" are divided into two kinds: "natural and ordinary" and "innuendo".

---

[6] [2011] 3 SCR 269.

[7] *Gatley on Libel and Slander*, 12th ed, (London: Sweet & Maxwell, 2013), para 6.13.

[8] Tugendhat and Christie, *The Law of Privacy and the Media*, 3rd Edn, para 15.34.

[9] *Lachaux & Ors v Independent Print Ltd* [2016] QB 402 at [15].

[10] For example, *Lait v Evening Standard Ltd* [2011] 1 WLR 2973 at [19].

Natural and ordinary meaning

5.17　The so-called "natural and ordinary meaning" is the meaning that would be placed upon the published material by the "ordinary reasonable reader" who does not have any special background knowledge.

5.18　The general principles to be applied in the determination of the natural and ordinary meaning of words complained of are well established. They are, for example, set out in an oft-quoted passage from the judgment of Sir Anthony Clarke MR in *Jeynes v News Magazines Ltd & Anor*[11] as follows:

> "The legal principles relevant to meaning … may be summarised in this way: (1) The governing principle is reasonableness. (2) The hypothetical reasonable reader is not naïve but he is not unduly suspicious. He can read between the lines. He can read in an implication more readily than a lawyer and may indulge in a certain amount of loose thinking but he must be treated as being a man who is not avid for scandal and someone who does not, and should not, select one bad meaning where other non-defamatory meanings are available. (3) Over-elaborate analysis is best avoided. (4) The intention of the publisher is irrelevant. (5) The article must be read as a whole, and any 'bane and antidote' taken together. (6) The hypothetical reader is taken to be representative of those who would read the publication in question. (7) In delimiting the range of permissible defamatory meanings, the court should rule out any meaning which, 'can only emerge as the produce of some strained, or forced, or utterly unreasonable interpretation…'…. (8) It follows that 'it is not enough to say that by some person or another the words might be understood in a defamatory sense'".

5.19　When a publication relates to alleged misconduct, there are three possible types of allegation which might be being made:

> "The sting of a libel may be capable of meaning that a claimant has in fact committed some serious act, such as murder. Alternatively it may be suggested that the words mean that there are reasonable grounds to suspect that he/she has committed such an act. A third possibility is that they may mean that there

---

[11] [2008] EWCA Civ 130 at [14].

are grounds for investigating whether he/she has been responsible for such an act."[12]

These three "levels" of meaning are referred to as "*Chase* Levels 1, 2 and 3."

Innuendo meaning

5.20 In a limited number of cases a statement may be defamatory on the basis of extrinsic facts known to some readers: this is known as an innuendo meaning.[13] This can be important in online cases where the words complained of may be very short and anodyne but may bear a defamatory meaning the context of an online debate which many readers will be aware of.

5.21 For example, the "Twitter libel" case of *Monroe v Hopkins*[14] concerned two tweets, the second of which read:

"Can someone explain to me – in 10 words or less – the difference between irritant @PennyRed and social anthrax @Jack Monroe"

Read in isolation, this conveyed the defendant's contempt for Ms Monroe but was not defamatory. However, in the light of the background facts concerning the vandalisation of a war memorial, a controversial tweet by @PennyRed and the defendant's condemnation of it, the judge held that the Tweet bore the "innuendo meaning" that Ms Monroe "condoned and approved of the fact that in the course of an anti-government protest there had been vandalisation by obscene graffiti of the women's war memorial in Whitehall, a monument to those who fought for her freedom." [48]

Meaning in online publication cases

5.22 There are no special principles applicable to the determination of meaning in internet publications. However, the court will take into account the context of publication. Words which are published on bulletins, blogs or social media are more akin to "slanders" and may be understood to be "vulgar abuse" and not to be taken seriously.[15]

5.23 In addition, the nature of the audience for a particular publication is taken into account when considering meaning. In the case of *McAlpine v Bercow*[16] the

[12] *Chase v News Group Newspapers Ltd* [2003] EMLR 11 at [45].

[13] See generally, *Gatley on Libel and Slander*, 12th Edn, para 3.21ff.

[14] [2017] 4 WLR 68; *McAlpine v Bercow* [2013] EWHC 1342 (QB) at [55].

[15] *Smith v ADVFN Plc & Ors* [2008] EWHC 1797 (QB) at [13] to [17].

[16] [2013] EWHC 1342 (QB) at [58].

judge said that "The hypothetical reader must be taken to be a reasonable representative of users of Twitter who follow the Defendant." The other tweets posted by the defendant can, therefore, be taken into account in determining the meaning of a particular tweet.

5.24 In the case of *Monroe*[17] Warby J considered the application of the well-established rules to publications on Twitter. He said that as this is a "conversational medium" it would be more fitting and appropriate to take an "impressionistic approach" which

> "must take account of the whole tweet and the context in which the ordinary reasonable reader would read that tweet. That context includes (a) matters of ordinary general knowledge; and (b) matters that were put before that reader via Twitter" [35].

5.25 In the same case, Warby J held that a matter can be treated as known to the ordinary reader if, for practical purposes, everybody knows it or if it is part of the information conveyed by the tweet itself [37]. Furthermore,

> "a matter can be treated as part of the context in which an offending tweet [is published] if it is on Twitter and sufficiently closely connected in time, content, or otherwise that it is likely to have been in the hypothetical reader's view, or in their mind, at the time they read the words complained of" [38].

5.26 The application of this approach may well mean that what might appear to be a statement of fact would, in the context of online debate, be treated as containing an "element of metaphor" and thus conveying an opinion rather than a factual allegation.[18]

Defamatory tendency

5.27 When the meaning of an allegation is determined it is then necessary to consider whether the allegation made is defamatory. This will only be the case if "the words tend to lower the claimant in the estimation of right-thinking members of society generally."[19] It is not enough that the words should damage the claimant in the eyes of a section of the public only. For example, in *Modi v Clarke*[20] it was accepted that it does not defame someone to say that he wishes to destroy the structure of world cricket, because that depends on

---

[17] [2017] 4 WLR 68.

[18] Ibid, at [43]; and the Canadian case of *Baglow v Smith* [2015] ONSC 1175.

[19] *Sim v Stretch* [1936] 2 All ER 1237 at 1240.

[20] [2011] EWCA Civ 937.

the views of that section of the public interested in the sport on the current structure.

5.28 It is important to distinguish between personal defamation, which involves imputations as to the character or attributes of an individual, and business or professional defamation, which involves imputations as to the way that profession or business was conducted.[21] The following definition of "defamatory" has been suggested:

> "the publication of which he complains may be defamatory of him because it substantially affects in an adverse manner the attitude of other people towards him, *or has a tendency so to do.*"[22]

Fourth element: serious harm to reputation

5.29 There is now a second stage in determining whether a publication is defamatory. This is set out in the Defamation Act 2013, s 1 ("the 2013 Act") which provides that:

> "(1) A statement is not defamatory unless its publication has caused or is likely to cause serious harm to the reputation of the claimant.

> (2) For the purposes of this section, harm to the reputation of a body that trades for profit is not 'serious harm' unless it has caused or is likely to cause the body serious financial loss".

5.30 There are two parts to this provision: s 1(1) applies to claims brought by individuals and bodies which do not trade for profit, s 1(2) applies to bodies which trade for profit.

5.31 The meaning of s 1(1) has been considered in a number of cases[23] over the past three years. The position has now been clarified by the decision of the Court of Appeal in *Lachaux & Ors v Independent Print Ltd*:[24] It was held that s 1(1) had the effect of giving statutory status to the definition of defamation in *Thornton v Telegraph Media Group*[25] but raising the threshold from one of substantiality to one of seriousness. In other words, a publication is

---

[21] *Thornton v Telegraph Media Group Ltd* [2011] 1 WLR 1985 at [34].

[22] Ibid, at [95].

[23] See espec *Cooke & Anor v Mirror Group Newspapers Ltd & Anor*, [2015] 1 WLR 895 and *Theedom v Nourish Training* [2016] EMLR 10.

[24] [2017] EWCA Civ 1334, at [82]; note that the decision is the subject of an application for permission to appeal to the Supreme Court.

[25] [2011] 1 WLR 1985.

defamatory if it "seriously affects" in an adverse manner the attitude of other people towards the claimant or has a tendency to do so. The common law presumption as to damage in cases of libel, the common law principle that the cause of action accrues on the date of publication, the established position as to limitation and the common law objective single meaning rule are all unaffected by s 1(1).

5.32   The Court of Appeal gave guidance as to how to deal with issues as to "serious harm":[26]

- If the admitted meaning (or the meaning ascertained by the Court) is seriously defamatory it will ordinarily then be proper to draw an inference of serious reputational harm, *Lachaux* [82(3)].
- Courts should ordinarily be slow to direct a preliminary issue, involving substantial evidence, on a dispute as to whether serious reputational harm has been caused or is likely to be caused by the published statement, *Lachaux* [82(4)].
- A defendant disputing the existence of serious harm may in an appropriate case, if the circumstances so warrant, issue a Part 24 summary judgment application – for example where it is plain that the number of publishees is very limited and no one thought less of the claimant by reason of the publication, *Lachaux* [79].
- A defendant could still issue a *Jameel* application: the *Jameel* jurisdiction continuing to be available after the 2013 Act as before (although there is potential degree of overlap with s 1(1)), *Lachaux* [79].

5.33   S 1(2) concerns claims by bodies that trade for profit. This is not defined but, presumably, will not cover charities or other corporate bodies which do not trade with the aim of producing profit for their shareholders.

5.34   A body which trades for profit must prove "serious financial loss". Although there is no guidance on the word "serious" in this context it must, presumably, mean substantial loss and must be relative to the size of the body.

5.35   There are two well established ways in which "serious financial loss" can be established:

- Direct financial loss – this is the paradigm case. The claimant may seek to prove direct losses caused by the impact of the libels on customers.

---

[26] See the summary, *Lachaux*, at [82]

These must be losses of profit, a reduction in turnover is not enough.[27] Such loss can, however, be inferred from relatively slim materials.[28]

- Money spent on mitigating the damage. For example, the costs of employing a PR consultant[29] or other costs of "counter-publicity", the costs of investigation identity of wrongdoers or the costs of removing republications from the internet.[30]

5.36   It is possible that "serious financial loss" could be established in other ways – although these remain untested and controversial. For example,

- Reduction in balance sheet goodwill. This would reflect damage to the corporate name and brand and would be a loss suffered by the company. In contrast, reduction in share price is not sufficient – share price is not an aspect of goodwill or an asset of the company.[31]
- Wasted management time – spent dealing with the problems caused by the libels. It is clear that the cost of time spent investigating wrong or mitigating its consequences is recoverable and that it is not necessary to show additional expenditure or loss of revenue or profit.[32] This "wasted management time", must however be "directly attributable" to the libel.

Defences

Introduction

5.37   There are a number of defences which apply only to defamation claims. Several of these have been codified by the 2013 Act. In this section we will consider six defences: truth, honest opinion, public interest, absolute privilege, qualified privilege and limitation.

---

[27] *Undre v Harrow LBC* [2017] EMLR 3.

[28] *Brett Wilson LLP v Persons Unknown* [2016] 4 WLR 69.

[29] *ReachLocal UK Ltd v Bennett* [2015] EMLR 7.

[30] See by analogy *Lisle-Mainwaring v Associated Newspapers Ltd & Anor* [2017] EWHC 543 (QB) at [131]–[180].

[31] *Collins Stewart v Financial Times Ltd* [2005] EMLR 5.

[32] *R+V Versicherung v Risk Insurance & Reinsurance Solutions SA & Ors* [2006] EWHC 42 (Comm).

Truth

5.38   The 2013 Act has codified the common law truth defence. Under s 2 a defendant has a complete defence if s/he can show that the imputation conveyed by the statement complained of is substantially true.

5.39   Some statements include two or more distinct imputations; for example, a publication stating that the claimant struck someone and sole their purse alleges violence and dishonesty. Where a defendant cannot show that one of the imputations is substantially true, s/he will still succeed with a truth defence if "having regard to the imputations which are shown to be substantially true, the imputations which are not shown to be substantially true do not seriously harm the claimant's reputation." It is likely that a defendant can rely on this element of the truth defence as long as the claimant has complained of the imputation that is substantially true.[33]

5.40   The defence of truth is inextricably linked to the meaning of a statement – it is the meaning decided upon by a court that must be shown to be true.

5.41   A defendant seeking to defend a *Chase* level 1 allegation as true will need to prove the primary facts relating to the conduct of a claimant; it is not sufficient to rely solely on what another body, e.g., the police, have said. A defendant seeking to prove that the claimant was actually guilty of misconduct may rely on events post-dating the publication.[34]

5.42   With a *Chase* level 2 meaning a defendant will have to prove some conduct which, objectively assessed, gives rise to grounds for suspicion. Relying on strong circumstantial evidence (rather than specific evidence of the claimant's conduct) may be sufficient in some cases.[35]

5.43   When justifying a *Chase* level 3 meaning as true it may be sufficient to rely on assertions made by third parties but this is not settled law.[36]

Honest opinion

5.44   The defence of honest opinion (formerly known as fair comment) is now set out in s 3 of the 2013 Act. A defendant relying on this defence has to satisfy a number of conditions:

---

[33] *Duncan & Neill on Defamation*, 4th ed (London: Butterworths, 2015), at 12.29.

[34] *Cohen v Telegraph Ltd* [1968] 1 WLR 916 (CA), at p 919; *Chase* at [52]–[55].

[35] *Musa King v Telegraph Group Ltd* [2005] 1 WLR 2282 at [22].

[36] *Gatley on Libel and Slander*, 12th ed, (London: Sweet & Maxwell, 2013), at 11.13.

(1) The statement complained of must be a statement of opinion. This question is determined by reference to whether a hypothetical ordinary reader/listener would regard it as such.[37] Opinion is something which "is or can reasonably be inferred to be a deduction, inference, conclusion, criticism, remark, observation, *etc*".[38] Generally it is helpful to ask whether the statement is one that is verifiable: statements of opinion will rarely be verifiable. There is no need for the opinion to be on a matter of public interest. The distinction between "fact" and "opinion" is similar to that drawn by the Court of Human Rights between "facts" and "value judgments".[39]

(2) The statement complained of must have indicated, whether in general or specific terms, the basis of the opinion. This has been held to be important for defendants publishing information online because the internet enables the publication of comments on matters which are often not generally known and whose readers may not be able to evaluate the opinions expressed.[40]

(3) The opinion must be one that an honest person could have held on the basis of either:

    i.   any fact which existed at the time the statement complained of was published, the truth of which a defendant has to prove. A defendant need not have been aware of the fact(s) but publishing in ignorance of such facts may go the question of whether the opinion was genuinely held (see below).[41] *or*

    ii. anything asserted to be a fact in a privileged statement (meaning that the person who made that statement would have had one of the defences listed)[42] published *before* the statement complained of. This too is an objective test but as Warby J reiterated in *Yeo v Times Newspapers* it is a generous test because:

---

[37] *Duncan and Neill on Defamation*, at 13.11.

[38] *Branson v Bower* [2001] EMLR 32 at [12].

[39] For example *Cumpănă and Mazăre v Romania* [GC] (2005) 41 EHRR 14 at [98].

[40] *Donovan v Gibbons* [2014] EWHC 3406 (QB) at [14] (per HHJ Richard Parkes QC).

[41] Gavin Millar and Andrew Scott, *Newsgathering: Law, Regulation and the Public Interest*, (Oxford: OUP, 2016), at 17.46.

[42] These are listed at s 3(7) of the 2013 Act as: a public interest defence under s 4, a statement published in a scientific or academic journal meeting the conditions in s 6, reports of court proceedings under s 14 of the Defamation Act 1996, reports protected by qualified privilege under s 15 of the 1996 Act.

"it protects any comment which could have been made honestly, even if only by a person who is prejudiced, or holds exaggerated or obstinate views."[43]

5.45   If these conditions are satisfied, a claimant can still defeat the defence if s/he can show that the opinion was not genuinely held or, if the defendant was not the author of the opinion, that s/he knew or ought to have known that the author did not reasonably hold it. This second qualification is likely to be relevant to the operator of a moderated online comments board on which defamatory opinions are published by others.

5.46   If the opinion was genuinely held it does not matter whether the publisher was motivated by spite or animosity towards the claimant (although such findings may go to the question of whether the opinion could honestly have been held).[44]

Public interest

Introduction

5.47   The public interest (or *Reynolds*[45]) defence was put onto a statutory footing by s 4 of the 2013 Act. A defendant must establish the following criteria:[46]

(1)   the statement complained of was, or formed part of, a statement on a matter of public interest; *and*

(2)   a reasonable belief that publishing the statement complained of was in the public interest.

5.48   The defence can be relied on both in regard to assertions of fact and opinion. Factual statements need not be demonstrated to be true in order to be covered by the s 4 defence; a publication may be wrong but fair.[47]

5.49   Although the s 4 defence is likely to be relied on primarily by media organisations,[48] it can be invoked by any defendant, including persons sued for statements provided to and then published by the media.[49]

---

43 *Yeo v Times Newspapers Ltd* [2017] EMLR 1 at [21] (per Warby J).

44 *Tse Wai Chun v Cheng* [2001] EMLR 31 at [79].

45 First recognised in *Reynolds v Times Newspapers & Anor* [2001] 2 AC 127. It is likely that the pre-2013 Act case law will remain relevant: *Yeo*, at [29] (per Warby J).

46 S 4 of the 2013 Act.

47 *Yeo*, at [175] (per Warby J); *Economou v De Freitas* [2017] EMLR 4 at [139(6)] (per Warby J).

48 *Flood v Times Newspapers Ltd* [2012] 2 AC 273 at [44] (per Lord Phillips).

49 *Economou*, at [246] (per Warby J).

A statement on a matter of public interest

5.50   Whether or not a statement was or formed part of a statement on a matter of public interest is an objective test to be determined by a court.[50] The subjective motives of the person publishing the information will not generally be relevant to whether the statement is on a matter of public interest.[51] Subject to the axiom that what is in the public interest is distinct from what is interesting to the public,[52] this first limb of the public interest test will not usually be difficult to satisfy.

Reasonable belief that publishing the statement was in the public interest

5.51   To determine this limb of the public interest defence a court will address the following question:

> "could whoever published the defamation, given whatever they knew (and did not know) and whatever they had done (and had not done) to guard so far as possible against the publication of untrue defamatory material, properly have considered the publication in question to be in the public interest?"[53]

5.52   Accordingly, to satisfy this requirement, a defendant must:

(1)   show that s/he in fact believed that publishing the statement was in the public interest,[54] and

(2)   demonstrate that this was a reasonable belief.[55]

5.53   The applicable principles for the assessment of whether a defendant has "reasonable belief" that the statement was in the public interest have recently been summarised as follows:[56]

(1)   The question in each case is whether the defendant behaved fairly and responsibly in gathering and publishing the information.

(2)   For this purpose "the information" is the particular defamatory information which is the subject of the claim.

---

[50] *Flood* at [201] (per Lord Dyson).

[51] Loc.cit.

[52] *Jameel (Mohammed) & Anor v Wall Street Journal Europe Sprl* [2007] 1 AC 359 at [147] (per Lady Hale).

[53] *Flood* at [113] (per Lord Brown).

[54] *Economou*, at [139(1)].

[55] *Economou*, at [139(2)].

[56] This list is adapted from the judgment of Warby J in *Yeo*, at [133].

(3)   Some latitude must be allowed for reasonable differences of view on precisely what the allegation is. More generally, the existence or otherwise of the public interest defence must be judged on the facts as they reasonably appeared to the defendant at the time.

(4)   Lord Nicholls' well-known non-exhaustive ten point list in *Reynolds*[57] is an important guide but not a set of tests which the publication has to pass; the standard of conduct must be applied in a practical and flexible manner. These factors include the gravity of the defamatory allegation(s), whether it/they have been put to the subject for comment, whether the publication contains the subject's comment and the urgency of the topic of the publication.

(5)   Thus, the nature and extent to which verification is required is a fact-sensitive issue (and will depend on the source and status of the information). The publisher must have taken the care that a responsible publisher would take to verify the information, but this depends on the nature and source of that information.

(6)   Further, a publication may be held protected by the public interest defence even if the journalistic exercise (or process by which the Defendant formed his/her reasonable belief) has in some respect fallen short of the standards to be expected of a responsible journalist.

(7)   Where the defamatory allegation is that the claimant is guilty of some misconduct, and the public interest lies in the fact that this is or may be true, a public interest defence is unlikely to "get off the ground" unless the journalist "honestly *and* reasonably believed" that the statement was true … The defence is not available where there is some indication that the professional judgment of the editor or journalist was made in a "casual, cavalier, slipshod or careless manner."

5.54   A defendant must have held the reasonable belief at the time of publication. This means that, generally, events that took place either after publication or before publication but which were unknown to the defendant are unlikely to be significant in the assessment of reasonable belief.[58] Post-publication conduct is, however, capable of being probative of a defendant's state of mind at the time of publication.[59]

5.55   What is required in terms in terms of pre-publication checks/steps (evidencing a reasonable belief that publication was in the public interest) may

---

[57] *Reynolds v Times Newspapers Ltd & Ors* [2001] 2 AC 127, at p204 (per Lord Nicholls).

[58] *Economou* [2017] EMLR 4 at [139(3) and (5)].

[59] *Economou* [2017] EMLR 4 at [139(3)] and [141].

depend on the status and role of a defendant, including whether s/he or it is, for instance, a large media organisation or a citizen journalist publishing articles online. In *Economou*, Warby J remarked that "the enquiries and checks that can reasonably be expected must be bespoke, depending on the precise role that the individual plays."[60] This defence is, however, little tested in the context of online publications by defendants who are not media organisations. It remains to be seen whether, for example, citizen journalists or small publishers may be held to less exacting standards when running a public interest defence.

5.56   A defendant's ability to rely successfully on a public interest defence may change over time. Defamatory allegations which could at one point be defended on the basis of a reasonable belief that publication was in the public interest may not remain defensible (within the limitation period) if, for example, information is made available vindicating a claimant.[61] This is particularly relevant to online publications which remain available.

Reportage

5.57   S 4(3) of the 2013 Act provides a subcategory of public interest defence, which was at common law known as "reportage". A defendant can rely on this defence where the statement complained of was, or formed part of, an *accurate and impartial account of a dispute* to which the claimant was a party. In such a case, the court can disregard any failure on the part of a defendant to verify the truth of the imputation conveyed by the statement.

5.58   In the pre-2013 Act case of *Roberts v Gable*, reportage was summarised in the following terms: "it is the neutral reporting without adoption or embellishment or subscribing to any belief in its truth of attributed allegations of both sides of a political and possibly some other kind of dispute" [53].

5.59   The precise parameters of reportage remain unclear. Having regard to s 4(3) and (5) and the pre-2013 Act case law the following points may be made:

- Reportage covers both statements of fact and opinion.
- Reporting must be of a dispute – whether that dispute must be ongoing and how exactly a dispute is defined remain uncertain.
- Reporting of the dispute must be accurate and impartial. The defence is likely to be lost if the person reporting a dispute adopts a

---

[60] *Economou*, at [246].

[61] See, for example, *Flood v Times Newspapers Ltd* [2013] EWHC 4047 (QB) at [71]–[78].

statement/allegation as her own and/or fails to report a dispute in a fair disinterested and neutral way.[62]

- The person publishing the statement is not required to verify the underlying allegations, s/he need only verify that they were in fact made.[63]

Absolute privilege

5.60   Where publication is subject to absolute privilege there is no liability in defamation regardless of the truth of a statement or whether it was published maliciously.

5.61   The most common instance of absolute privilege is fair and accurate reports of proceedings before any national or international court or tribunal, as long as those reports are published contemporaneously.[64] A report may refer both to things said in court as well as matters referred to by a court/tribunal sitting in public.[65] For a report to be *fair* and *accurate* it must present a summary of the cases put by both sides and contain no substantial inaccuracies, while allegations should be attributed quotes. A report will be regarded as *contemporaneous* if it published as soon as practicable – this will vary depending on the type of publication.

Qualified privilege

5.62   A defendant has a defence to a defamation claim if the statement complained of is covered by qualified privilege unless the defendant is malicious. Qualified privilege ("QP") is either conferred by statute or by the common law.

5.63   At common law, a statement may be protected by qualified privilege in circumstances in which the publisher had a legal, moral or social duty or a legitimate interest in making the statement to a recipient who had a corresponding interest or duty in receiving it. This is an objective test. Subject to a publication satisfying this test, common law QP is capable of applying to an unlimited range of publications/situations. Well-known examples include employment or academic references, allegations of misconduct against a fellow employee, and information supplied by credit reference agencies. This type of privilege is capable of attaching to both "private" communications

---

[62] *Roberts v Gable* [2008] QB 502 at [61(5)].

[63] S 4(3) and *Flood*, at [77] (per Lord Phillips).

[64] Defamation Act 1996, s 14 (as amended by s 7 of the 2013 Act).

[65] *Duncan and Neill on Defamation*, at 16.37.

made online through e.g., messaging services or email and publications to a wider public on e.g., Twitter or Facebook.

5.64   Fair and accurate reports/copies/extracts of the following (non-exhaustive categories of information)[66] will be protected by QP as long as they are on a matter of public interest and published without malice:[67]

- Reports of proceedings in public of a legislature anywhere in the world.
- A copy or extract from matter published by or on the authority of a government or legislature anywhere in the world.
- Reports of proceedings or of copy or extract from matter published anywhere in the world by an international organisation or an international conference (note that international conference is referred to here in a narrow sense, meaning an official interstate forum such as the Conference on Disarmament).

5.65   Reports containing the following categories[68] of document/information will be protected by qualified privilege if they fulfil the requirements set out above and the defendant has not refused or neglected to publish a letter or statement by way of explanation or contradiction when requested to do so by the claimant (in the case of an online publication this would entail the defendant publishing the explanation/contradiction on the same platform):[69]

- A copy of or extract from or summary of a document made available by a court anywhere in the world.
- Reports of proceedings at any public meeting or sitting in the United Kingdom of, inter alia, a local authority or local authority committee or an inquiry.
- Reports of proceedings at any public meeting (bona fide and lawfully held for the furtherance or discussion of a matter of public interest) held anywhere in the world.
- Reports of proceedings at a general meeting of a listed company.
- A copy of or extract from any document circulated to members of a UK public company by, for example, the board of directors or auditors.

5.66   S 6 of the 2013 Act provides a new form of QP for statements published in peer-reviewed scientific and academic journals. A defendant has to satisfy two conditions. First, the statement must relate to a scientific or academic matter.

---

[66] See further the Pt 1 of Sch 1 to the 1996 Act.

[67] S 15 of the 1996 Act.

[68] For a full list, see Pt 2 of Sch 1 to the 1996 Act (as amended by s 7 of the 2013 Act).

[69] S 15(2) of the 1996 Act.

Second, before the statement was published in the journal, an independent review of the statement's scientific or academic merit must have been carried out by the editor of the journal, and one or more persons with expertise in the scientific or academic matter concerned. Privilege extends to assessments of the merits of such statements published in the same journal. Where a statement is protected by this form of privilege, s 6(5) provides that the publication of a fair and accurate copy of, extract from or summary of the statement or assessment is also privileged.

Limitation

5.67   The limitation period for claims in defamation (and malicious falsehood) is one year from the date on which the cause of action accrued.[70] That will usually be the date on which the material complained of was first published.

5.68   At common law, a new cause of action arises every time a defamatory statement is republished – publications remaining online were treated as being republished on an ongoing basis. This means that, if a statement is published online, a claim could be brought in respect of the period of one year prior to issue of the claim during which it was available online.[71]

5.69   The position has, however, been changed by s 8 of the 2013 Act, which provides that where a statement is published and there is a subsequent publication by the same person which is substantially the same, the cause of action is to be treated as having accrued on the date of first publication. This does not apply if the manner of the subsequent publication is materially different from the manner of the first publication.[72] In deciding this issue, the court shall have regard to the level of prominence of the statement and the extent of the subsequent publication.[73]

5.70   The court has a discretion to extend the time limit in the Limitation Act 1980, s 4A.[74] The court must have regard to any prejudice that would be caused to either side. It has been long recognised that the exercise of that discretionary jurisdiction is exceptional because, for reasons of public policy, time is treated as being of the essence in the defamation context.[75]

---

[70] Limitation Act 1980, s 4A.

[71] *Loutchansky v Times Newspapers Ltd & Ors* [2002] QB 783 at [51]–[76].

[72] S 8(4) of the 2013 Act.

[73] S 8(5) of the 2013 Act.

[74] S 32A of the 1980 Act.

[75] *Steedman v BBC* [2002] EMLR 17; *Austin v Newcastle Chronicle and Journal Ltd* [2001] EWCA Civ 834; *Bewry v Reed Elsevier* [2015] 1 WLR 2565 at [5]–[8].

Defamation Act 2013, s 9[76]

5.71   Where a defendant is not domiciled in the UK, EU or a Lugano Convention state, s/he may be able to rely on s 9 of the 2013 Act to defeat a defamation claim. This section prevents the court from exercising jurisdiction over a claim brought against such persons/organisations unless it is satisfied that "of all the places in which the statement complained of has been published, England and Wales is clearly the most appropriate place in which to bring an action."

5.72   This requires the court to look at all of the jurisdictions in which the statement complained of has been published and to have regard to considerations such as: the claimant's reputation in England and Wales as compared to elsewhere; the extent to which the publication targeted a readership/audience here; and whether there is reason to think that the claimant would not receive a fair hearing elsewhere.[77] s 9 may be deployed against claimants who are resident/domiciled in this jurisdiction and those who are not. It is, however, likely to be easier for a claimant domiciled in this jurisdiction to establish that England and Wales is the most appropriate place to bring their defamation claim.[78]

Jameel abuse

5.73   Defendants may also be able to contend that a claim should be dismissed as an abuse of process on the basis that there has been no real and substantial tort (so-called *Jameel*[79] abuse).

5.74   While *Jameel* abuse arguments can be relied on against any claimant, they are most likely to be relevant where a defendant is not domiciled in this jurisdiction and there has been minimal publication of the defamatory statement here. For example, it might be argued that there has been no real and substantial tort where a claimant sues the English publisher of an online article in circumstances in which the article has been viewed (published) in England on very few occasions and/or the claimant is unknown here. There will often be an overlap between the matters relied on by a defendant seeking to get a libel action dismissed on the basis that it amounts to *Jameel* abuse and those relied on to dispute serious harm to reputation.

---

[76] For a more detailed discussion, see para 4.48.

[77] *Ahuja v Politika Novine I Magazini DOO & Ors* [2016] 1 WLR 1414 at [41] and [31].

[78] *Ahuja* at [31].

[79] *Jameel (Yousef) v Dow Jones & Co Inc* [2005] QB 946 at [48]–[71].

MALICIOUS FALSEHOOD

Introduction

5.75 The tort of malicious falsehood – sometimes known as "slander of goods" or "trade libel" – applies to false statements which are published maliciously and which cause damage. This tort is, therefore, concerned not with reputation but with protecting the economic interests of claimants against damage caused by false statements.

5.76 A malicious falsehood claim faces a much higher hurdle than one in a defamation: the claimant cannot rely on the presumption of falsity and takes on the positive burden of providing malice on the part of the defendant. The "serious harm" test does not, however, apply to such claims.

Elements of tort

5.77 In order to establish a claim in the tort of "malicious falsehood" it must be proved:

(1)   the defendant has made a false statement;

(2)   referring directly or indirectly to the claimant, his business, property or economic interests;[80]

(3)   published maliciously; and

(4)   which caused the claimant pecuniary damage or which was calculated to cause such damage.[81]

5.78 In relation to the first element, the "single meaning rule" is not applied.[82] The Court has to consider the reasonably available meanings – those which a substantial number of people would have understood the words to bear – and then decide the issue of falsity in relation to each one.[83]

5.79 It seems likely that the same approach will be applied to the second element: did a substantial number of people understand the statement as referring to the claimant?

5.80 The third element is malice. The claimant must show that the defendant knew that the words were false or was reckless as to their truth or falsity. The test is a subjective one and must, therefore, be assessed with reference to the

---

[80] *Marathon Mutual Ltd & Anor v Waters* [2010] EMLR 3 at [9].

[81] The first alternative is the position at common law, the second is provided for by the Defamation Act 1952, s 3(1).

[82] *Ajinomoto Sweeteners Europe SAS v ASDA Stores Ltd* [2011] QB 497.

[83] *Cruddas v Calvert* [2014] EMLR 5 at [30].

meaning that the defendant believed the words to bear:[84] "a defendant should only be liable for malicious falsehood if the falsehood represents one of the possible correct meanings of the defendant's words and the defendant intended to convey that falsehood".[85]

5.81 Malice is the most difficult element to prove. There must be some cogent evidence that the defendant knew that the statement was false (or was reckless as to its truth or falsity). If the evidence is equally consistent with malice or lack of malice then the claim must fail.[86]

5.82 The final element is damage. At common law "special damage" (that is, actual financial loss) is an essential element of the tort of malicious falsehood. This strict rule was relaxed by the Defamation Act 1952, s 3(1) which provides that:

> "In an action for slander of title, slander of goods or other malicious falsehood, it shall not be necessary to allege or prove special damage –
>
> (a) if the words upon which the action is founded are calculated to cause pecuniary damage to the claimant and are published in writing or other permanent form; or
>
> (b) if the said words are calculated to cause pecuniary damage to the claimant in respect of any office, profession, calling, trade or business held or carried on by him at the time of the publication".

5.83 In this provision "calculated to" means "more likely than" not.[87] The assessment of whether words are "calculated" to cause damage is made at the time of publication. If words are "calculated" to cause damage of the kinds identified then the claimant is not required to evidence actual financial loss.[88] All the claimant has to do is to identify the nature of the loss and the way in which it is likely to be sustained. [89]

---

[84] *Loveless v Earl & Anor* [1999] EMLR 530.

[85] *Cruddas v Calvert* [2015] EMLR 16 at [114] (per Jackson LJ).

[86] *Telnikoff v Matusevich* [1991] 1 QB 102, at 120.

[87] *Tesla Motors Ltd v BBC* [2013] EWCA Civ 152 at [27].

[88] *Joyce v Sengupta & Anor* [1993] 1 WLR 337.

[89] *Tesla Motors Ltd v BBC* [2011] EWHC 2760 (QB) at [37].

HARASSMENT

Introduction

5.84   Under the ECHR, art 8 the State has a positive obligation to secure respect for private life "even in the sphere of the relations of individuals between themselves".[90] This requires maintenance and implementation of an adequate legal framework. In respect of less serious acts between individuals which may nonetheless violate psychological integrity, the obligation may be to have in place civil law remedies capable of affording sufficient protection.[91]

5.85   In domestic law this framework is provided by the Protection from Harassment Act 1997, which prohibits a "course of conduct" which a person knows or ought to know amounts to harassment of another.[92] A "course of conduct" must involve conduct on at least two occasions.[93] Harassment is both a crime and a civil wrong.[94]

Nature of harassment

5.86   The 1997 Act does not provide a comprehensive definition of "harassment" but provides that it includes conduct which alarms a person or causes the person distress.[95]

5.87   The 1997 Act has been considered by the civil and criminal courts on many occasions over the past two decades. A number of points can be derived from the case law:

(1)   Conduct that causes distress or alarm becomes harassment when it ceases to be merely unattractive or unreasonable and becomes oppressive and unacceptable.[96] To cross the boundary from the regrettable to the unacceptable the gravity of the misconduct must be of an order which would sustain criminal liability under s 2.[97]

---

[90] For example, *Bărbulescu v Romania* [2016] IRLR 235 at [52].

[91] For example, *A & Ors v Latvia* (App No. 30808/11) at [151].

[92] S 1(1) of the 1997 Act.

[93] S 7(3)(a) of the 1997 Act.

[94] S 2 (criminal offence) and s 3 (civil remedy) of the 1997 Act.

[95] S 7(2) of the 1997 Act.

[96] *Majrowski v Guy's and St Thomas's NHS Trust* [2007] 1 AC 224 at [30]; see also *Ferguson v British Gas Trading Ltd* [2010] 1 WLR 785 at [17].

[97] *Majrowski,* loc.cit.

(2)   When the conduct relied on consists of statements or publications, the defendant's right to freedom of expression under the ECHR, art 10 must be taken into account.[98]

(3)   The fact that statements made are true does not prevent them from constituting harassment.[99]

(4)   The conduct must be targeted at an individual but such targeting can be direct or indirect.[100] A claim can be brought either by that individual or by other persons who are foreseeably, and directly, harmed by the course of targeted conduct.[101]

Online harassment

5.88   The 1997 Act has been applied to remarks on internet forums[102] and to an internet based campaign.[103] It has been held that publication on a website of the name of an individual in the knowledge that such publication will inevitably come to their attention on more than one occasion and on each occasion cause them alarm or distress may constitute harassment.[104]

5.89   In *S v Director of Public Prosecutions*[105] the Divisional Court considered a case where a picture of the complainant had been placed online with an offensive caption. It was contended that the harassment, alarm or distress had not been caused to the complainant by the defendant's act because the complainant had not seen the photograph until shown it by a Police Officer. The Divisional Court dismissed the appeal. Maurice Kay LJ stated that:

> "Once the defendant with the requisite intent had posted the image to the … website he took the chance that the intended harassment, alarm or distress would be caused to the complainant" ([13]).

[98] For example, *EDO MBM Technology Ltd v Campaign To Smash EDO & Ors* [2005] EWHC 837 (QB) at [51], and *AstraZeneca v Vincent* [2014] EWHC 1637 (QB) at [18].

[99] See generally, *Merlin Entertainments Plc v Cave* [2015] EMLR 3 at [40].

[100] For example, *Mitton & Ors v Benefield & Anor* [2011] EWHC 2098 (QB) (finding of harassment based entirely on allegations which had been made to third parties).

[101] *Levi & Anor v Bates* [2016] QB 91 at [34].

[102] *Cray v Hancock* [2006] EWCA Civ 302 (see 5RB case comment).

[103] *Petros & Ors v Chaudhari & Anor* [2004] EWCA Civ 458.

[104] *Law Society v Kordowski* [2014] EMLR 2 at [61] and [75].

[105] [2008] 1 WLR 2847.

In the case of *AMP v Persons Unknown*[106] it was held that disseminating the digital photographic naked images of the claimant amounted to harassment.

5.90   It nevertheless remains difficult for a claimant to establish that a course of online conduct constitutes harassment. The threshold for harassment is a high one. A defendant's point of departure will often be that the impugned conduct was not, when objectively judged, oppressive and unacceptable in the sense that it would justify criminal liability.[107]

Harassment by "journalism"

5.91   Many alleged acts of online harassment (such as abusive messaging or posts on a private Facebook page) may not fall into even the broadest categories of journalism because they may not involve disclosing information to the public at large.[108] However, where a defendant can argue that his/her online publications amount to journalism, the following dicta suggests that a claimant will face difficulties in succeeding with a claim for harassment.

5.92   In *Thomas v News Group Newspapers Ltd*[109] Lord Phillips MR held that:

> "before press publications are capable of constituting harassment, they must be attended by some exceptional circumstance which justifies sanctions and the restriction on the freedom of expression that they involve. It is also common ground that such circumstances will be rare" [35].

This observation was built upon by Tugendhat J in *Trimingham*:[110]

> "It would be a serious interference with freedom of expression if those wishing to express their own views could be silenced by, or threatened with, claims for harassment based on subjective claims by individuals that they feel offended or insulted" [267].

5.93   In the case of *Lisle-Mainwaring v Associated Newspapers Ltd & Anor*[111] it was held that the contents of a series of articles concerning the claimant were capable of constituting actionable harassment in that some of them were defamatory and they contained various inaccuracies. The court declined to

---

106 [2011] Info TLR 25.

107 See the summary of the law in *Calland v Financial Service Authority* [2015] EWCA Civ 192 at [5] (per Lewison LJ).

108 See by analogy: *University of Oxford v Webb* [2006] EWHC 2490 (QB) at [72] (per Irwin J).

109 [2002] EMLR 4137.

110 [2012] EWHC 1296 (QB).

111 [2017] EWHC 543 (QB).

grant summary judgment to the defendant and directed that the matter should go to trial.

Defences

Introduction

5.94   S 1(3) of the 1997 Act provides three defences to a claim for harassment; a defendant may assert that the conduct complained of:

(a) was pursued for the purpose of preventing or detecting crime,

(b) was pursued under any enactment or rule of law or to comply with any condition or requirement imposed by any person under any enactment, or

(c) the pursuit of the course of conduct was reasonable in the circumstances.

5.95   The first (preventing and detecting crime defence) and third (reasonableness defence) of these defences are most likely to be invoked by a defendant sued for things written or posted online.

Preventing or detecting crime

5.96   This defence can be relied upon by individuals taking it upon themselves to enforce the law.[112] A defendant need not show that the course of conduct embarked upon for preventing or detecting crime was objectively reasonable. The Supreme Court has held that a defendant's "purpose" in this context is a subjective state of mind but this is subject to a rationality test. This means that a defendant will need to have acted in good faith and there has to be a logical connection between the evidence and the reasons for her decision to pursue the course of conduct.[113] In *Hayes v Willoughby*, it was held that, in what is not a demanding test to satisfy, a defendant

> "must have thought rationally about the material suggesting the possibility of criminality and formed the view that the conduct [...] was appropriate for the purpose of preventing or detecting [crime]."[114]

---

[112] *Hayes v Willoughby* [2013] 1 WLR 935 at [13] (per Lord Sumption).

[113] *Hayes*, at [13] – [14].

[114] *Hayes*, at [15].

"Reasonableness"

5.97   By contrast to s 1(3)(a), the defence in s 1(3)(c) requires an objective assessment of reasonableness.[115] Where online publications for the purposes of journalism are said to amount to harassment, the question of reasonableness must "be answered by reference to the right of the press to freedom of expression."[116] In *Trimingham*, Tugendhat J held (interpreting *Thomas*) that:

> "[A court] must hold that a course of conduct in the form of journalistic speech is reasonable under PHA s 1(3)(c) unless, in the particular circumstances of the case, the course of conduct is so unreasonable that it is necessary (in the sense of a pressing social need) and proportionate to prohibit or sanction the speech in pursuit of one of the aims listed in Art 10(2), including, in particular, for the protection of the rights of others under Art 8."[117]

5.98   Where a claimant seeks to rely on art 8 and art 10(2), the court will need to undertake the balancing set out below in relation to the tort of misuse of private information – applying the ultimate balancing test to the pursuit of the course of conduct (see Chapter 8).[118] However, in many cases of alleged harassment by way of online publication, art 8 will either not be engaged or art 8 rights will be relatively weak.

5.99   Finally, it is no defence to a claim for harassment by publication to show that the information published is already in the public domain.[119] Similarly, it is irrelevant whether the facts published are true or whether any opinions expressed are reasonably held.

---

[115] *EDO Technology & Anor v Campaign to Smash EDO & Ors* [2005] EWHC 2490 (QB) at [23] (per Walker J).

[116] *Thomas v News Group Newspapers* [2002] EMLR 4 at [32].

[117] *Trimingham v Associated Newspapers Ltd* [2012] 4 All ER 717 at [53].

[118] Ibid, at [55].

[119] *WXY v Gewanter & Ors* [2012] EWHC 1601 (QB) at [100] (per Slade J).

CHAPTER 6: LIABILITY FOR ONLINE PUBLICATION: BREACH OF CONFIDENCE, MISUSE OF PRIVATE INFORMATION, DATA PROTECTION

Chapter Synopsis

- Looks at liability for online publication for claims in: breach of confidence, misuse of private information, and breach of data protection laws.
- An action for breach of confidence is designed to protect the confidential information of an individual or company. It has most often been used to protect confidential commercial information but can also be used to protect confidential personal information.
- Misuse of private information has developed out of the equitable cause of action for breach of confidence, although it is now established as a separate tort – in part based upon the requirements of ECHR, art 8.
- The Data Protection Directive has the object of protecting the fundamental rights and freedoms of natural persons and in particular, their right to privacy with respect to the processing of personal data. The Data Protection Act 1998, was passed to implement it in UK law.

Introduction

6.1   In this Chapter we consider claims in relation to internet publications which infringe one or more of the following rights:

  (1)   Right to confidential information – protected by an action for breach of confidence;

  (2)   Right to privacy – protected by the tort of misuse of private information;

  (3)   Right to the fair and lawful processing of personal data.

All of these claims potentially arise in cases based on online publication. We will give a brief outline of the law in relation to each of these.

Breach of Confidence

Introduction

6.2   The action for breach of confidence is designed to protect the confidential information of an individual or company. It has most often been used to protect confidential commercial information – sometimes referred to as "trade secrets" – but can also be used to protect confidential personal information. The action to protect personal confidential information has a very high degree of overlap with the action for misuse of private information (see paras 6.16–33).

6.3 An action for breach of confidence can be brought to restrain the threatened disclosure of confidential information or, after disclosure has taken place, to recover damages for breach of confidence and to prevent its further dissemination. It is now clear that damages for breach of confidence cover not only financial losses (or an account of profits made from the misuse) but also "general damages". The latter category covers both damages for distress (in the case of individuals) and "general damages for breach" in the case of companies.

Elements of the claim

6.4 The cause of action for breach of confidence requires the establishment of three elements:

(1)   the relevant information had the "necessary quality of confidence";

(2)   it had been imparted in circumstances imposing a duty of confidence; and

(3)   there has been (or is likely to be) an unauthorised use of that information.[1]

6.5 In relation to the second element, it has been said that a duty of confidence arises "when information comes to the knowledge of a person in circumstances where he has notice, or is held to have agreed, that the information is confidential".[2] More recently it has been said that a "good test" in considering whether a claim for breach of confidence is well founded is whether the claimant has a "reasonable expectation of confidentiality" in the information in question.[3]

6.6 Information may lose the "necessary quality of confidence" by virtue of its being in the public domain with the result that no claim in breach of confidence can be brought.[4] Whether confidence is lost by virtue of information being in the public domain will depend on the degree to which

---

[1] *Coco v AN Clark (Engineers) Ltd* [1969] RPC 41 at 47–48 (per Megarry J).

[2] *Terry v Persons Unknown* [2010] EMLR 16 at [49].

[3] *Imerman v Tchenguiz & Ors* [2011] Fam 116 at [66].

[4] *Attorney General v Guardian Newspapers (No 2)* [1990] 1 AC 109, at 282 (per Lord Goff).

the information has been made available to third parties.[5] When information is posted on the internet it is likely to lose its confidential character – but very limited or partial dissemination in some remote or expert site which is not generally available to the public without a great deal of effort may not result in a loss of confidentiality.[6]

6.7 Information is capable of being confidential if it is available to one person (or a group of people) and not generally available to others, provided that the person (or group) who possesses the information does not intend that it should be available to others.[7]

6.8 In deciding whether a claimant has a reasonable expectation of confidentiality in information, all the circumstances of the case are considered, in particular:

(a) any relationship between the claimant and the confidant within which the information was acquired, the relationship need not be contractual;

(b) how far access to the information was limited to a restricted group of people – the information must not be available to the public generally;

(c) the nature of the information and, in particular, its subject matter, form and sensitivity for the claimant; and

(d) whether the information has been communicated for a specific purpose.[8]

Defences

Introduction

6.9 A number of defences to breach of confidence claims have been suggested:

- Public interest.
- Disclosure under or required by statute.
- Disclosure to protect legitimate interests.
- Limitation – it is now generally accepted that the applicable limitation period is 6 years (that is, the period applicable to claims in

---

[5] *Franchi v Franchi* [1967] RPC 149 at p152–153.

[6] *Barclays Bank Plc v Guardian News and Media Ltd* [2009] EWHC 591 (QB) at [22].

[7] *Douglas & Ors v Hello! Ltd & Ors (No 3)* [2006] QB 125 at [55].

[8] See generally, P Stanley, *Law of Confidentiality* (2008), at §2, pp.7ff.

tort)[9] – which can be extended in cases of "fraud, concealment or mistake."[10]

6.10   This section will deal only with the first of these defences as the others are likely to be of limited relevance in online publication cases.

Public interest

6.11   This defence amounts to an assertion that disclosure is *required* in the public interest and that while there is a public interest that confidences be protected, there is a countervailing public interest favouring disclosure.[11] This requires a court to balance these competing public interests.

6.12   The test to be applied when considering whether it is necessary to restrict freedom of expression in order to prevent disclosure of information received in confidence is whether, in all the circumstances, it is in the public interest that the duty of confidence should be breached.[12] It is not enough that there is a public interest in disclosure, this must be sufficiently strong to outweigh the public interest in the observance of duties of confidence.[13] This approach is consistent with the approach of the European Court of Human Rights.[14]

6.13   The defence is not limited to disclosures revealing iniquity or misconduct; there need not necessarily have been any wrongdoing on the part of a claimant.[15] The categories of information whose disclosure is likely to be regarded as being in the public interest is open-ended.

6.14   The public interest in disclosure has been held to outweigh the public interest in confidentiality in cases such as the following:

- Serious danger or harm to the public. Examples have included an event or practice that is dangerous to the public, such as a threat to security, a pending disaster or a dangerous medical practice,[16] use by police of faulty breathalysers with the risk of wrongful convictions.[17]

---

[9] Limitation Act 1980, s 2.

[10] s 32 of the 1980 Act.

[11] *Attorney General v Guardian Newspapers (No 2)* [1990] 1 AC 109, at 282 (per Lord Goff).

[12] *Associated Newspapers Ltd v HRH Prince of Wales* [2008] Ch 57 at [68].

[13] *Brevan Howard Asset Management v Reuters* [2017] EWCA Civ 950 at [69].

[14] Ibid, at [66].

[15] *Lion Laboratories v Evans & Ors* [1985] QB 526, at 550; also *Brevan Howard* at [69].

[16] *Beloff v Pressdram* [1973] 1 All ER 241, at 260; *Malone v Commissioner of Police (No 2)* [1979] Ch 344, at 362.

[17] *Lion Laboratories v Evans & Ors* [1985] QB 526.

- Misleading the public. If a person has made false public statements or presented a false image to the public then there is a public interest in setting the record straight. But the individual must have set out to present a false picture.[18]

6.15   The audience to which information is published in breach of confidence is relevant to whether a public interest defence will succeed. This is important for online publications because it is very easy to publish to an unlimited audience through, for example, a blog post or tweet. Depending on the nature of information disclosed, such broad publication may not be covered by the public interest defence. The starting point is that the recipients must have a "proper interest" in receiving the information.[19] Generally allegations of criminal misconduct are to be disclosed to the police or an appropriate regulator/professional body[20] and civil wrongs to the wronged party. However, where the information disclosed affects the community/society at large or there is clearly a wider public interest in the information it is more likely to be reasonable for it to be published to everyone. Examples have included alleged wide-scale corruption in racing[21] and questions of value for money in large-scale public procurement,[22] allegations of corrupt dealings between a company director and a local authority official,[23] and the risk of unsafe convictions arising from faulty breathalysers.[24]

MISUSE OF PRIVATE INFORMATION

Introduction

6.16   Private information includes information that is personal to the person who possesses it and that he or she does not intend shall be imparted to the general public.[25]

6.17   The cause of action of misuse of private information has developed out of the equitable cause of action for breach of confidence, although it is now

---

[18] *PJS v News Group Newspapers Ltd* [2016] EMLR 17 at [38].

[19] *Initial Services Ltd v Putterill & Anor* [1968] 1 QB 396, at 405–406.

[20] For example, *Francombe & Anor v Mirror Group Newspapers Ltd & Ors* [1984] 1 WLR 892; *Imutran Ltd v Uncaged Campaigns Ltd* [2001] 2 All ER 385.

[21] *Jockey Club v Buffham* [2003] QB 462, at 475–479.

[22] *London Regional Transport v Mayor of London* [2003] EMLR 4.

[23] *Cream Holdings Ltd & Ors v Banerjee & Anor* [2005] 1 AC 253.

[24] *Lion Laboratories v Evans & Ors* [1985] QB 526.

[25] See the cases cited in *Lord Browne of Madingley v Associated Newspapers Ltd* [2008] QB 103 at [24].

established as a separate tort.[26] The tort is in part based upon the requirements of European Convention for the Protection of Human Rights and Fundamental Freedoms, art 8. This imposes a positive obligation on the state to respect and promote the interests of private and family life. This is achieved by the courts articulating and enforcing that state obligation in actions between private individuals in breach of confidence[27] and now under the tort of misuse of private information. Given its Convention origins, the rules governing the tort of misuse of private information are based on the jurisprudence of arts 8 and 10, which form the content of the domestic tort.[28]

6.18   There are two elements to a claim for misuse of private information:

(1)   Is the information private in the sense that it is, in principle, protected by art 8? If "no", that is the end of the case. If "yes";

(2)   In all the circumstances, must the interest of the person to whom the private information relates yield to the right of freedom of expression conferred on the publisher by art 10?[29] This involves balancing the art 8 rights of the claimant against the art 10 rights of the defendant, looking at the relative strength of each, and then striking the "ultimate balance" between them.[30]

6.19   If the balance is struck in favour of the claimant then there is a claim for misuse of private information. If the balance is struck in favour of the defendant then the claim fails. Strictly speaking, there are no "defences" to a claim – matters such as public domain and consent are taken into account at the first stage of the analysis and public interest at the second stage.

6.20   It is important to note that in a misuse of private information case the issue is whether the information is private, not whether it is true or false. As the Court of Appeal said in *McKennitt & Ors v Ash & Anor*[31]:

"The truth or falsity of the information is an irrelevant inquiry in deciding whether the information is entitled to be protected and judges should be chary of becoming side-tracked into that irrelevant inquiry".[32]

---

[26] *Vidal-Hall & Ors v Google Inc* [2016] QB 1003.

[27] *McKennitt & Ors v Ash & Anor* [2008] QB 73 at [10]–[11].

[28] Ibid, at [12].

[29] Ibid, at [11].

[30] Per Lord Steyn *In Re S (A Child) (Identification: Restrictions on Publication)* [2005] 1 AC 59 at [17].

[31] [2008] QB 73.

[32] Ibid, at [86].

The "first stage"

General

6.21   In relation to the "first stage", the question is whether there is a "reasonable expectation" that the information in question will remain private. This extends to every occasion on which a person can be said to have a reasonable expectation that there will be no interference with the broader right of personal autonomy.[33]

6.22   The question whether there is a reasonable expectation of privacy is a broad one, which takes account of all the circumstances of the case. These include:

- the attributes of the claimant;
- the nature of the activity in which the claimant was engaged;
- the place at which it was happening;
- the nature and purpose of the intrusion;
- the absence of consent and whether it was known or could be inferred;
- the effect on the claimant;
- the circumstances in which and the purposes for which the information came into the hands of the publisher. [34]

6.23   Photographs taken of adults taken in public places engaging in ordinary activities ("popping out for a pint of milk"[35]) are unlikely to attract a reasonable expectation of privacy.[36] The position will, however, be different if there are obviously private or embarrassing aspects to the behaviour of the adult in public. Photographs of children taken in public places are likely to attract a reasonable expectation of privacy.[37]

6.24   There can, in appropriate circumstances, be a reasonable expectation of privacy in the *fact* of a relationship or other private event as well as the details as to what took place.[38]

---

[33] *R (Catt) v Association of Chief Police Officers of England, Wales and Northern Ireland & Anor* [2015] AC 1065 at [4].

[34] *Murray v Big Pictures Plc & Anor* [2009] Ch 481 at [36].

[35] Per Baroness Hale *Campbell v Mirror Group Newspapers Ltd* [2004] 2 AC 457 at [154].

[36] For example *John v Associated Newspapers Ltd* [2006] EMLR 27.

[37] *Weller & Ors v Associated Newspapers Ltd* [2016] 1 WLR 1541, at in particular [39]–[41] (per Lord Dyson MR); *PJS v News Group Newspapers Ltd* [2016] AC 1081 at [72]–[74] (per Lady Hale).

[38] *ZYT v Associated Newspapers Ltd* [2015] EWHC 1162 (QB) at [12].

Public figures

6.25　The fact that a person is a "public figure" means that, in relation to certain aspects of private life there is a reduced expectation of privacy. Public figures are persons holding public office and/or using public resources and, more broadly speaking, all those who play a role in public life, whether in politics, the economy, the arts, the social sphere, or sport.[39] This "reduced expectation of privacy" only relates, however, to aspects of a public figure's private life which are relevant to the public functions which the individual performs.[40] In particular, being a public figure doesn't make the entire history of that person's private life public property.[41]

Public domain

6.26　In contrast to a claim for breach of confidence, demonstrating that private information is already in the public domain is unlikely to be sufficient for a defendant to prevail. A reasonable expectation of privacy may not be vitiated by the information being in the public domain. This is because the tort protects not only the secrecy or confidence of information but also the intrusion associated with the publication of private information, even if that information is already public.[42] Such considerations may be especially relevant where private information is published through an internet platform that will reach large numbers of people, is likely to remain online quasi-permanently and will appear in search results.

The "second stage"

6.27　The second stage involves an "intense focus on the comparative importance of the specific rights being claimed".[43] The court must apply what has been called the "new methodology": looking at the art 8 and art 10 rights of the parties and others (and at any other Convention rights which may be engaged), conducting a "parallel analysis" of the justification for the interference with each of the rights and applying a proportionality test. This is sometimes known as the "ultimate balancing" exercise.

---

[39] *Spelman v Express Newspapers* [2012] EWHC 355 (QB) at [44]–[52].

[40] *Rocknroll v News Group Newspapers Ltd* [2013] EWHC 24 (Ch) at [17].

[41] *AMC v News Group Newspapers Ltd* [2015] EWHC 2361 (QB) at [19].

[42] *PJS v News Group Newspapers Ltd* [2016] AC 1081, at [32] (per Lord Mance), at [57]–[58] (per Lord Neuberger).

[43] *Re S (A Child)* [2005] 1 AC 593 at [17].

6.28   The art 8 rights of a claimant's children are of particular importance in this balancing exercise.[44] They have independent privacy interests which must be taken into account.[45]

6.29   When striking this balance, it must be borne in mind that neither art 8 nor art 10 has "presumptive priority". This position is not altered by the Human Rights Act 1998, s 12.[46] The balancing exercise involves, in particular, considering the strength and importance of the "freedom of expression rights" involved as against the strength and importance of the "privacy rights" involved.

6.30   When arts 8 and 10 are being balanced, the Grand Chamber of the European Court of Human Rights has identified six criteria which are especially relevant – the first of which is described as the "initial essential criterion":[47]

(a) Does the information concerned contribute to a debate of general interest?

(b) How well known is the person concerned and what is the subject of the publication?

(c) Prior conduct of the person concerned.

(d) Method of obtaining the information and its veracity.

(e) Content, form and consequences of the publication.

(f) Severity of the sanction imposed.

6.31   The "decisive factor at the second stage" concerns the contribution that the publication of the information in the article would make to a debate of general interest.[48] What is required is an actual contribution to a debate which is of general interest in a democratic society. A distinction must be drawn between reporting facts – even if controversial – capable of contributing to a debate of general public interest in a democratic society, and making tawdry allegations about an individual's private life.[49] A publication whose sole purpose is to satisfy the curiosity of an audience regarding a person's private life is not to be regarded as contributing to a debate of general interest.[50]

---

[44] See generally, *K v News Group Newspapers Ltd* [2011] WLR 1827.

[45] *PJS v News Group Newspapers Ltd* [2016] AC 1081 at [72] (per Lady Hale).

[46] *PJS v News Group Newspapers Ltd* [2016] AC 1081 at [19]–[20] (per Lord Mance), at [51] (per Lord Neuberger).

[47] *Couderc & Anor v France* (2015) 40 BHRC 436 at [93].

[48] For example, *K v News Group Newspapers Ltd* [2011] 1 WLR 1827 at [23].

[49] *Mosley v United Kingdom* (2011) 53 EHRR 10 at [114].

[50] *Couderc* (2015) 40 BHRC 436 at [100]; *Von Hannover v Germany* (2005) 40 EHRR 1 at [65]–[66].

Specific "public interest" considerations

6.32   A number of "public interest" considerations which may justify interfering with privacy rights have been considered in the case law, including:

- The high level of protection that art 10 affords to the right to freedom of expression when exercised by the media/journalists, which is intimately linked to the right of the public to receive information.[51]
- The mere fact that a claimant is a public or well-known figure is insufficient to justify publication of private information in the public interest. Art 10 rights are only likely to prevail where the information published has a bearing on or is relevant to the conduct of her official role/participation in public life.[52]
- Whether the publication of information is necessary to put the "record straight" where a person has made false public statements or presented a false image to the public.[53] However, this doctrine has important limits: the fact that at some point in the past a person has made a statement which could be interpreted as being inconsistent with some private conduct of his is not of itself sufficient to generate a "public interest" in disclosure of the private conduct. The weight attached to this consideration will vary depending on, for example, if and how the original image was deliberately portrayed, whether the person set out to present a false image,[54] the passage of time,[55] and whether there is a public interest in setting the record straight.
- "The supposed right to criticise conduct": it is not enough for a defendant to rely on a right to criticise a person's conduct.[56]

The assessment of public interest

6.33   Art 10 recognises that some weight should be accorded to journalistic/editorial judgment or latitude in assessing whether it is in the public interest to publish particular information and how it should be

---

[51] *Jersild v Denmark* (App No. 15890/89), at [31].

[52] See for example: *Standard Verlags Gmbh v Austria No 2* (2009) (App No. 21277/05), at [48] – [54]; *Axel Springer AG v Germany* (GC) (2012) 55 EHRR 6, at [91]; *Campbell v Mirror Group Newspapers Ltd* [2004] 2 AC 457 at [148] (per Baroness Hale).

[53] *Ferdinand v Mirror Group Newspapers Ltd* [2011] EWHC 2454 (QB).

[54] *PJS v News Group Newspapers Ltd* [2016] EMLR 17 at [38] (per Jackson LJ).

[55] *AMC v News Group Newspapers Ltd* [2015] EWHC 2361 at [24].

[56] *PJS v News Group Newspapers Ltd* [2016] AC 1081 at [21] (per Lord Mance); see also *AMC v News Group Newspapers Ltd* [2015] EWHC 2361.

presented.[57] There is an unresolved question as to the relevance in the ultimate balancing exercise of the publisher's subjective belief in the public interest in publication.[58]

DATA PROTECTION

The Directive

6.34   The Data Protection Directive has the object of protecting the fundamental rights and freedoms of natural persons and in particular, their right to privacy with respect to the processing of personal data. It applies whatever a person's nationality or residence (see Recital (2)).

6.35   The provisions of the Directive must themselves be construed purposively and "in the light of the aim pursued by the directive and the system it establishes".[59] The provisions are *"necessarily relatively general"* since they have to be applied in a large number of different situations.

6.36   In *Google Spain SL v Agencia Espanola de Proteccion de Datos & Anor* ("*Google Spain*")[60] the Court of Justice of the European Union referred on a number of occasions to the objective of the Directive when construing its provisions:

> "Furthermore, in the light of the objective of [the Directive] of ensuring effective and complete protection of the fundamental rights and freedoms of natural persons, and in particular their right to privacy, with respect to the processing of personal data, those words [in article 4(1)(a)] cannot be interpreted restrictively" [53]

6.37   Further, the Directive must be interpreted in light of the rights now set out in the Charter of Fundamental Rights of the European Union.[61]

Data Protection Act 1998 and the Directive

Introduction

6.38   The Data Protection Act 1998 was passed to implement the Directive. It therefore falls within the ambit of EU law and has to be understood and

---

[57] *Jersild v Denmark* (App No. 15890/89), at [31].

[58] See the discussion in *Terry v Persons Unknown* [2010] EMLR 16 at [70]–[73].

[59] *Tietosuojavaltuutettu v Satakunnan Markkinaporssi Oy & Anor* [2008] ECR I-9831 at [51].

[60] [2014] QB 1022.

[61] Ibid, at [68]–[69].

applied in accordance with the general principles of EU law. This in effect creates a further obligation on national courts, as explained by the CJEU:

"Consequently, it is for the authorities and courts of the member states not only to interpret their national law in a manner consistent with Directive 95/46 but also to make sure they do not rely on an interpretation of it which would be in conflict with the fundamental rights protected by the Community legal order or with the other general principles of Community law, such as inter alia the principle of proportionality." [62]

The 1998 Act should, therefore, be interpreted, so far as possible, in the light of, and to give effect to, the provisions of the Directive.[63]

Personal data

6.39   For the purposes of the Directive "personal data" means

"any information relating to an identified or identifiable natural person ('data subject'); an identifiable person is one who can be identified, directly or indirectly, in particular by reference to an identification number or to one or more factors specific to his physical, physiological, mental, economic, cultural or social identity" (art 2).

6.40   This is transposed into English law by s 1(1) of the 1998 Act, which provides that

""personal data" means data which relate to a living individual who can be identified–

(a) from those data, or

(b) from those data and other information which is in the possession of, or is likely to come into the possession of, the data controller."

It is important to note that the 1998 Act does not apply to companies or other "artificial persons" or to the dead.

6.41   In assessing whether a particular piece of information is personal data, there are two questions to be considered: whether a living individual is "identifiable" from that data and whether that data "relates to" the individual

---

[62] *Criminal Proceedings Against Lindqvist* [2004] QB 1014 at [87].

[63] *Durant v Financial Services Authority* [2004] FSR 28 at [3].

in question. Comprehensive guidance is provided by the ICO in a document entitled *Determining what is personal data.*

6.42   As to the first question, a name will be sufficient to identify someone but it is not necessary. All the means reasonably available to the data controller or other persons will be taken into account. [64]

6.43   As to the second question, it is clear that mere mention of the data subject in a document is not necessarily personal data[65] but it will be sufficient if this is linked to, for example, an email address or telephone number or information about working conditions or hobbies.[66] When assessing whether a particular piece of information "relates" to an identifiable individual it is necessary to consider factors such as[67]

- Is the data obviously "about" an individual, providing particular information about that individual?
- Is the data used to inform or influence decisions affecting the individual?
- Does the data has biographical significance for the individual?
- Does the data concentrate on the individual (rather than on some other person, object transaction or event)?
- Does the data have a potential to impact on the individual?
- If the answer to any of these questions is "yes" then the data is likely to be personal data of that individual.

6.44   The Directive makes special provision in relation to personal data "revealing racial or ethnic origin, political opinion, religious or philosophical beliefs, trade union membership and the processing of data concerning health or sex life" (art 8(1)). In the 1998 Act this is known as "sensitive personal data" which is defined in s 2 as:

"personal data consisting of information as to–

(a) the racial or ethnic origin of the data subject,

(b) his political opinions,

(c) his religious beliefs or other beliefs of a similar nature,

---

[64] *Determining what is personal data*, pp.8–9 and see generally, *Vidal-Hall & Ors v Google Inc* [2016] QB 1003, at [110]–[133].

[65] *Durant*, at [28]; and *Ittihadieh v 5-11 Cheyne Gardens RTM Company Ltd & Ors* [2017] EWCA Civ 121 at [63]–[66].

[66] See *Determining what is personal data* (ICO) at p.7, n.8.

[67] Ibid.

(d) whether he is a member of a trade union (within the meaning of the Trade Union and Labour Relations (Consolidation) Act 1992),

(e) his physical or mental health or condition,

(f) his sexual life,

(g) the commission or alleged commission by him of any offence, or

(h) any proceedings for any offence committed or alleged to have been committed by him, the disposal of such proceedings or the sentence of any court in such proceedings."

Processing

6.45   Processing is given an extremely wide definition by art 2(b) of the Directive which states that:

"'processing of personal data' ('processing') shall mean any operation or set of operations which is performed upon personal data, whether or not by automatic means, such as collection, recording, organization, storage, adaptation or alteration, retrieval, consultation, use, disclosure by transmission, dissemination or otherwise making available, alignment or combination, blocking, erasure or destruction".

6.46   This is transposed into in s 1(1) of the 1998 Act which provides that processing includes:

"obtaining, recording or holding the information or data or carrying out any operation or set of operations on the information or data" and specifically "disclosure of the information or data by transmission, dissemination or otherwise making available".

This includes making material available online.[68]

Data controller

6.47   A "data controller" is defined as a person who (either alone or jointly or in common with other persons) determines the purposes for which and the

---

[68] *Criminal Proceedings against Lindqvist* [2004] QB 1014 at [27]; *Law Society v Kordowski* [2014] EMLR 2 at [76].

manner in which any personal data are, or are to be, processed (s 1(4)). The administrator of any website will be a data controller in relation to the data which appears on that website.

Data Protection Principles

6.48   s 4(4) of the 1998 Act provides that:

"Subject to s 27(1), it shall be the duty of a data controller to comply with the data protection principles in relation to all personal data with respect to which he is the data controller."

S 27(1) refers to various exemptions set out in Part IV of the 1998 Act. These are considered below (see para 6.60ff).

6.49   The Directive sets out a number of "Principles relating to Data Quality" (art 6). These are transposed into the "Data Protection Principles" set out in the Part I of Sch 1 to the 1998 Act:

- First Principle: Personal data shall be processed fairly and lawfully and, in particular, shall not be processed unless (a) at least one of the conditions in Sch 2 is met, and (b) in the case of sensitive personal data, at least one of the conditions in Sch 3 is also met." (see generally, the ICO Guidance on this principle).
- Second Principle: Personal data shall only be obtained for specified lawful purposes and shall not be processed in a manner incompatible with them (see generally, the ICO Guidance on this principle).
- Third Principle: Personal data shall be adequate, relevant and not excessive in relation to the purposes for which they are processed (see generally, the ICO Guidance on this principle).
- Fourth Principle: Personal data shall be accurate and, where necessary, kept up to date (see generally, the ICO Guidance on this principle).
- Fifth Principle: Personal data processed for any purpose shall not be kept for longer than is necessary for that purpose (see generally, the ICO Guidance on this principle).
- Sixth Principle: Personal data shall be processed in accordance with the rights of data subjects under the DPA (see generally, the ICO Guidance on this principle).
- Seventh Principle: Appropriate technical and organisational measures shall be taken against unauthorised or unlawful processing of personal data and against accidental loss or destruction of, or damage to, personal data (see generally, the ICO Guidance on this principle).

- Eighth Principle: Prohibits the transfer of personal data to a country outside the EEA unless it has an adequate level of protection in relation to data processing (see generally, the ICO Guidance on this principle).
- Guidance on the principles is provided in Part II of Sch 1, paras 1 to 15.

6.50   Claims in most cases are likely to be based on breaches of the First Data Protection Principle. Attention is drawn to the following:

- The data must be processed "lawfully" – it will not be if the data is being processed in breach of confidence, or is defamatory or harassing.[69] The ICO has provided guidance on "lawful processing".
- The data must be processed "fairly" and, in particular, specified information must be provided to the data subject. The ICO has provided guidance on "fair processing".
- at least one condition in Sch 2 and in the case of sensitive personal data, Sch 3 must be satisfied. The ICO has provided guidance on "Conditions for Processing".

6.51   There are six "conditions" in Sch 2 in relation to the processing of personal data generally. The most relevant for present purposes are likely to be:

- Para 1: the data subject has given consent.
- Para 6: the processing is necessary for the purposes of legitimate interests pursued by the data controller or by the third party or parties to whom the data are disclosed, except where the processing is unwarranted in any particular case by reason of prejudice to the rights and freedoms or legitimate interests of the data subject.

6.52   There are eleven conditions in Sch 3, in relation to the processing of sensitive personal data. The most relevant are likely to be:

- Para 1: the data subject has given *explicit* consent.
- Para 5: the information in the data has been made public as a result of steps deliberately taken by the data subject.
- Para 6: processing the data is necessary for the purposes of establishing or defending legal rights.
- Para 10: for purposes specified in the Data Protection (Processing of Sensitive Personal Data) Order 2000, in particular para 3 – which require the demonstration of a "substantial public interest", is in

---

[69] *Law Society v Kordowski* [2014] EMLR 2 at [78].

connection with the commission of an unlawful act, dishonesty or mismanagement and is for a journalistic purpose.

Rights and remedies under the DPA

6.53   The 1998 Act confers a number of distinct rights on data subjects. For present purposes, we draw attention to four to these.

6.54   First, s 7 of the 1998 Act confers a "right of access" to data subjects: this is a right to be informed if data is being processed, to be given a description of those data and a copy of those data. The data controller must carry out a search for this data.[70] This is an extremely powerful and wide-ranging right and is not expressly limited to reasonable or proportionate searches. It has, however, been held that the principle of proportionality limits the scope of the efforts which the data controller must take in response (although it cannot justify a blanket refusal to comply).[71]

6.55   Secondly, there is a right under s 10 of the 1998 Act to compel a data controller to cease or not start processing personal data of which an individual is the data subject on the ground that the processing is causing or is likely to cause substantial damage and distress which would be unwarranted. There is no need to show that the processing is in breach of any data protection principle. A notice must be served giving the data controller 21 days to comply with the request. The data subject can seek a court order requiring compliance.

6.56   S 10 appears to impose a "different and narrower test" than that imposed by the Directive.[72] S 10 of the 1998 Act should be interpreted so that it corresponds to the right guaranteed by the Directive.

6.57   Thirdly, there is the right under s 14(1) to "Rectification, blocking, erasure and destruction" of inaccurate personal data (or personal data which contain an expression of opinion and appear to be based on inaccurate data). This reflects art 12(b) and (c) of the Directive.

6.58   Lastly, there is a right under s 13 of the 1998 Act[73] to compensation for individuals who suffer damage as result of any contravention of any of the

---

[70] *Dawson-Damer v Taylor Wessing LLP* [2017] EWCA Civ 74, at [71] to [79].

[71] *Ittihadieh v 5-11 Cheyne Gardens RTM Company Ltd & Ors* [2017] EWCA Civ 121, at [100].

[72] R Jay, *Data Protection: Law and Practice,* 4th Edn, 2012, para 12.28.

[73] Art 23 and Recital (55) of the Directive.

requirements of the DPA. It is no longer necessary to show financial damage[74] – "damage" includes damages for distress.

6.59   In proceedings brought against a person by virtue of s 13 of the 1998 Act "it is a defence to prove that he had taken such care as in all the circumstances was reasonably required to comply with the requirement concerned" (s 13(3)). This notion of "reasonable care" is uniquely applicable to questions of compensation.

Exemptions

Introduction

6.60   Part IV of the 1998 Act sets out a range of "exemptions" from compliance with various provisions of the Act. This section focuses on the two that are most likely to be relevant to internet publications.

S 32: Journalism, literature and art

6.61   S 32 of the 1998 Act provides an exemption for any data controller processing personal data for the purposes of journalism, literary or artistic activities. The exemption covers all the data protection principles except the seventh (the security of data processing), and also ss 7 (subject access requests), 10 (right to prevent processing likely to cause distress), and 14(1)–(3) (rectification, blocking and erasure of inaccurate data).

6.62   "Journalism, literature and art" are not defined in the 1998 Act but s 32(1)(a) states that the processing may be done by "any person," making it clear that reliance on s 32 does not depend on the identity of a defendant. The CJEU has held that reliance on the journalism exemption (and by analogy the other exemptions) depends not on the status of a defendant but on whether s/he engaged in journalism.[75] The Information Commissioner's Office (ICO) has emphasised that these terms are to be interpreted broadly. Journalism covers "most of the day-to-day business of media organisations, and may also cover some activities of others" (e.g., citizen bloggers or civil society groups) as well as non-media organisations whose "purpose in processing the specific

---

[74] Note that s 13(2) has been disapplied by the Court of Appeal on the grounds that it was incompatible with the EU Charter of Fundamental Rights, art 47; see *Vidal-Hall & Ors v Google Inc* [2016] QB 1003 at [95].

[75] *Tietosuojavaltuutettu v Satakunnan Markkinapörssi Oy & Anor* [2008] ECR I-9831 at [58] and [61].

information is to publish information, opinions or ideas for general public consumption."[76]

6.63 Strictly speaking, s 32 does not absolve a defendant from liability for damages for a breach of the 1998 Act causing damages or distress. Instead, a defendant should contend that they s/he is exempt from complying with one or more provisions of the 1998 Act by operation of s 32.

6.64 To rely successfully on s 32, a defendant has to meet the following conditions:

 (1) the data is processed only for journalism, art or literature,
 (2) with a view to publication of some material,
 (3) with a reasonable belief that publication is in the public interest, and
 (4) with a reasonable belief that compliance is incompatible with journalism.

These will be considered in turn.

6.65 In relation to the first condition it is a question of fact as to whether data is being processed *only* for one of these purposes. It is likely that a journalist or media organisation will be able to satisfy this requirement in any case where information is being collected, stored and edited for the purpose of publishing articles.

6.66 In relation to the second condition the data controller must show that the personal data was processed with a view to the publication of *any* journalistic, artistic and literary material. In other words, what has to be contemplated is not the publication of the data in question but the publication of *some* journalistic, artistic or literary material. The publication need not be by the data controller. The exemption applies both before and after publication.[77]

6.67 In relation to the third condition the position is more complex: it has two "limbs", public interest and reasonable belief. If a defendant is a media organisation and subject to one or more codes of practice, a court will have regard to compliance with such codes.[78] The ICO's Guide on s 32 states that "if an organisation is subject to one of these codes and has clearly complied with its provisions on the public interest, this will be a strong indication that the belief that publication was in the public interest was reasonable."[79] This is

---

[76] Information Commissioner's Office, *Data Protection and Journalism: A guide for the media* (2014), at 29–30.

[77] *Campbell v Mirror Group Newspapers Ltd* [2004] 2 AC 457 at [127]–[129] (per Lord Phillips MR).

[78] The relevant codes of practice are set out in the schedule to Data Protection (Designated Codes of Practice) (No 2) Order 2000 (SI 2000/1864).

[79] *Data Protection and Journalism: A guide for the media*, at p.36.

analogous to the responsible journalism assessment applicable to the public interest defence under the Defamation Act 2013, s 4.

6.68 In relation to the fourth condition the position is also complex. The data controller must reasonably believe that, in relation to each of the relevant provisions of the 1998 Act, compliance with that provision is "incompatible with the special purposes". The ICO's Guide suggests that this means that the data controller must reasonably believe that it is "impossible both to comply with a particular provision" and fulfil the journalistic purpose. Non-compliance must be justified in relation to each data protection principle that has not been complied with. [80] This can be contrasted with the approach of the Court of Appeal in *Campbell v Mirror Group Newspapers Ltd*[81] where the test was said to be "not appropriate" or "impractical".

6.69 It is likely to be easier to rely successfully upon s 32 if a data controller defendant has procedures in place for decision-making on invoking the exemption and keeps records documenting such matters.[82]

6.70 ss 32(4) and (5) contain provisions to protect those processing data for the purposes of "journalism, literature and art" from pre-publication claims. If data protection proceeding are brought against a data controller and it is shown that the data is being processed only for the special purposes and with a view to publication then the proceedings must be stayed. It has been held that these provisions are compatible with EU law.[83]

S 36: Domestic purposes

6.71 s 36 of the 1998 Act provides an exemption from compliance with data protection principles in regard to personal data processed by an individual only for the purposes of that individual's personal, family or household affairs, including recreational purposes. The purpose of the processing and the identity of the data processor are the key factors determining whether s 36 applies.

6.72 s 36 does not, in the ICO's view, apply to organisations which either post personal data on third party's websites or host fora on which personal data

---

[80] *Data Protection and Journalism: A guide for the media*, at pp.36–37.

[81] [2004] 2 AC 457 at [117], [121]–[122].

[82] Rosemary Jay, *Data Protection Law and Practice* (2012), at 17–28; *Data Protection and Journalism: A guide for the media*, at 36.

[83] *Stunt v Associated Newspapers Ltd* [2017] EMLR 18.

may be posted by others.[84] Nor does it apply to individuals posting personal data for anything other than domestic or recreational purposes, e.g., a journalist posting a comment article. Further, it would appear that it would not apply where data is posted on e.g., a Facebook group set up by a sports club whose purpose is not regarded as being wholly domestic. Although this will depend on how formal the group is and the extent to which it is distinct from its individual members.[85]

6.73   It appears that s 36 does not cover the processing of personal data by an individual publishing it on the internet to an unlimited audience. The CJEU has interpreted the equivalent provision of the Directive narrowly, holding that a church warden posting information about members of the congregation online fell outside this exemption.[86] In such cases the purpose of the publication is critical.

---

[84] Information Commissioner's Office, *Social networking and online forums – when does the DPA apply?* (2014), at 4.

[85] *Social networking and online forums – when does the DPA apply?* (2014), at 5.

[86] *Criminal Proceedings against Lindqvist* [2004] QB 1014 at [47] (interpreting art 3(2) of the Directive; and approach approved in *Rynes v Urad pro ochranu osobnich udaju* [2015] 1 WLR 2607.

CHAPTER 7: DEFENCES SPECIFIC TO INFORMATION SOCIETY SERVICE PROVIDERS

CHAPTER SYNOPSIS

- Deals with the safe harbours available to ISSPs under the E-Commerce Directive. The effect of the safe harbours is that, when the requisite conditions are met, they protect ISSPs from any form of legal liability arising from any civil or criminal claim.
- Looks at the background to the E-Commerce Directive, and provides a general overview of its provisions. Outlines the transposition into UK law of the safe harbours: mere conduit, caching and hosting.
- Touches on the availability of injunctions, and the general and specific monitoring of content.
- Lastly, looks at the European Convention for the Protection of Human Rights and intermediary liability, including a discussion of the Grand Chamber decision in *Delfi v Estonia*, and other case law.

INTRODUCTION

7.1   This Chapter deals with the safe harbours available to Information Society Service Providers ("ISSPs") under the Directive 2000/31/EC on electronic commerce[1] (the "E-Commerce Directive"). The critical feature of these safe harbours is that, when the requisite conditions are met, they protect ISSPs from any form of legal liability arising from any civil or criminal claim. The primary protection is against liability in damages, and ISSPs remain subject to the power of domestic courts to grant certain types of injunction, although under art 15 of the E-Commerce Directive such injunctions must not impose on ISSPs a general obligation to monitor their own content.

7.2   The E-Commerce Directive was enacted by the European Parliament and Council of Ministers in 2000, as an attempt to shield Europe's fledgling e-commerce industry from potentially unlimited secondary liability arising as a result of processing, communicating or publishing third party content online. The policy behind the legislation was that ISSPs should in general be shielded from liability to pay damages for unlawful content generated by third parties, providing that they took appropriate steps to remove access to it following notice.

---

[1] Directive 2000/31/EC on certain aspects of information society services, in particular electronic commerce, in the Internal Market.

7.3   The E-Commerce Directive was implemented into UK law by the Electronic Commerce (EC Directive) Regulations 2002, SI 2002/2013, although the implementation of the provisions relating to injunctions is unsatisfactory, and art 15 of the E-Commerce Directive (the prohibition on monitoring) was not implemented at all.

E-COMMERCE DIRECTIVE: GENERAL PROVISIONS

Information society services and service providers

7.4   The E-Commerce Directive applies to providers of "information society services" and the definition adopted is that contained in art 2(1) of the Technical Standards Directive,[2] as follows:

"any service normally provided for remuneration, at a distance, by electronic means and at the individual request of a recipient of services.

For the purposes of this definition:

(i)   'at a distance' means that the service is provided without the parties being simultaneously present,

(ii) 'by electronic means' means that the service is sent initially and received at its destination by means of electronic equipment for the processing (including digital compression) and storage of data, and entirely transmitted, conveyed and received by wire, by radio, by optical means or by other electromagnetic means,

(iii) 'at the individual request of a recipient of services' means that the service is provided through the transmission of data on individual request."

7.5   This definition is very broad. Recital 18 to the E-Commerce Directive states that "information society services span a wide range of economic activities which take place online", giving as examples activities that consist in selling goods online but making it clear that they are not restricted to services giving rise to online contracting but also, "in so far as they represent an economic activity extend to services which are not remunerated by those who receive them". Examples of the latter include services "offering online information

---

[2] Directive (EU) 2015/1535, laying down a procedure for the provision of information in the field of technical regulations and of rules on Information Society services.

or commercial communications, or those providing tools allowing for search, access or retrieval of data".

7.6   It is clear therefore that in addition to information society service providers that sell goods and services online such as online retailers like Amazon UK, eBay, Apple, Netflix and Tesco, the definition embraces service providers who are remunerated through advertising not through any contract with the consumer, including online entertainment providers like YouTube, social media such as Facebook and search engines. This has been confirmed by UK and European case law, holding that such services as Google's Blogger.com blog-hosting service,[3] Google's search engine[4] and Google's AdWords service[5] all fall within the definition – in the language of the recital these are "services hosting information provided by a recipient of the service".

7.7   Other ISSPs that are covered include "services which consist of the transmission of information via a communications network", e.g. email providers like Microsoft Outlook and "services providing access to a communication network", which include telecommunications companies providing internet access such as BT and Virgin Media. Providers of Wi-Fi services may also meet this definition.[6]

7.8   As the definition of ISSPs is very broad, it is flexible enough to embrace new types of online service that may come into existence in the future, and is not limited to the types of information society services that happened to exist when the E-Commerce Directive was enacted in 2000.

7.9   Recital 18 also gives examples of certain activities that are not "information society services" by reason of not including one or more elements of the definition. Television and radio broadcasting services are not "information society services" as they are not provided at individual request, but video-on-demand services do meet the definition. Commercial communications by email are information society services, but not email communications conducted between persons outside of any business or professional context. Examples of information-related services that are not provided at a distance and that don't fall within the definition include public libraries and internet cafes.

---

[3] *Davison v Habeeb & Ors* [2012] 3 CMLR 6.

[4] *Metropolitan International Schools Ltd v DesignTechnica & Ors* [2011] 1 WLR 1743.

[5] *Google France SARL v Louis Vuitton SA* [2011] Bus LR 1.

[6] *McFadden v Sony Music Entertainment Germany GmbH* [2017] Bus LR 430.

The scope of the E-Commerce Directive

7.10 The E-Commerce Directive only applies to ISSPs that are established on the territory of an EU Member State and not to ISSPs located in other parts of the world.[7] The term "established service provider" is defined as

"a service provider who effectively pursues an economic activity using a fixed establishment for an indefinite period".[8]

The key issue is where the enterprise carries on its business, not where any IT infrastructure or other technology is physically located.[9]

7.11 The concept of "establishment" is an autonomous concept under EU law and recital 19 makes it clear that the place at which an ISSP is established should be determined in accordance with the case law of the CJEU. It seems likely that the broad interpretation of establishment given in the *Google Spain SL & Anor v Agencia Española de Protección de Datos & Anor* [10] judgment in the context of the Data Protection Directive would also apply under the E-Commerce Directive (see para 2.6).

7.12 The E-Commerce Directive seeks to harmonise certain aspects of EU law as they relate to e-commerce including the liability of ISSPs (this is known as the "coordinated field"), but it does not seek to regulate all aspects of the law relating to ISSPs. For example, the substantive law determining whether an ISSP is liable for any civil or criminal claim is decided by reference to the national law of the country concerned, not the Directive. Likewise, although the prohibition of a general obligation to monitor qualifies the powers of national courts to grant injunctions against ISSPs, their power to grant injunctions generally and the procedures by which such injunctions are granted are determined by national law.

7.13 A number of matters that could potentially come within the scope of the E-Commerce Directive are specifically excluded from it, for example issues relating to taxation, questions relating to agreements or practices governed by cartel law and gambling activities, including online betting and lotteries.[11]

---

[7] Art 3(1), recital 58.
[8] Art 2(c).
[9] Art 2(c).
[10] [2014] QB 1022.
[11] Art 1(5).

Relationship with Data Protection Directive

7.14   One important issue for potential claims based on data protection is the relationship between the E-Commerce Directive and the Data Protection Directive.[12] Art 5 of the E-Commerce Directive states that it shall not apply to

> "questions relating to information society services covered by Directives 95/46/EC and 97/66/EC" (the Data Protection Directive and the Directive on the Processing of Personal Data in the Telecommunications Sector).[13]

Recital 14 of the E-Commerce Directive states that "the protection of individuals with regard to the processing of personal data is solely governed . . . " by the Data Protection Directive and Directive on the Processing of Personal Data in the Telecommunications Sector.

7.15   The point arose for decision in *CG v Facebook Ireland Ltd*,[14] where the claimant contended that the E-Commerce Directive did not apply in data protection cases (with the result, if correct, that Facebook could not rely on the safe harbours). This argument was rejected by the Northern Ireland Court of Appeal, which held at [95] that:

> "the starting point has to be the matter covered by the E-commerce Directive which is the exemption for information society services from the liability to pay damages in certain circumstances. The provisions do not interfere with any of the principles in relation to the processing of personal data, the protection of individuals with regard to the processing of personal data or the free movement of such data. The provisions do, however, provide a tailored solution for the liability of information society services in the particular circumstances outlined in the E-commerce Directive. We do not consider that this is a question relating to information society services covered by the earlier Data Protection Directives and accordingly do not accept that the scope of the exemption from damages is affected by those Directives."

---

[12] Dir 95/46/EC.

[13] Reg 3(1)(b) of the E-Commerce Regulations.

[14] [2017] 2 CMLR 29.

7.16   The same conclusion was reached by the Italian Supreme Court in *Italian Prosecutor's Office v Drummond*.[15] That case concerned a video that had been uploaded by an internet user to Google Video that showed a child with Down's syndrome being teased by other children. A number of Google executives were prosecuted and convicted for data protection offences, even though they had no prior knowledge of the video's publication and it had been removed on the day of notification. The Supreme Court held that the two Directives were intended to operate "in harmony" with each other and that the E-Commerce safe harbours operated alongside, and were not affected by, the Data Protection Directive. Accordingly, the Google executives successfully defended themselves under the hosting exemption.

7.17   The point is addressed in the General Data Protection Regulation ("GDPR"),[16] Recital 21 of which states that:

> "This Regulation is without prejudice to the application of Directive 2000/31/EC of the European Parliament and of the Council, in particular of the liability of intermediary service providers in Articles 12 to 15 of the Directive. That Directive seeks to contribute to the proper functioning of the internal market by ensuring the free movement of information society services between Member States."

Art 2 of the GDPR concerns its material scope and art 2(4) provides that:

> "This Regulation shall be without prejudice to the application of Directive 2000/31/EC, in particular of the liability of intermediary service providers in Articles 12 to 15 of the Directive."

7.18   This makes it clear that the GDPR is "without prejudice" to the application of the E-Commerce Directive and in particular the safe harbours given to internet intermediaries in arts 12–15. It therefore provides the much needed clarity on the relationship between the data protection regime and the e-commerce regime, making it clear that the safe harbours for internet intermediaries continue to apply and are unaffected by the Regulation.

---

[15] Judgment No 3672, Italian Supreme Court, 17 December 2013.

[16] Reg (EU) 2016/679.

CONDUITS, CACHING AND HOSTING

Conduits

7.19 The Electronic Commerce (EC Directive) Regulations 2002, reg 17 ("E-Commerce Regulations") transposes art 12 of the E-Commerce Directive into domestic law. It provides as follows:

> "(1) Where an information society service is provided which consists of the transmission in a communication network of information provided by a recipient of the service or the provision of access to a communication network, the service provider (if he otherwise would) shall not be liable for damages or for any other pecuniary remedy or for any criminal sanction as a result of that transmission where the service provider–
>
> (a) did not initiate the transmission;
>
> (b) did not select the receiver of the transmission; and
>
> (c) did not select or modify the information contained in the transmission.
>
> (2) The acts of transmission and of provision of access referred to in paragraph (1) include the automatic, intermediate and transient storage of the information transmitted where:
>
> (a) this takes place for the sole purpose of carrying out the transmission in the communication network, and
>
> (b) the information is not stored for any period longer than is reasonably necessary for the transmission."

7.20 Telecommunications companies that provide email services and internet access are prime examples of ISSPs that are "mere conduits". In the case of an email, for example, the "recipient of the service" or service user initiates the email or call, decides on the recipient and chooses the content of the message. The ISSP plays a purely passive role by facilitating the communication of the information without in any way being responsible for it; hence the rationale for protecting it against incurring any liability for damages in any civil or criminal claim. Providers of Wi-Fi services are also mere conduits; they merely provide access to the network and are not responsible for selecting the content that third parties may choose to send to the network.[17]

---

[17] *McFadden v Sony Music Entertainment Germany GmbH* [2017] Bus LR 430.

7.21   In *Bunt v Tilley & Ors*,[18] the claimant brought claims for defamation against three individuals who had published statements on websites and also against their three ISPs, AOL UK Ltd, Tiscali UK Ltd and British Telecommunications Plc. Eady J held that the three ISPs were not publishers at common law as they did not have any knowing involvement in publication of the relevant words (see paras 3.60–3.61). He also held that the ISPs were protected variously by the mere conduit, caching and hosting exemptions under the E-Commerce Regulations, with e.g. AOL's caching of Google Groups benefitting from the caching exemption and BT's hosting of Usenet newsgroups benefitting from the hosting exemption.

7.22   A service provider that takes an active role in initiating transmissions, selecting recipients or influencing the contents of communications ceases to be a mere conduit and will not be able to rely on the exemption. In similar vein, recital 44 of the E-Commerce Directive states that:

> "A service provider who deliberately collaborates with one of the recipients of his service in order to undertake illegal acts goes beyond the activities of 'mere conduit' or 'caching' and as a result cannot benefit from the liability exemptions established for these activities."

7.23   The requirement that the Internet Service Provider (ISP) must not "modify" the information does not prevent it from applying technical procedures that make transmission of the information more efficient, providing that the actual content of the information is not affected. This is made clear by recital 43 that states that the requirement not to modify:

> "does not cover manipulations of a technical nature which take place in the course of the transmission as they do not alter the integrity of the information contained in the transmission."

7.24   The mere conduit exemption, unlike the caching and hosting exemptions, is not qualified by any provision relating to actual knowledge or awareness of relevant facts and does not have a Notice and Take Down procedure. The notice and takedown model is inappropriate because the exemption is confined to information that is temporarily transmitted by the ISP, and that must not be stored for any period longer than is necessary for the transmission, so the ISP will not have retained any information that could be the subject of notice and takedown.[19]

---

[18] [2007] 1 WLR 1243.

[19] *McFadden*, at [63].

Caching

7.25   Reg 18 of the E-Commerce Regulations transposes into UK law art 13 of the E-Commerce Directive and provides as follows:

"Where an information society service is provided which consists of the transmission in a communication network of information provided by a recipient of the service, the service provider (if he otherwise would) shall not be liable for damages or for any other pecuniary remedy or for any criminal sanction as a result of that transmission where–

(a) the information is the subject of automatic, intermediate and temporary storage where that storage is for the sole purpose of making more efficient onward transmission of the information to other recipients of the service upon their request, and

(b) the service provider–

(i) does not modify the information;

(ii) complies with conditions on access to the information;

(iii) complies with any rules regarding the updating of the information, specified in a manner widely recognised and used by industry;

(iv) does not interfere with the lawful use of technology, widely recognised and used by industry, to obtain data on the use of the information; and

(v) acts expeditiously to remove or to disable access to the information he has stored upon obtaining actual knowledge of the fact that the information at the initial source of the transmission has been removed from the network, or access to it has been disabled, or that a court or an administrative authority has ordered such removal or disablement."

7.26   Caching is the process of storing data in a cache, which is a temporary storage area used for the purpose of making retrieval of recently accessed files swifter and more efficient. For example, if a person looks at a particular webpage a temporary copy of that page is stored in his hard drive. When the user returns to that recently-viewed page, the browser can retrieve the file from the cache rather than the original server, saving the user time and saving the network the burden of additional traffic.

7.27 ISSPs may engage in caching on a large scale ("network caching") to process the millions of requests for information that they receive from service users, setting up farms of proxy servers that replicate the content on the original servers, thereby enabling their users to access the content as quickly as possible through retrieval from the network cache. The most important kind of ISSP covered by the caching exemption is a search engine.[20] Reg 18 of the E-Commerce Regulations seeks to protect such ISSPs from legal liability in damages and certain types of injunctions when engaging in network caching, providing certain conditions are met.

7.28 First, the activity must meet the E-Commerce Directive definition for caching that involves the automatic, intermediate and temporary storage of information.

7.29 Secondly, the provider must not modify the information. As noted above in connection with mere conduits, the requirement not to modify does not cover

"manipulations of a technical nature which take place in the course of the transmission as they do not alter the integrity of the information contained in the transmission" (recital 43).

7.30 For example, if in the course of transmission a file were to be converted into a different format e.g. a full image into a thumbnail image, for the purpose of making its onward transmission more efficient, this should not be regarded as modification of the information.[21]

7.31 The requirements at reg 18(b)(ii) and 18(b)(iii) of the E-Commerce Regulations refer to industry caching rules that enable websites to be programmed so that they are not cached (e.g. news websites that are updated very frequently will often not permit caching), as well as industry rules governing updating of cached information. Likewise, reg 18(b)(iv) requires ISSPs not to interfere with technologies that permit service providers to evaluate how data is being used e.g. how many hits a particular website receives.

7.32 Reg 18(b)(v) applies where the provider acts expeditiously to remove or disable access to the cached information on obtaining actual knowledge of the fact that the information at the initial source of the transmission (i.e. the original file) has been removed from the network, or access to it has been disabled, or a court or administrative authority has ordered such removal or disablement. This notice and takedown provision seeks to ensure that where an original file has been, or will be, removed or rendered inaccessible, that the

---

[20] Mosley v Google Inc [2015] EMLR 11.

[21] Ibid, at [41].

cached copy will also be removed or rendered inaccessible by the ISSP. To date, there have been no English cases on this provision.

7.33   The meaning of "actual knowledge" and acting "expeditiously" are considered in the section on the hosting exemption below.

Hosting

Introduction

7.34   Reg 19 of the E-Commerce Regulations transposes into UK law art 14 of the E-Commerce Directive and provides as follows:

> "Where an information society service is provided which consists of the storage of information provided by a recipient of the service, the service provider (if he otherwise would) shall not be liable for damages or for any other pecuniary remedy or for any criminal sanction as a result of that storage where–
>
> (a) the service provider–
>
>   (i) does not have actual knowledge of unlawful activity or information and, where a claim for damages is made, is not aware of facts or circumstances from which it would have been apparent to the service provider that the activity or information was unlawful; or
>
>   (ii) upon obtaining such knowledge or awareness, acts expeditiously to remove or to disable access to the information, and
>
> (b) the recipient of the service was not acting under the authority or the control of the service provider."

7.35   In practical terms, the hosting exemption is likely to be the most important of the three exemptions for ISSPs. This is because it is typically through the hosting of information provided by third parties that ISSPs make accessible to the general public information that may become the subject of complaints or legal proceedings.

7.36   The owners of big social media websites such as Facebook, YouTube, Twitter, Instagram, Google+ and Snapchat and blogs such as Google Blogger, are therefore the most likely ISSPs to find themselves responding to removal requests or seeking to defend themselves against claims for damages. The hosting exemption will also be relevant to news websites that permit members of the public to post their own comments on articles, as for these purposes the news provider will be a host of the third party information.

7.37   The first condition for the art 14 of the E-Commerce Directive exemption is that the ISSP is providing a service that "consists of the storage of information provided by a recipient of the service" i.e. the ISSP must be hosting information provided by its service users, typically either members of the public accessing the service or advertisers advertising on the service.

7.38   The hosting exemption, as the above examples illustrate, is therefore limited to storage of third party content and will not protect an ISSP from liability in respect of its own content. This was confirmed by the CJEU in *Papasavvas v O Fileleftheros Dimosia Etairia Ltd*,[22] where a newspaper that sought to defend one of its own articles based on the exemptions was held not to be an intermediary service provider because it had created the content.

7.39   However, this does not prevent a newspaper publisher from relying on the hosting exemption as it applies to comments about an article made by third parties. In *Karim v Newsquest Media Group Ltd*,[23] for example, the claimant sued a newspaper for defamation over an article and the public's comments on that article on the newspaper's website. The newspaper could not rely on the exemption in respect of the allegedly defamatory article (for which it had a substantive defence), but successfully relied on the hosting exemption in relation to comments that members of the public had posted about the article.

7.40   There have been several cases where ISSPs have successfully relied on the hosting exemption, for example:

- *Bunt v Tilley & Ors*: BT successfully invoked the hosting exemption in relation to its hosting of postings on Usenet discussion groups;[24]
- *Davison v Habeeb & Ors*[25] and *Tamiz v Google*:[26] Google Inc successfully relied on the hosting exemption for its hosting of postings on Blogger.com;
- *Karim v Newsquest Media Group Ltd*: a newspaper publisher successfully defended readers' comments about an online article based on the hosting exemption;[27]

---

[22] [2015] 1 CMLR 24.

[23] [2009] EWHC 3205 (QB).

[24] [2006] EWHC 407 (QB).

[25] [2012] 3 CMLR 6.

[26] [2012] EMLR 24.

[27] *Mosley v Google,* above.

- *McGrath & Anor v Dawkins & Ors*: Amazon successfully used the hosting exemption to strike out a libel claim concerning comments about a book;[28]
- *Gestevision Telecinco SA & Anor v YouTube LLC*: YouTube successfully used the hosting exemption to defend itself against intellectual property claims;[29]
- *Italian Public Prosecutor's Office v Drummond*: Google used the hosting exemption to defend itself in relation to criminal proceedings brought against Google executives relating to a video posted by a member of the public;[30]
- *CG v Facebook Ireland*: Facebook Ireland was largely successful in relying on the hosting exemption for hosting profile pages on Facebook that were held to have misused the claimants' private information, although the safe harbour was lost for some information as a result of Facebook failing to remove it sufficiently promptly following notification.[31]

7.41   However, where an ISSP goes beyond mere hosting of third party content by including its own content in the information provided to internet users, or influencing that content to any significant degree, the hosting exemption may not be available. For example, the CJEU held in *L'Oreal SA & Ors v eBay International AG & Ors*[32] that eBay was unable to rely on the hosting exemption in relation to advertisements for L'Oreal products that it had promoted, while in *Google France SARL & Anor v Louis Vuitton Malletier SA*[33] the CJEU held that while Google's advertisements service (AdWords) generally fell within the hosting exemption, that protection might be lost depending on the extent to which Google was involved in the drafting of commercial messages or in selecting keywords.

Notification and loss of safe harbour protection

7.42   The hosting safe harbour affords hosts protection subject to two conditions. The first is that the provider does not have actual knowledge of unlawful

---

[28] [2012] Info TLR 72.

[29] [2014] 2 CMLR 13.

[30] Judgment No 3672, Italian Supreme Court, 17 Dec 2013.

[31] [2017] 2 CMLR 29.

[32] [2012] Bus LR 1369.

[33] [2011] Bus LR 1.

activity or information and, as regards to claims for damages, is not aware of facts or circumstances from which the unlawful nature of the activity or information would have been apparent (the lack of knowledge requirements). The second condition is that the provider, upon obtaining such knowledge or awareness, acts expeditiously to remove or to disable access to the information (the swift removal requirement).

7.43   Conversely, an ISSP that comes to know about illegal activity or information and fails to disable access to it or to remove it expeditiously may lose safe harbour protection, entitling a claimant to claim damages against it.

7.44   Reg 22 of the E-Commerce Regulations ("Notice for the purpose of actual knowledge") provides as follows:

> "In determining whether a service provider has actual knowledge for the purposes of regs 18(b)(v) and 19(a)(i), a court shall take into account all matters which appear to it in the particular circumstances to be relevant and, among other things, shall have regard to–
>
> (a) whether a service provider has received a notice through a means of contact made available in accordance with reg 6(1)(c), and
>
> (b) the extent to which any notice includes–
>
> (i) the full name and address of the sender of the notice;
>
> (ii) details of the location of the information in question; and
>
> (iii) details of the unlawful nature of the activity or information in question."

7.45   Reg 22 is relevant to the first stage of the enquiry, namely whether an ISSP has actual knowledge of the unlawful activity or information. Reg 22 requires a court to take into account all relevant factors and in particular to have regard to whether the ISSP has received a notice through its notice and takedown procedure and the extent to which that notice includes the sender's name and address, "details of the location of the information in question" and "details of the unlawful nature of the activity or information in question".

7.46   The "details of the location of the information in question" focuses on the location of the specific information about which complaint is made. The most precise way of identifying the location of information on the internet is by reference to its URL (Uniform Resource Locator), also known as its web address. In *Davison v Habeeb & Ors* the court accepted that "location of information" in reg 22(b)(ii) of the E-Commerce Regulations means the URL.[34]

7.47   In most cases complainants should be required to provide the URL or URLs of which complaint is made. But whether providing every single URL should be treated as a necessary condition in all cases is questionable. On Twitter, for example, every tweet has its own URL. There can be thousands or in some cases tens of thousands of tweets and re-tweets on a given subject. Furthermore, information that has been made public online can be simultaneously available on many different URLs and its removal on some URLs may simply mean that other URLs feature more highly up the search engine's results. Furthermore, in cases of harassment, where an individual is deliberately putting unlawful information online, an ISSP may remove some URLs only for the offender to re-post it to others. In such situations, requiring claimants to identify all of the relevant URLs all of the time is likely to be oppressive and disproportionate.

7.48   In such cases it is arguable that the requirements of reg 22 will be satisfied when the complainant has provided sufficient information to enable the ISSP to identify the information in question having regard to the technologies available to it. Often the URL will be the best way of identifying the location, but in cases where there are many changing URLs it may be reasonable to expect ISSPs to provide more proactive assistance. This issue is considered further in relation to monitoring below.

7.49   The "details of the unlawful nature of the activity or information in question" is an important safeguard as the ISSP must be fixed with actual knowledge of "unlawful activity or information". In the case of a publication giving rise to tortious liability, the publisher will usually have potential defences available to it e.g. a statement may be defamatory without being unlawful if the publisher has a truth defence. As Eady J observed in *Bunt v Tilley & Ors*, in those circumstances for an ISSP to be fixed with actual knowledge of unlawful activity it "must know something of the strength and weakness of relevant defences".

7.50   Removals following notification are to be undertaken "in observance of the principle of freedom of expression" (recital 46 of the E-Commerce Directive). The need for an ISSP to be provided with sufficient information to enable it to evaluate whether a given publication is unlawful is vital, because the ISSP will usually have no idea whether the original publisher has a defence to the allegation. If for example, there is a link on a Facebook page to an

---

[34]   [2011] EWHC 3031 (QB) at [58].

article on a newspaper's website that makes a defamatory allegation, Facebook will have no idea about the available defences; it is the newspaper that will have made the decision to publish, which will have given thought to potential defences and that will be in possession of any supporting evidence. The ISSP cannot be expected to decide whether the publication is unlawful without a substantial amount of information from the complainant.

7.51   Both in the UK and in Europe the courts have consistently held that actual knowledge of unlawful activity requires the complainant to provide sufficient information to the ISSP for it to make a meaningful evaluation of the lawfulness of the publication. In both *Davison v Habeeb & Ors* and *Tamiz v Google,* the claims failed *inter alia* on the issue of notification because the ISSPs were not put in a position to decide whether the information was unlawful, in *Davison* because there were competing claims that the ISSP couldn't adjudicate, and in *Tamiz* because there was nothing more than a bare assertion of unlawfulness.

7.52   Likewise, in *L'Oreal v eBay* the CJEU held that the mere fact of notification of unlawful activity or information is not sufficient; the notification must be sufficiently precise and sufficiently substantiated before an ISSP may be deprived of the protection of the hosting exemption. The CJEU held that:

> "… such a notification admittedly cannot automatically preclude the exemption from liability provided for in art 14 of Directive 2000/31, given that notification of allegedly illegal activities or information may turn out to be insufficiently precise or inadequately substantiated, the fact remains that such notification represents, as a general rule, a factor of which the national court must take account when determining, in the light of the information so transmitted to the operator, whether the latter was actually aware of facts or circumstances on the basis of which a diligent economic operator should have identified the illegality." ([122])

7.53   The concept of what a "diligent economic operator" should do in circumstances where it has been provided with some information about a claim but not enough for it to have actual knowledge of unlawful information formed the basis of the Court of Appeal of Northern Ireland's finding that Facebook was liable for misuse of private information in *CG v Facebook Ireland.* In that case, although most of the letters sent by the plaintiff's solicitor were held not to amount to effective notification (because they referred to inapplicable causes of action and failed to identify the only actionable private information) one letter of complaint was held to be effective even though it made no reference to misuse of private information (it referred only to defamation) and did not provide Facebook with the relevant URLs, on the grounds that it did identify the particular information that was unlawful. The Court held that the letter contained sufficient information that Facebook should, as a "diligent economic operator", have appreciated that the information was unlawful.

Expeditious removal

7.54   The second key requirement for avoiding liability for damages is "expeditious removal" of unlawful content. This is linked to the requirement placed on complainants to provide a sufficiently precise and substantiated claim, as what it is reasonable to expect of an ISSP in terms of the speed of its response depends in large part on how clearly and fully the claim has been set out. The speed with which the ISSP must act to remove unlawful material was considered in *Tamiz v Google Inc*, where a leisurely 5 weeks was held to be within reasonable bounds. By contrast, in *CG v Facebook Ireland,* Facebook was held liable (without any discussion in the judgment) for the 6 day period between notification of the claim and removal from its website, in spite of the lack of clarity in the original complaint. This judgment may suggest that Courts expect large and wealthy global corporations like Facebook to evaluate and act on complaints very swiftly if they are to avail themselves of safe harbour protection.

The position of search engines

7.55   Unlike the Digital Millennium Copyright Act 1998, the E-Commerce Directive does not create a specific exemption for search engines. As a consequence, a large number of European countries, when transposing the Directive into national law, have legislated to create a specific exemption for them.[35] In countries such as Britain and France that have transposed the rest of the Directive but without creating a specific exemption for search engines, the question has arisen as to which safe harbour protection is available.

7.56   As noted above, search engines are expressly referred to in the recitals of the E-Commerce Directive as an example of an information society service and, as Advocat-General Maduro observed in *Google France v Louis Vuitton*, their inclusion is consistent with the aims pursued by the Directive. As search engines are the primary means by that members of the public find information online, it could be argued that they are the paradigm of an information society

---

[35] The relevant countries were identified in *Metropolitan International Schools Ltd v Designtechnica Corp & Anor* as Austria, Spain, Portugal, Hungary, Liechtenstein, Bulgaria and Romania.

service that requires safe harbour protection. However, the wording of the three safe harbours in the E-Commerce Directive, that are essentially functional, does not fit particularly well with what search engines actually do.

7.57   In *Google France v Louis Vuitton*,[36] Advocate-General Maduro took the view that search engines fall within the caching exemption. Search engines crawl the web and then create an index of web pages that are cached, to make their retrieval swifter and more efficient. But some websites are programmed to prevent caching, so search engines cannot cache those websites and search results must link to the original server (this is typically the case with news websites). In addition, in presenting information to internet users in response to search terms, search engines undertake steps that go beyond caching. For example, search engines match search terms to relevant websites, rank them for relevance and present the ranked results to internet users. None of these steps is "caching" as defined by art 13 and it is not clear whether, if caching is present but only part of a more extended range of activities, protection can be claimed for the wider activities that go beyond the definition.

7.58   The CJEU held that Google's advertising on its search engine (AdWords) falls within the hosting exemption. The exemption as defined refers to "the storage of information provided by a recipient of the service" and in this context the Court treated Google as storing information that had been provided by advertisers before making it available in response to related search requests. However, the Court did not consider the position of natural search results. Unlike advertisements, natural search results are not provided by internet users for storage in a conventional sense, although it could be argued that by allowing a search engine's web crawler to link to a given website the website's host is permitting Google to store that information for the purpose of making it available in search results.

7.59   In *Metropolitan International Schools Ltd v Designtechnica Corp & Ors*,[37] Eady J held that Google's search engine was not a publisher at common law as it did not have any knowing involvement in publication of the relevant words. But Eady J was also invited to consider whether Google could defend the claim on the basis of the E-Commerce exemptions. Although his observations were strictly *obiter*, Eady J expressed doubts as to whether the mere conduit, caching or hosting exemptions were available to Google's search engine and stated that in his view statutory intervention would be needed for Google to be able to

---

[36] [2011] Bus LR 1, Advocate-General Opinion.

[37] [2011] 1 WLR 1743.

rely on the hosting defence.[38] However, as noted above, in *Mosley v Google Inc*[39] Mitting J accepted that Google's search engine was covered by the caching exemption.

THE AVAILABILITY OF INJUNCTIONS

Introduction

7.60   All three of the safe harbours – mere conduit, caching and hosting – are expressly qualified to make it clear that they do not affect the powers of courts or administrative authorities to require "the service provider to terminate or prevent an infringement" i.e. to grant injunctions. This is unsurprising as other aspects of EU law require Member States to make injunctive remedies available e.g. to protect against copyright infringement.

7.61   Recital 45 also states as follows:

> "The limitations of the liability of intermediary service providers established in this Directive do not affect the possibility of *injunctions of different kinds;* such injunctions can in particular consist of orders by courts or administrative authorities requiring the termination or prevention of any infringement, including the removal of illegal information or the disabling of access to it." (emphasis added)

7.62   It is arguable that where an ISSP can bring itself within reg 19 of the E-Commerce Regulations (art 14 of the Directive), the ISSP is exempted from all forms of legal liability (including in the form of injunctive relief), with the exception of what in recital 45 to the Directive are referred to as "injunctions of different kinds" (such as for example, *Norwich Pharmacal* orders that do not depend upon establishing legal liability on the part of the ISSP).[40] On this basis, the correct analysis would be that the ISSP can be ordered to bring an end to the unlawful activity *of another* but cannot itself be held legally liable by way of injunction if the safe harbour applies.[41]

---

[38] At [97]–[114].

[39] [2015] EMLR 11.

[40] See the explanation of the operation of the E-Commerce Directive by Kenneth Parker J in *R (British Telecommunications Plc) & Anor v Secretary of State for Business Innovation and Skills & Ors* [2011] 3 CMLR 5 at [102]; approved by the Court of Appeal in that case at [2012] Bus LR 1766 at [53]; and see *Mosley v Google Inc* [2015] EMLR 11 at [35]–[37].

[41] See *CG v Facebook Ireland* [2017] EMLR 12 at [37].

General and specific monitoring of content

7.63 The power to grant injunctions is not, however, unlimited and is itself qualified by art 15 of the E-Commerce Directive that provides as follows:

"Member States shall not impose a general obligation on providers, when providing the services covered by arts 12, 13 and 14, to monitor the information which they transmit or store, nor a general obligation actively to seek facts or circumstances indicating illegal activity."

7.64 The prohibition on general monitoring is not intended, however, to prevent courts from imposing on ISSPs any monitoring obligation, only a "general obligation" that does not exclude monitoring obligations in a specific case. This is made clear by recital 47, which is as follows:

"Member States are prevented from imposing a monitoring obligation on service providers only with respect to obligations of a general nature; this does not concern monitoring obligations in a specific case and, in particular, does not affect orders by national authorities in accordance with national legislation."

7.65 Although art 15 was not transposed into UK law in the E-Commerce Regulations, the Court must nonetheless exercise any power to grant an injunction (including under s.37 of the Supreme Court Act 1981) consistently with art 15 of the Directive.[42]

7.66 Art 15 only applies in relation to ISSPs when providing the services covered by arts 12, 13 and 14 of the Directive (regs 17, 18 and 19 of the E-Commerce Regulations), so it is a condition precedent for the operation of art 15 that the ISSP can rely on one of the safe harbours.

7.67 Art 15 has two elements. The first is that it prevents courts from imposing on ISSPs a "general obligation . . . to monitor the information which they transmit or store". Secondly, ISSPs may not be placed under a "general obligation actively to seek facts or circumstances giving rise to illegal activity."

7.68 The prohibition against placing ISSPs under general monitoring obligations and general obligations actively to seek out unlawful activity is the other side of the same coin as notification, namely the intermediary liability regime putting the onus on complainants to notify ISSPs, clearly and precisely, of the existence and location of unlawful activity or information. It is for complainants, not ISSPs, to identify the unlawful activity and information.

---

[42] See *Cartier International AG & Ors v British Sky Broadcasting Ltd & Ors* [2015] Bus LR 298 at [140]–[141] per Arnold J, upheld on appeal at [2017] Bus LR 1.

Once the information has been drawn to their attention the onus falls on ISSPs who wish to avail themselves of the safe harbours to investigate such complaints and to act promptly to remove unlawful information. That is how the scheme for intermediary liability is intended to work. Absent precise notification of unlawful activity or information, ISSPs would be required to engage in general monitoring of their content.

7.69   Both the CJEU and national courts have given important judgments on whether applications for injunctions brought against ISSPs fall foul of the prohibition on general monitoring. The Belgian society of authors, SABAM, brought proceedings against Scarlet Extended (an ISP) and Netlog (an online social networking platform), seeking injunctions to prevent them from allowing their services to be used for the peer-to-peer sharing of copyright-protected works.[43]

7.70   The injunctions sought did not seek to identify any specific infringing content or provide the URLs for any infringing content but would have required the ISSPs to install a filtering system and to actively monitor the data of all of their customers in order to prevent any future infringement of intellectual property rights. The CJEU concluded that:

> "the injunction imposed on the ISP concerned requiring it to install the contested filtering system would oblige it to actively monitor all the data relating to each of its customers in order to prevent any future infringement of intellectual-property rights. It follows that that injunction would require the ISP to carry out general monitoring, something which is prohibited by Article 15(1) of Directive 2000/31."[44]

7.71   Similarly, in *Gestevision Telecinco SA v YouTube LLC*,[45] the case concerned a claim brought by a television broadcaster alleging infringement of intellectual property rights against YouTube. The Madrid Court of Appeal held that YouTube did not have actual knowledge so as to take it outside the hosting exemption, because the notifications sent to it by the complainant were of a general nature and did not specify precisely the location of the material complained of. The Court of Appeal of Madrid thus upheld the decision of the court below at [20] that:

---

[43] *Scarlet Extended SA v Société belge des auteurs, compositeurs et éditeurs SCRL (SABAM) & Ors* [2011] ECR I-11959; *Belgische Vereniging van Auteurs, Componisten en Uitgevers CVBA (SABAM) v Netlog NV* [2012] 2 CMLR 18.

[44] *Scarlet Extended* at [40].

[45] [2014] 2 CMLR 13.

"YouTube cannot be obliged to monitor and control in advance and in a general manner the content loaded onto its servers, the appellants must cooperate with it, bringing to its attention 'in an individual and specific manner' those contents which may breach its rights."

7.72   By way of contrast, applicants for injunctions have been successful where those injunctions have been sufficiently specific in identifying the websites or webpages where the unlawful information is located. For example, in *UPC Telekabel Wien GmbH v Constantin Film Verleih GmbH & Anor*,[46] rightholders who owned copyright in films succeeded in obtaining an injunction against the ISSP to prohibit it from providing its customers with access to a specific website that was streaming copyright-infringing material.

7.73   Likewise, in *Twentieth Century Fox Film Corp & Ors v British Telecommunications Plc*,[47] the claimant rightholders successfully obtained an injunction against BT requiring it to apply certain technology to block its subscribers from accessing a specific website that was sharing copyright-infringing material. BT, as a mere conduit, had argued that the injunction amounted to a general obligation to monitor the information it transmitted. That argument was rejected by Arnold J, who held that although art 15 of the E-Commerce Directive prevents the general active monitoring of all the data of all the customers of an ISSP, it does not prevent courts from ordering specific monitoring in particular cases. In *McFadden*,[48] the CJEU held that an individual who provided access to a free Wi-Fi network (which had been used by a third party to download copyright-infringing content), could be ordered to put in place a password system which required users to provide their names, to protect the copyright owners' material.

7.74   One area for the future is the extent to which ISSPs may be required to utilise existing technologies to prevent unlawful information from appearing on their search engines or social media platforms once it has been drawn to their attention. For example, Google and Bing have taken steps to prevent certain words from being used as search terms to bring up child abuse imagery, while technologies also exist that permit ISSPs to create digital fingerprints of images and then to prevent them from being made available (again, these technologies are deployed against child abuse imagery). If such technologies already exist, it would seem to be open to claimants to argue that in appropriate cases they should also be utilised for their benefit e.g. to prevent

---

[46] [2014] Bus LR 541.

[47] [2012] Bus LR 1461.

[48] [2017] Bus LR 430.

re-publication of an unlawful image. Whether such proactive measures would amount to general or specific monitoring is an issue the courts are likely to have to decide in future cases.

THE EUROPEAN CONVENTION ON HUMAN RIGHTS AND INTERMEDIARY LIABILITY

7.75   By the Human Rights Act 1998, s 2 the English Courts must take into account the relevant case law of the European Court of Human Rights ("ECtHR"). This means that in considering issues of intermediary liability the recent case law of that court on the subject needs to be considered.

7.76   The ECtHR was first called upon to examine issues of intermediary liability in *Delfi v Estonia*.[49] The applicant was Delfi, an Estonian news website, which had published an article about the destruction of an ice road by a ferry company. The Grand Chamber accepted that the article was balanced, was on a matter of public interest and was not contended to be unlawful under domestic law. The article was accompanied, however, by a comments section, in which a number of anonymous internet users had posted racist and abusive comments about the company's owner. The comments were made available online by Delfi for 6 weeks, but were removed by Delfi on the same day that it was notified of them. Delfi was held liable by the Estonian courts and ordered to pay a fine.

7.77   The Grand Chamber held that there was no violation of Article 10 of the Convention. The Court's reasoning followed that of the Estonian Supreme Court, which treated Delfi as if was a publisher of the comments, on the ground that it was a commercial enterprise which made a profit out of the website and its comments section and that on this basis it should be treated as a commercial publisher of the comments, not a true internet intermediary. The Estonian Supreme Court found that as Delfi had control over the comments section it was proportionate to hold it liable for having failed to remove the user comments at its own initiative prior to notification. This reasoning was criticised by the dissenting minority as being inconsistent with the hosting safe harbour under the E-Commerce Directive (to which Estonia was a party).

7.78   The Grand Chamber looked at five factors when balancing the Article 10 rights of the applicant and the Article 8 rights of those who are subject to the comments:

- The context and content of the impugned comments;

---

[49] (2016) 62 EHRR 6 (GC).

- The liability of the authors of the comments;
- Measures taken by the applicants and the conduct of the injured party;
- Consequences of the comments for the injured party;
- Consequences for the applicant.

7.79   These factors have been considered in two subsequent cases, in both of which the internet company was successful:

- In *MTE and Index.Hu v Hungary*,[50] the applicants were a regulatory body and an internet company who challenged a court ruling that they should be held liable for articles and user comments made on websites that they hosted. The claimant company had not notified the applicants about the comments, but as soon as it issued proceedings the comments were removed. The Hungarian courts held that the applicants were responsible for the publications and could not avail themselves of the hosting defence. They were ordered to pay court fees, but not damages. The European Court of Human Rights held that this amounted to a violation of Article 10 of the Convention, accepting that holding internet intermediaries liable for third-party comments would be likely to have a chilling effect on freedom of expression online, for example by encouraging them to close comment spaces altogether.

- In *Pihl v Sweden*,[51] a blog post on a small website run by a non-profit organisation accused the applicant of being involved in the Nazi party. He responded saying the comment was wrong and should be immediately removed. This was done the following day. The applicant's claims were rejected by the domestic courts. His complaint that his Article 8 rights had been violated was inadmissible. The post did not amount to hate speech or incitement to violence.

---

[50] [2016] ECHR 135.

[51] App No 74742/14. Decision of 9.3.17.

CHAPTER 8: REMEDIES

CHAPTER SYNOPSIS

- Deals with the remedies open to a person who has been – or who may be – the victim of the types of online conduct outlined in Chapters 5 and 6.
- Sets out interim remedies available where a claimant wishes to take steps to prevent conduct from happening or continuing. Interim injunctions can be obtained at the pre-publication stage to prevent threatened online publications that have not yet taken place. Such can be granted to restrain future breaches of confidence or misuse of private information. They can also be used to prevent future online harassment in certain circumstances.
- Discusses the impact of the Human Rights Act 1998, s 12, the "*Spycatcher* principle", and injunctions with a foreign element. Also outlines other interim remedies and orders.
- Looks at final remedies, where the claimant is seeking a remedy in respect of past wrongdoing and to prevent its repetition in future. Examines: damages (in defamation, privacy, under the Data Protection Act 1998, in harassment and special damages for "internet clean up); and final injunctions (in defamation, privacy and harassment, orders under the 1998 Act, orders to remove a statement or cease distribution).

INTRODUCTION

8.1   This Chapter deals with the remedies available to a person who has been the victim of unlawful online conduct. These remedies will be sought at two stages:

- When the claimant first learns of the threatened or actual online conduct and wishes to take steps to prevent it from happening or continuing (interim remedies).
- At the conclusion of an action in respect of the unlawful conduct, where the claimant is seeking a remedy in respect of past wrongdoing and to prevent its repetition in future (final remedies).

8.2   This Chapter will deal with interim and final remedies for the various causes of action outlined in Chapters 5 and 6 above. In practice, most issues in relation to interim remedies concern breach of confidence, misuse of private information and harassment.

INTERIM INJUNCTIONS

Introduction

8.3   An interim injunction is a remedy that is available at the start or during the course of proceedings and will only be granted pending trial and the final determination of the case. A claimant will have to provide an "undertaking in damages" to the defendant in the event that a final injunction is not ordered at trial to compensate the defendant for any loss and damage caused as a result of the interim injunction having been ordered.

8.4   Interim injunctions can be obtained at the pre-publication stage to prevent threatened online publications that have not yet taken place. This type of injunction is known as a "quia timet" injunction. The circumstances in which such injunctions available are limited and they are very rarely granted in defamation or malicious falsehood cases or under the Data Protection Act 1998.

8.5   Most importantly, such injunctions can be granted to restrain future breaches of confidence or misuse of private information. They can also be used to prevent future online harassment, provided that the defendant has already committed or is threatening to commit a course of conduct amounting to harassment against the claimant.

8.6   While pre-publication injunctions can be granted in advance of a legal wrong being committed, it is not enough for a claimant simply to have concerns that the defendant is going to publish something about them. It is necessary to show a threat of imminent publication which will infringe their rights: "it is not sufficient to say 'I fear', the claimant must aver and prove that what is going on is calculated to infringe his rights."[1] A court does not grant injunctions on the principle that they would do no harm to the defendant, if he does not intend to commit the act in question, there need to be grounds to make one.[2] Incentive to do a wrong does not equate to a real risk of wrongdoing.[3]

8.7   The Practice Guidance: Interim Non-Disclosure Orders that was issued in August 2011 by the (then) Master of the Rolls, Lord Neuberger, set out

---

[1] *Attorney General for Dominion of Canada v Ritchie Contracting and Supply Co Ltd* [1919] AC 999 (PC) at 1005. For example, *ERY v Associated Newspapers Ltd* [2017] EMLR 9 at [41].

[2] *Coffin v Coffin* (1821) 37 ER 776.

[3] *Rafael Defense Systems Ltd v Mectron Engenharia, Industria e Comercio SA* [2017] EWHC 597 (Comm).

recommended practice when seeking interim injunctions. This is considered further in Chapter 9.

Human Rights Act 1998, s 12

8.8   Where an injunction might affect the exercise of the art 10 right to freedom of expression the Court must consider the Human Rights Act 1998, s 12. There are three relevant sub-sections.

8.9   Firstly, s 12(2) provides that, if the respondent is not present or represented no relief shall be granted unless the Court is satisfied that the applicant has taken all practicable steps to notify them, or that there are compelling reasons why they should not be notified.

8.10   This provision is mirrored by the provisions of the CPR. CPR 25.3(1) and (3) and CPR PD 25A, para. 4.3(3), which requires the defendant to be put on notice of an interim application "except in cases where secrecy is essential". The Practice Guidance: Interim Non-Disclosure Orders makes it clear that failure to provide advance notice can only be justified, on clear and cogent evidence, by compelling reasons e.g. in a blackmail case where there is a real prospect that if the defendant were to be notified they would take steps to defeat the court's purpose.[4]

8.11   Secondly, s 12(3) provides that no relief will be granted to restrain publication before trial unless the court is satisfied that the applicant is likely to establish that publication should not be allowed. This normally means that success at trial must be shown to be more likely than not.[5] However in some cases it may be just to grant an injunction where the prospects of success fall short of this standard; for instance, if the damage that might be caused is particularly severe, or where a short-lived injunction is needed to enable the court to hear and give proper consideration to an application for interim relief pending trial or an appeal.[6] But ordinarily a claimant must show that he will probably succeed at trial, and the court will have to form a provisional view of the merits on the evidence available to it at the time of the interim application.[7]

8.12   Thirdly, s 12(4) states that the court must have "particular regard to the importance of the Convention right to freedom of expression". This does not

---

[4] Practice Guidance: Interim Non-Disclosure Orders, at paras 21.

[5] *Cream Holdings Ltd & Ors v Banerjee & Anor* [2005] 1 AC 253.

[6] *Cream* at [22].

[7] *YXB v TNO* [2015] EWHC 826 (QB) at [9].

result in any enhanced weight being given to art 10 when it is in conflict with another right (usually art 8). The Court must apply the following test[8]:

(1) neither article has preference over the other,

(2) where their values are in conflict, what is necessary is an intense focus on the comparative importance of the rights being claimed in the individual case,

(3) the justifications for interfering with or restricting each right must be taken into account, and

(4) the proportionality test must be applied.

8.13   S 12(4) also provides that where the proceedings relate to material which the respondent claims, or which appears to the court, to be journalistic, literary or artistic material (or to conduct connected with such material) then the Court must consider the extent to which the material has, or is about to, become available to the public; or it is, or would be, in the public interest for the material to be published; and any relevant privacy code.

8.14   The fact that a publication is only available online and steps have been taken to remove or limit access to it is a relevant factor when considering the extent to which journalistic material "has, or is about to, become available to the public". The Supreme Court explained that this factor does not preclude the court from having regard to:

• the nature of the journalistic material involved and the medium in which it is, or is to be, expressed, and

• the extent to which it is already available in that medium and the extent to which steps are being or can be taken to remove or limit access to any other publication in that or any other medium.[9]

Interim injunctions: "*Spycatcher* principle"

8.15   A party who has notice of an interim injunction is at risk of being in contempt of court if he does something that effectively flouts or undermines the injunction.[10] This is usually referred to as the "*Spycatcher* principle" or effect. It means that a claimant who obtains an interim injunction can serve it on third parties who are then, in practice "bound", by its terms. Accordingly, a claimant who has obtained a pre-publication injunction against one

---

[8] *In re S (A Child) (Identification: Restrictions on Publication)* [2005] 1 AC 593, para 17 (per Lord Steyn); *PJS v News Group Newspapers Ltd* [2016] AC 1081 at [20].

[9] *PJS v News Group Newspapers Ltd* [2016] AC 1081 at [33].

[10] *Attorney General v Times Newspapers Ltd* [1992] 1 AC 191 at 223–224; *Attorney General v Punch Ltd* [2003] 1 AC 1046 at 1066.

publication can serve it on other media bodies so that they are aware of it and cannot act in any way contrary to it.

8.16   As pre-publication orders restrict the exercise of the art 10 convention right, the court is required to take particular care to provide active case management. If it appears that a trial is unlikely to take place between the parties to the proceedings, the court should either dismiss the substantive actions, proceed to summary judgment or enter judgment by consent[11].

8.17   The High Court has stated that the Spycatcher principle only applies to interim injunctions and not to final injunctions[12], however the Court of Appeal has stated that it cannot be safely assumed that this conclusion would be approved by it if the issue came before it.[13]

Interim injunctions with a foreign element

8.18   In an online publication case a claimant may wish to seek orders against a foreign defendant (e.g. operators of websites) to prevent publication abroad or against a defendant in England and Wales requiring them to cease publishing abroad. Neither case gives rise to difficulties of principle.

8.19   In granting injunctions the Court operates *in personam*. The person to whom its orders are addressed must be within the reach of the Court or amenable to its jurisdiction but its jurisdiction is independent of the locality of the act to be done.[14] Injunctions can be granted against defendants abroad who have been properly served in accordance with the CPR.[15] The Court may grant an injunction against a defendant within the jurisdiction ordering them to do acts abroad or against a properly served defendant outside the jurisdiction ordering them to do an act abroad.[16]

8.20   But it is important to note that the power to grant an injunction is discretionary and a court will not grant an injunction which is ineffectual. An injunction can always, in principle, be enforced against a defendant present in England. The position is more difficult if the defendant is abroad. In such a

---

[11] Practice Guidance: Interim Non-Disclosure Orders, at paras 37 and 41; *Caterpillar Logistics Services (UK) Ltd v Huesca de Crean* [2012] 3 All ER 129 at [71]–[73]; *Caterpillar Logistics Services (UK) Ltd v Huesca de Crean* [2011] EWHC 3154 (QB) at [58]–[61]; and *Spelman v Express Newspapers* [2012] EWHC 239 (QB).

[12] *Jockey Club v Buffham* [2003] QB 462.

[13] *Hutcheson v Popdog Ltd & Anor* [2012] WLR 782 at [26].

[14] *In re Liddell's Settlement Trust* [1936] Ch 365.

[15] See generally, *Re J (a child) (contra mundum injunction)* [2014] EMLR 7 at [44] to [56].

[16] Ibid, at [55].

case there must be a real prospect that the order would be enforceable. The Court will need evidence as to whether the court of the jurisdiction where the defendant is present would be likely to enforce the order.[17] Bearing in mind the protections of the First Amendment in the United States it is highly unlikely that an English court would grant an injunction to restrain publication by a US defendant in the United States.[18]

Interim injunctions in particular cases

Breach of confidence and misuse of private information

8.21 Breach of confidence and misuse of private information are the most common causes of action relied upon by claimants when seeking pre-publication injunctions. These causes of action can be used to prevent both hard copy and online publications.

8.22 In order to succeed in a breach of confidence injunction a claimant will need to have standing to complain[19] and to show:

(1) that the information had the "necessary quality of confidence";

(2) that it had been imparted in circumstances imposing a duty of confidence; and

(3) that it had been (or was to be) disclosed in breach of confidence by the confidant.[20]

Information that is in the public domain and no longer "secret" will fail the test at the first hurdle.

8.23 In contrast, there is no such bright line in privacy cases and it may be possible to obtain a pre-publication privacy injunction even if the information is in the public domain and is no longer secret. A claimant may still have a reasonable expectation of privacy protection as this right encompasses not just the protection of "secrets" but also the right to prevent "intrusion" (see para 6.26).

8.24 Whether a privacy claim can succeed in the face of previous publicity, however, is likely to be a matter of fact and degree in each case. In *PJS v News Group Newspapers Ltd*[21] the Supreme Court refused to discharge an injunction

---

[17] Ibid, at [62]–[63].

[18] *Adelson v Anderson* [2011] EWHC 2497 (QB) at [67].

[19] At to this issue, see Toulson & Phipps, *Confidentiality*, 3rd Edn, 3-182 to 3-191.

[20] *Coco v AN Clarke (Engineers) Ltd* [1969] RPC 41. See too *Imerman v Tchenguiz & Ors* [2011] Fam 116 at [67]–[71].

[21] [2016] AC 1081.

preventing publication in the newspapers and related websites even though the information was already widely available online. The Supreme Court held that there was a qualitative difference in exposure to hard copy media and associated internet sites (which would occur if the story were not injuncted) and the publication of information on the internet (which had already occurred) and considered that further intrusion would be caused as a result of publications in hard copy newspapers[22].

Harassment

8.25   Online publications are capable of constituting harassment[23] and a pre-publication injunction can be obtained as a remedy under the Protection from Harassment Act 1997, s 3. A claimant would need to show that the defendant has carried out a course of conduct amounting to harassment of the claimant (see para 5.84ff).

8.26   Publications on a website can cause harassment even if only one statement targeting an individual has been made if it was made in the knowledge that such a publication would inevitably come to the individual's attention on more than one occasion and on each occasion would cause them alarm and distress constituting harassment under the 1997 Act.[24]

Defamation

8.27   The so-called "Rule in *Bonnard v Perryman*"[25] is that a court will not grant a pre-publication injunction in defamation if the publisher asserts that the words complained of are true or they have another clear defence. A defendant who seeks to resist an injunction against the publication of defamatory words should, at the minimum, identify the defamatory meanings that he intends to justify in a witness statement verified with a statement of truth. Where a defendant fails to do this an injunction may be granted until those basic requirements are complied with, at which point the defendant could apply to vary or discharge the injunction.[26]

---

[22] Ibid, per Lord Mance at [35] and per Lord Neuberger at [65].

[23] *Law Society v Kordowski* [2014] EMLR 2.

[24] *Law Society v Kordowski*, at [61], [64] and [75]; *Coulson & Ors v Wilby* [2014] EWHC 3404 (QB) at [49].

[25] [1891] 2 Ch 269.

[26] *Sunderland Housing Company Ltd v Bains & Ors* [2006] EWHC 2359 (QB) at [18].

8.28   In *Greene v Associated Newspapers Ltd*[27] the Court of Appeal considered the way in which the balance was struck between ECHR, arts 8 and 10 in defamation proceedings at this stage and decided that the balance was consistent with the convention. Consequently a claimant faced with the threat of publication of false and defamatory information about them can usually only prevent the publication if their claim can be properly formulated in terms of another cause of action.

8.29   If, however, the claim based on some other cause of action is in reality a claim brought to protect reputation, and the reliance on the other cause of action is merely a device to circumvent the rule, the application will fail. Examples of the court dismissing applications for this reason include:

- *Service Corporation International & Anor Plc v Channel Four Television & Anor*[28] in which an application for an interim injunction based on copyright to restrain a broadcast was refused as the initial basis of the complaint – which had been defamation – was considered to have been the true complaint.
- *Tillery Valley Foods v Channel Four Television & Anor*[29] in which a food company sought to restrain a broadcast on the basis of confidentiality unless it was given a right of informed reply. The application was refused because, although the claim was brought in confidentiality it was "really a defamation action in disguise".
- *Terry v Persons Unknown*[30] in which a well-known footballer failed in his application for an interim injunction which he based on misuse of confidential information, as the judge held that the nub of his complaint was the protection of reputation and not any other aspect of his private life.

Data Protection Act 1998

8.30   If data protection proceedings are brought against a data controller and it is shown that the data is being processed only for the purposes of journalism literature and art and with a view to publication then the proceedings must be

---

[27] [2005] QB 972.

[28] [1999] EMLR 83.

[29] [2004] EWHC 1075 (Ch).

[30] [2010] EMLR 16.

stayed.[31] This prevents claimants in most situations from applying for pre-publication orders under the 1998 Act.

OTHER INTERIM REMEDIES AND ORDERS

Delivery up and Preservation Orders

8.31   An application can be made under CPR 25.1(1)(e) for an order under the Torts (Interference with Goods) Act 1977, s 4 to deliver up goods. This section provides that the court shall have the power, in such circumstances as may be specified in the rules, to make an order for delivery up of any goods "which are or may become the subject matter of subsequent proceedings in the court, or as to which any question may arise in proceedings". Preservation Orders can be applied for pursuant to CPR 25.1(1)(c), which allows the court to order an interim remedy for "the detention, custody or preservation of relevant property".

8.32   These interim remedies can be sought in relation to property in respect of which a claimant has a claim in breach of confidence, misuse of private information, or breach of the 1998 Act. A court may grant such an application whether or not there has been a claim for a final remedy of that kind.[32] An order for delivery up can only be obtained in relation to "goods" – this would include electronic devices or storage media but not the information that they contain.[33]

8.33   The Court may also make an order for the "preservation" of property which is the subject of a claim (under CPR 25.1(1)(c)(i)) or for the inspection of such property (under CPR 25.1(1)(c)(ii)). The latter power includes the power to order the inspection of a database or access to a party's computer or the provision of a forensic image of a database.[34]

8.34   An order may be made at any time including before proceedings are started (i.e. before a claim form is issued), provided that the matter is urgent; or where it is otherwise desirable to do so in the interests of justice.[35]

8.35   On an interim application the court may make an order after being satisfied to a lower standard than would be required at trial. However, if an interim

---

[31] *Stunt v Associated Newspapers Ltd* [2017] EMLR 18.

[32] CPR 25.1(4).

[33] *Environment Agency v Churngold Recycling Ltd* [2015] Env LR 13 at [15]; see also *Your Response Ltd v Datateam Business Media Ltd* [2015] QB 41.

[34] For example, *Patel v Unite* [2012] EWHC 92 (QB).

[35] CPR 25.2(2)(1)(a) and CPR 25.2 (2)(b).

mandatory injunction is being sought the court will need to feel "a high degree of assurance that the claimant will be able to establish this right at trial"[36], as opposed to the test in *Cream Holdings Ltd & Ors v Bannerjee & Anor*[37] of whether a claimant was likely to succeed at trial.

8.36 The reason for the higher threshold in "mandatory order" cases was set out in *Zockoll Group* case as follows:

> "First, this being an interlocutory matter, the overriding consideration is which course is likely to involve the least risk of injustice if it turns out to be 'wrong' in the sense described by Hoffmann J [in *Films Rover Ltd v. Cannon Film Sales Ltd* [1987] 1 WLR 670].
>
> Secondly in considering whether to grant a mandatory injunction, the court must keep in mind that an order which requires a party to take some positive step at an interlocutory stage, may well carry a greater risk of injustice if it turns out to have been wrongly made than an order which merely prohibits action, thereby preserving any status quo.
>
> Thirdly, it is legitimate, where a mandatory injunction is sought, to consider whether the court does feel a high degree of assurance that the plaintiff will be able establish this right of trial. That is because the greater the degree of assurance the plaintiff will ultimately establish his right, the less would be the risk of injustice if the injunction is granted."[38]

8.37 It will therefore be necessary for a claimant who is seeking delivery up of documents from a defendant on the basis of confidentiality to demonstrate that the ingredients for that cause of action are satisfied including, for example, that the documents are the subject of a duty of confidence owed to that particular claimant.[39]

Other interim orders

8.38 CPR 25.1(1) also sets out other interim remedies which may be relevant in cases involving publications on the internet but which are not invoked as

---

[36] *Zockoll Group Ltd v Mercury Communications Ltd* [1998] FSR 354 at 366.

[37] [2005] 1 AC 253.

[38] [1998] FSR 354, at 366. The quote is from *Nottingham Building Society v Eurodynamics Systems* [1993] FSR 468 at 474 (per Chadwick J), cited with approval in *Zockoll Group*.

[39] *Bains & Ors v Moore & Ors* [2017] EMLR 20 at [51].

frequently as those mentioned above. The fact that a particular kind of interim remedy is not listed in CPR 25.1(1) does not affect any power that the court may have to grant that remedy.[40]

8.39   There are two particular types of order that are sought in "online publication" cases:

- An order requiring an anonymous defendant responsible for publishing material complained of to disclose his/her identity to the claimant's solicitors (see Chapter 3).

- An order requiring a person who has published or is threatening to publish private or confidential information to provide the claimant's solicitors with details of any third party to whom the information has been passed and any internet sites on which it has already been posted.[41]

Declaration of falsity

8.40   A declaration can only be sought in relation to an existing legal right[42]. Under the Summary Procedure set out in the Defamation Act 1996, s 8, if a court disposes of a claim, it has the power to make a declaration of falsity under s 9 of the 1996 Act.[43] A claimant is obliged to prove falsity if s/he seeks such a declaration.[44]

8.41   In cases involving the internet, where the publication in this jurisdiction may represent a fraction of the worldwide publications, the court may decide that the publication of a public judgment and an apology (which are also remedies under the summary procedure) is sufficient and there is no need for a declaration of falsity.[45]

8.42   It is also possible to seek a declaration of falsity pursuant to s 8(1) of the Human Rights Act 1998 against defendants that are public authorities, on the basis that by publishing and refusing to withdraw allegations which are false

---

[40] CPR 25.1(3).

[41] Such a mandatory order was made at a without notice hearing in *JPH v XYZ & Ors* [2015] EWHC 2871 (QB) at [11].

[42] *Nixon v Attorney General* [1930] 1 Ch 566; and *Loutchansky v Times Newspapers Ltd (No 6)* [2002] EMLR 44.

[43] For example *Mahfouz & Ors v Ehrenfeld & Anor* [2005] EWHC 1156 (QB) and *Smith v Unknown Defendant, Pseudonym 'Likeicare' & Ors* [2016] EWHC 1775 (QB).

[44] *Adelson v Anderson* [2011] EWHC 2497 (QB) at [77].

[45] *Mahfouz & Anor v Brisard & Anor* [2006] EWHC 1191 (QB) at [22]–[24].

the defendant has acted incompatibly with the claimant's rights under ECHR, art 8 which is contrary to s 6 of the 1998 Act.[46]

FINAL REMEDIES

Introduction

8.43   If a claimant succeeds at trial there are a number of "final remedies" which the Court can grant. We will consider the following:

- Damages;
- Injunctions;
- Orders under the 1998 Act; and
- Orders for the publication of a summary of the judgment.

These will be considered in turn.

Damages

Defamation

8.44   A person who proves they have been libelled is entitled to recover a sum in damages that is enough to compensate them for the wrong suffered. The sum performs three functions, namely:

(1)   compensates them for the damage to their reputation;
(2)   vindicates their good name; and
(3)   takes account of the distress, hurt and humiliation caused by the publication.

8.45   The main factors to take into account when assessing damages are:

- the gravity of the libel;
- the extent of publication;
- the need for vindication of reputation;
- any additional injury caused to the claimant's feelings by the defendant's conduct of the action including whether or not the defendant has persisted in maintaining the truth of what was said;[47]

---

[46] *McLaughlin & Ors v London Borough of Lambeth & Anor* [2011] EMLR 8.

[47] *John v Mirror Group Newspapers Ltd* [1997] QB 586 at 607–608 (per Sit Thomas Bingham MR).

- the fact that a reasoned award may help to vindicate a reputation;[48] and
- the status of the claimant: public figures such as politicians are expected to be more robust than others, whatever the actual position may be.[49]

8.46　Malice can be relied upon in aggravation of damages. If so the issue is not the actual state of mind of the defendant. It is whether the claimant has suffered additional injury to feelings as a result of the defendant's outward behaviour. If the defendant has behaved in a way which leads the claimant reasonably to believe s/he acted maliciously that is enough.[50]

8.47　There is an overall ceiling on defamation awards, currently about £300,000.[51] That sort of award is only suitable for the gravest of libels such as widespread publication of allegations of genocide, terrorism, or murder.

8.48　Libel damages awards in online publication cases vary greatly depending on the nature of the allegation, the scale of publication and the other factors referred to above. By way of example:

- In *Cairns v Modi*,[52] the Court of Appeal upheld an award of £75,000 for a tweet sent by the defendant to 65 people which accused the claimant of match-fixing.
- In *Monroe* v *Hopkins*,[53] Warby J awarded the claimant a total of £24,000; £16,000 for the first tweet that meant the claimant "condoned and approved of scrawling on war memorials, vandalising monuments commemorating those who fought for her freedom" and £8,000 for the second tweet that meant she "condoned and approved of the fact that in the course of an anti-government protest there had been vandalisation by obscene graffiti of the women's war memorial in Whitehall, a monument to those who fought for her freedom".
- In *Sloutsker v Romanova*,[54] Warby J awarded libel damages of £110,000 to a former Russian senator and President of the Israel Jewish

---

[48] *Purnell v Business F1 Magazine Ltd & Anor* [2008] 1 WLR 1, *Cairns v Modi* [2013] 1 WLR 1015 at [31].

[49] *Barron & Anor v Vines* [2016] EWHC 1226 (QB) at [86].

[50] Ibid, at [22].

[51] *Rai v Bholowasia & Anor* [2015] EWHC 382 (QB) at [179] (per HHJ Parkes QC).

[52] [2013] 1 WLR 1015.

[53] [2017] 4 WLR 68.

[54] [2015] EMLR 27.

Congress against Russian journalist Olga Romanova for allegations published in an online blog written by Ms Romanova which included that the claimant had put a contract out for the murder of Alexei Kozlov, which was to be carried out whilst Mr Kozlov was being transferred to prison.

Privacy

8.49   Privacy damages have significantly increased since the cases in the early 2000s in which the awards were modest. Indeed, until 2008 the largest ever privacy award was the £60,000 awarded in *Mosley v News Group Newspapers Ltd*.[55] The issues were fully examined by Mann J in the leading case of *Gulati v Mirror Group Newspapers Ltd*.[56] He awarded the claimants damages of between £260,250 (Sadie Frost) and £72,500 (Lucy Alcorn) for misuse of private information in the "phone hacking" cases. This compensated them not only for distress they suffered but also for "the right to control the dissemination of information about one's private life" [111]. The damages awarded moved away from the "single sum" approach adopted in previous cases and included e.g. separate compensation for the phone hacking itself, for the use of private investigators and for articles containing private information derived from phone hacking. Mann J's approach was upheld by the Court of Appeal.[57]

8.50   In *TLT & Ors v Secretary of State for the Home Department & Anor*,[58] the claimants were all asylum seekers whose personal data was erroneously made available on the internet for a limited period of time in the context of the Home Office's publication of data on family returns process. The defendants conceded that their actions amounted to a misuse of private information, a breach of confidence and breaches of the 1998 Act, but maintained that the distress suffered was not such that it sounded in damages. Mitting J rejected the defendants' contention and awarded the claimants damages of between £2,500 and £12,500 each at trial. In determining the quantum the judge took into account the fact that this was an erroneous breach and that, in contrast with the phone hacking cases, the private information was not being exploited for commercial profit. He did include an award for "loss of control" of the information.

---

[55] [2008] EMLR 20.

[56] [2016] FSR 12, upheld on appeal *Representative Claimants v Mirror Group Newspapers Ltd* [2017] QB 149.

[57] *Representative Claimants*.

[58] [2016] EWHC 2217 (QB).

8.51   In *Brown v The Commissioner of Police of the Metropolis*,[59] HHJ Luba QC awarded the claimant a total of £9,000 for breach of privacy and breach of the 1998 Act. The claim arose as a result of a Metropolitan Police Officer seeking information to use in a potential disciplinary process about the claimant's private holiday, taken while on sick leave, from the National Border Targeting Centre (which was managed by the Greater Manchester Police). The information obtained included the claimant's name and date of birth; her nationality; her passport number; the country which issued the passport; the expiry date of that passport; details of 15 flights taken by the claimant between 2005 and 2011; and details of the family member who accompanied her on her holiday. The award was apportioned between the defendants with the MPS ordered to pay £6,000 and the GMP ordered to pay £3,000. In making the award the judge took into account the fact that the material was "not sought for gain, was not widely disseminated and was not of the sensitive nature of being concerned with medical matters, financial matters or personal relationships" [71].

8.52   In *Weller v Associated Newspapers*,[60] the well-known singer, Paul Weller, brought a claim against the publishers of Mail Online over seven paparazzi photos which were published on the internet by Mail Online in October 2012 under the headline *A family day out: Paul Weller takes wife Hannah and his twin sons out for a spot of shopping in the hot LA sun.* Dingemans J awarded his three children a total of £10,000 damages for misuse of private information and breach of the 1998 Act. The award was upheld by the Court of Appeal[61].

Data Protection Act 1998

8.53   The ability for claimants to obtain compensation under the 1998 Act has been radically altered as a result of the decision of the Court of Appeal in *Vidal-Hall & Ors v Google Inc.* That decision provided that what was required in order to make s 13(2) compatible with EU law is "the disapplication of s 13(2), no more and no less" [105]. The consequence of this decision is that compensation would be recoverable under s 13(1) for *any* damage suffered as a result of a contravention by a data controller of any of the requirements of the 1998 Act.

---

[59] Judgment of HHJ Luba QC dated 7 October 2016 (unreported).

[60] [2014] EMLR 24.

[61] *Weller & Ors v Associated Newspapers Ltd* [2016] 1 WLR 1541.

8.54   This decision potentially has very wide ramifications as there is no requirement that it has to be the data subject who is applying for compensation under s 13(1). This section provides:

> "*An individual who suffers damage* by reason of *any* contravention by a data controller of *any* of the requirements of this Act *is entitled to compensation* from the data controller for that damage." (emphasis added)

8.55   The issue of whether a claimant can recover the same level of quantum as may be possible in a libel or misuse of private information claim is yet to be determined. There is little guidance on quantum of damages for breach of data protection action alone, as the cause of action is often deployed along with other causes of actions (see the *TLT, Weller* and *Brown* cases at paras 8.50–8.52). To date data protection damages have been low. In *Douglas & Ors v Hello! Ltd & Ors (No 6)* Lindsay J awarded Michael Douglas and Catherine Zeta-Jones £50 each as nominal damages for breaches of the 1998 Act.[62] In the more recent decision of *Woolly v Akram*,[63] Sheriff Ross awarded damages of £8,634 to each of the pursuers in a dispute between neighbours involving CCTV footage. The filming of the pursuers property, which had taken place for 912 days, was found to have been in breach of the 1998 Act and the compensation was calculated by awarding £10 per day minus 4 weeks a year for holidays.

8.56   A data controller can avoid having to pay compensation under s 13 if they can prove that they took reasonable care having regards to all of the circumstances.

Harassment

8.57   Damages are available under the 1997 Act, s 3(2) for "(among other things) any anxiety caused by the harassment and any financial loss resulting from the harassment".

8.58   In *Hourani v Thomson & Ors*,[64] Warby J awarded the claimant damages for harassment of £10,000 (as against the first defendant); £15,000 (as against the second defendant) and £30,000 (as against the fifth defendant) as a result of a campaign of street protest, online publication, and sticker distribution conducted in 2014. The campaign involved targeting three individuals and

---

[62] [2004] EMLR 2 at [12(ii)]. See too *Douglas & Ors v Hello! Ltd & Ors (No 3)* [2003] 3 All ER 996 at [278].

[63] [2017] SC EDIN 7.

[64] [2017] EWHC 432 (QB).

denouncing them as murderers, responsible for the torture, drugging, beating and sexual assault of a young woman, Anastasiya Novikova, and her subsequent death, in Beirut, in 2004.

Special Damages: internet "clean up" costs

8.59   A claimant may take steps to mitigate their loss and to recover the cost of doing so from the defendant as special damage. The standard of reasonableness to which the victim of loss will be held, in seeking to mitigate, is not a high one. It has been held that there is no possible reason why a claimant should not be able to take steps to take down reasonably foreseeable internet repetitions and republications of a defamatory article, and to recover the reasonable cost of doing so from the defendant.[65] Such special damages are also available when an offer of amends has been made; however any such claim would need to have been properly pleaded to make clear the full extent of their claim so that a defendant can offer to make amends on an informed basis.[66]

8.60   There is no reason in principle why such "clean up" costs for removing reasonably foreseeable third party internet repetitions of an unlawful publication should be limited to defamation claims and not also be available in other causes of action, such as misuse of private information or breach of confidence.

Injunctions

Introduction

8.61   An injunction is a discretionary remedy which is not granted "as of right". The Court should consider whether there is any ground for apprehending the repetition of the wrongful act. If there is not then no injunction should be granted.[67] As with interim injunctions, final injunctions can be granted to restrain a defendant from carrying out acts abroad and, if there is evidence that the injunction is enforceable, against foreign defendants (see paras 8.18–8.20).

---

[65] *Lisle-Mainwaring v Associated Newspapers Ltd & Anor* [2017] EWHC 543 (QB) at [166] (per HHJ Parkes QC).

[66] Ibid, at [173].

[67] *Proctor v Bayley* (1889) 42 Ch 390, at 401.

Final injunctions and third parties

8.62   There is first instance authority to the effect that the "*Spycatcher* principle" (see para 8.17) does not apply in relation to final injunctions.[68] However, it is difficult to find a principled basis for excluding the principle from final injunctions and the Court of Appeal has held that it cannot safely be assumed that this conclusion would be approved on appeal.[69] The point, therefore, remains open and a third party should be very cautious in taking steps which have the effect of undermining a final injunction.

8.63   The Court does, however, have jurisdiction to grant a final injunction *contra mundum,* that is binding on the whole world. Such an injunction can be granted whenever it is necessary and proportionate to protect Convention rights.[70] Such an injunction can, in an appropriate case, be granted to restrain the publication of private information. For example, in *OPQ v BJM,*[71] a final *contra mundum* injunction was granted to restrain the publication of intimate photographs and other information which had been the subject of an attempted sale to a newspaper and blackmail.

8.64   There is no objection in principle to such an injunction being granted against foreign-based internet website providers.[72] However the court is likely to require the applicant to give an undertaking that no attempt will be made to enforce the order outside England and Wales without the permission of the court and to include a so-called *Babanaft* proviso in the order[73] – that is a proviso persons outside England and Wales would not be affected by the order unless certain conditions are fulfilled.[74] In practice, it is likely that *contra mundum* orders will only be granted against foreign defendants in exceptional circumstances.

Defamation

8.65   It is well established that if a court finds that the defendant has published false and defamatory words about the claimant online, the claimant will be entitled to an injunction to have the words complained of taken down and, if there is

---

[68] *Jockey Club v Buffham* [2003] QB 462, at [23]–[27].

[69] *Hutcheson v Popdog Ltd & Anor* [2012] 1 WLR 782, at [26](iv)(b).

[70] *OPQ v BJM* [2011] EMLR 23, at [18].

[71] Ibid.

[72] *Re J (a child) (contra mundum injunction)* [2014] EMLR 7 at [47].

[73] Ibid, at [64]–[65].

[74] *Babanaft International Co SA v Bassatne* [1990] Ch 13.

a threat of republication, an injunction to prevent any threat of the same or any similar words being republished. In *Monroe*,[75] Warby J said there was no need for an injunction as he did not think there was any evidence of a threat or risk of repetition. In deciding this he took into account the fact that the first tweet sent by Ms Hopkins was a mistake, it was not fully retracted but there had been no attempt to prove the truth of what was suggested and that Ms Hopkins would realise that to repeat the same message would be likely to result in a substantial damages award.

8.66   A final injunction will not be granted unless a court is satisfied that the words are false. In *Law Society v Kordowski*,[76] Tugendhat J did not grant a perpetual libel final injunction in respect of the "solicitors from hell" website as he did "not think it just, or in accordance with the Human Rights Act 1998, s 12, to grant it simply on the basis of the presumption of falsity" [139]. Conversely mandatory and prohibitory final injunctions were granted on the claimant's application for summary disposal in respect of allegations that he was a child rapist and paedophile made by unknown persons on a website.[77]

Privacy

8.67   The general principle that an injunction should not be granted unless there is an apprehension of repetition of the wrong applies. However, a court may require a defendant to give an undertaking to the Court that there will be no further publication and, in the absence of such an undertaking, grant an injunction to restrain further publication.[78]

Harassment

8.68   If it is found that the defendant has been pursuing a course of conduct amounting to harassment under the 1997 Act without any justification and the defendant does not give an undertaking not to continue such conduct in future, a final injunction can be ordered. As these include a restraint on art 10 rights, such orders are usually for a set period of time with provision for the claimant to apply for an extension if appropriate, rather than for an indefinite period.

---

[75] [2017] 4 WLR 26.

[76] [2014] EMLR 2.

[77] *Smith v Unknown Defendant, Pseudonym 'Likeicare' & Ors* [2016] EWHC 1775 (QB).

[78] *Weller & Ors v Associated Newspapers Ltd* [2016] 1 WLR 1541 at [88].

Orders under the Data Protection Act 1998

Data Protection Act 1998, s 10

8.69   Under s 10 of the 1998 Act, a data subject can at any time issue a written notice to a data controller requiring it to cease, or not commence, processing of their personal data if the processing of those data is causing or is likely to cause substantial damage or substantial distress to him or to another and that distress is or would be unwarranted. Although this right has to be invoked by the data subject in respect of any personal data of which they are the data subject, they do not necessarily have to be the ones that have been caused substantial distress or damage. Thus if an online blog containing a father's personal data was, or was likely to, cause substantial distress to his child which was unwarranted, the father would have a basis for invoking the section even if the father himself was not distressed by the processing.

8.70   A data controller in receipt of a notice has 21 days in which to comply or give reasons as to why the notice is unjustified. If a data controller does not comply, a data subject may make an application to court for a s 10(1) order requiring compliance.

8.71   The Data Protection Act 1998, s 10 can be a very powerful tool in preventing the unlawful processing of personal data online. It can be used on an individual basis, or, if there is a website which is unlawfully processing the data of all the individuals named, as in the "solicitors from hell" case, on a representative basis to obtain an injunction to take down the whole website. As Tugendhat J noted in that case:

> "The procedural remedy of representative proceedings, coupled with an injunction, may be the best that the law can offer at present to protect the public from the unjustifiable dissemination of false information about the suppliers of goods and services. It is also the means by which the court may protect its limited resources in time and judiciary from having to deal with large numbers of claims by different claimants against the same individual on the same or similar facts." [182]

Data Protection Act 1998, s 14

8.72   Under s 14 of the 1998 Act a data subject can apply for a court order requiring the data controller to rectify, block, erase or destroy those data and any other personal data which contain an expression of opinion which appears to the court to be based on the inaccurate data if (1) the data is shown to be inaccurate or (2) the data subject can establish damage (now including distress) entitling him/her to compensation under s 13. s 70(2) provides that data are inaccurate if they are "incorrect or misleading as to any matter of fact".

8.73   Under this section it is possible that a court could order the correction of an article published online and even the publication of a supplementary statement setting out true facts.

Publication of a summary of the judgment

8.74   The Defamation Act 2013, s 12 provides that where a court gives judgment for the claimant in an action for defamation it may order the defendant to publish a summary of the judgment. If the parties cannot agree on the wording of the summary then the wording is to be settled by the court. This avenue could be used by claimants to include a statement that "the words were false", certainly in respect of claims where a defence of "truth" has failed.

Order to remove a statement or cease distribution

8.75   An author, editor or publisher may not always be in a position to remove or prevent further dissemination of material which has been found to be defamatory. However, pursuant to s 10 of the 2013 Act a claimant must, unless it is not reasonably practicable, bring a defamation claim against the author, editor or publisher as the court will not otherwise have jurisdiction to hear and determine the claim (see para 3.78).

8.76   S 13 of the 2013 Act applies to this situation and provides that where a court gives judgment for the claimant in an action for defamation the court may order "the operator of a website on which the defamatory statement is posted to remove the statement", or "any person who was not the author, editor or publisher of the defamatory statement to stop distributing, selling or exhibiting material containing the statement".

8.77   There is no definition in the Act of "website" or "operator"; these terms are also used in s 5 of the 2013 Act and the same interpretive provisions should apply (see paras 3.75–3.77).

8.78   "Author", "editor" and "publisher" have the same meaning as in s 1 of the 1996 Act i.e.

- "author" means the originator of the statement, but does not include a person who did not intend that his statement be published at all;
- "editor" means a person having editorial or equivalent responsibility for the content of the statement or the decision to publish it; and

- "publisher" means a commercial publisher, that is, a person whose business is issuing material to the public, or a section of the public, who issues material containing the statement in the course of that business.

8.79 A person is not considered to be the "author", "editor" or "publisher" of a statement if he is only involved in:

- processing, making copies of, distributing or selling any electronic medium in or on which the statement is recorded, or in operating or providing any equipment, system or service by means of which the statement is retrieved, copied, distributed or made available in electronic form;[79]
- as the broadcaster of a live programme containing the statement in circumstances in which he has no effective control over the maker of the statement;[80]
- as the operator of or provider of access to a communications system by means of which the statement is transmitted, or made available, by a person over whom he has no effective control.[81]

8.80 The purpose of this provision is to "close any possible loophole" in cases where the operators of a website or a person who is not the "author, editor or publisher" of the defamatory statement refuses to remove or cease distributing material which has been found to be unlawful.

8.81 It seems that the order will be available when the court makes a final determination of the issue of liability in the claimant's favour. A court will then have the discretion to make such an order if appropriate and can order the removal of the material during or shortly after the conclusion of proceedings.[82] Although the section makes no provision for the giving of notice to the third party a court would obviously want to give them an opportunity to be heard before making an order under s 13 of the 2013 Act.

8.82 Although s 13 is silent on the point, it is possible that an order under this provision could be made in relation to operators of websites outside the jurisdiction. The purpose of the section, which is to enable successful claimants to obtain a more effective and cost-effective remedy to prevent future publications, would be greatly diminished if its application was limited

---

[79] Defamation Act 1996, s 1 (3)(c).

[80] s 1 (3)(d) of the 1996 Act.

[81] S 1 (3)(e) of the 1996 Act.

[82] Explanatory Notes to s 13 of the 2013 Act.

to operators of websites in this jurisdiction. Operators of websites frequently require orders of the court before they can comply with any takedown requests under their terms and conditions. If the operator of a website in a foreign jurisdiction refuses to comply with the Order then a claimant may have to seek recognition of the Order and enforcement in the jurisdiction concerned. However, the caution of the Courts in granting injunctions with extra territorial reach (see paras 8.18–8.20 above) means that such an order may be refused as a matter of discretion.

8.83   S 13(3) provides that the section does not affect the courts' existing powers to grant relief; the explanatory notes state that this ensures that the provision does not have any wider effect on the jurisdiction of the court to grant injunctive relief.

CHAPTER 9: BRINGING A CLAIM, PRACTICAL ISSUES

CHAPTER SYNOPSIS

• Deals with the practical issues which may arise in relation to legal proceedings about potentially unlawful online conduct: whether such proceedings are likely to benefit the person who is subject to the online conduct in issue and what steps should be taken to ensure that claims are progressed in an effective and efficient way.
• Examines in detail: whether to bring a claim; choosing the cause of action; choosing the defendant; preparing and issuing the claim; practical matters relating to interim remedies; procedure "between Issue and Trial"; and the enforcement of injunctions and judgments/committal proceedings.

INTRODUCTION

9.1   When a person discovers that they are the subject of potentially unlawful online conduct a number of immediate practical issues arise:

• Is it possible to resolve the matter informally by contacting the author, webmaster or ISSP?
• Can steps be taken to have the material removed by using the "takedown" procedures of the site on which the material appears? This is dealt with in Chapter 1.
• Can steps be taken to have the material "delisted" by search engines? This is the subject of Chapter 2.
• Can the author and the publisher of the online material be identified? If the author is anonymous then it will be necessary to seek an order identifying him or her. This is dealt with in Chapter 3.

9.2   After these issues have been considered, then the question arises as to whether a legal claim is available in the Courts of England and Wales. This is the subject of Chapter 4. If these courts do have jurisdiction then consideration can be given to the types of claims available in law (see Chapters 5 and 6).

9.3   This Chapter deals with the practical issues which may arise in relation to legal proceedings: whether such proceedings are likely to benefit the person who is subject to the online conduct in issue and what steps should be taken to ensure that claims are progressed in an effective and efficient way.

9.4   The practical issues which arise will be considered under seven headings:

209 | ONLINE PUBLICATION CLAIMS: A PRACTICAL GUIDE

- Whether to bring a claim;
- Choosing the cause of action;
- Choosing the defendant;
- Preparing and issuing the claim;
- Interim remedies;
- Between issue and Trial;
- Enforcing injunctions and judgments.

WHETHER TO BRING A CLAIM

9.5   The first issue to consider is the extent of the publication of the online material complained of. There is a very wide range of possibilities:

- At one end of the scale, some online communications only reach a very limited number of people. An email may only have a single recipient, a chat forum or blog may only be accessed by a very small number of people. If the number of publishees of a particular post is low then there may be considerable difficulties in bringing a defamation claim (see paras 5.29–5.36, 5.73–5.74).
- At the other end of the scale, there are established international "media" websites which have millions of visitors a day and individual posts may have tens or hundreds of thousands of hits.

It is important for the claimant to ascertain at the outset, with as much precision as possible, the number of people who have accessed the material about which complaint is to be made (cf para 1.57ff).

9.6   In many cases it will be possible to resolve matters informally, by approaching the author, webmaster or Information Society Service Providers (ISSP) and drawing attention to the problems arising from the publication of the material. A reasonable approach by email seeking, for example, takedown and an undertaking not to repost, may produce satisfactory results. A "legal letter" may be counter-productive. A careful assessment of the position needs to be carried out at the outset.

9.7   ISSPs have "terms of use" and obviously defamatory, private or abusive posts are likely to be in breach of these. An approach to the ISSP may, therefore, enable matters to be resolved at an early stage. However, this is often unsuccessful as it is usually very difficult to make direct contact with a human being at an ISSP and emails are often met with "automated responses". Many of the large ISSP companies are based in the United States where they are generally immune from civil suit and their "default position" usually strongly favours continued publication.[1]

9.8   If an informal approach does not work or is, for whatever reason, inappropriate, careful consideration needs to be given to the advantages and disadvantages of bringing a legal claim. The benefits of removing online material must be balanced against the costs and the risk of spreading the material more widely by legal action.

9.9   There are a number of considerations which are "special" to online cases:

- If there has been limited online publication then the bringing of an action might result in a much wider publication of the material complained about as other online publishers take it up and republish. This is sometimes referred to as the "Streisand Effect".

- The speed at which online material can spread means it will often be necessary to pursue numerous "republishers" in a number of jurisdictions. Effective action to prevent such republications can be time consuming and expensive.

- Action against anonymous publishers is unlikely to be cost effective in that, unlike "mainstream media" publishers, they are unlikely to comply with orders for damages or costs.

9.10   If the author of the material complained about is an identified person then it may be possible to obtain an interim order requiring that person to take the material down. In other cases, the most effective remedies will often be those against the ISSPs or search engines. However, these entities have a number of "special defences" to proceedings (see Chapter 7). In addition, these entities may be large and well-resourced international corporations who may defend proceedings "as a matter of principle".

9.11   The potential effectiveness of legal action depends on a careful analysis of the facts of each case. Consideration should be given to the nature of the material objected to, the extent of the damage being caused and what is known about the identity, characteristics and geographical location of the "author".

9.12   At one end of the scale, claims against identifiable persons in the United Kingdom or the EU may achieve positive results for a claimant. At the other end of the scale claims against unidentified and difficult to identify individuals outside the EU may not be viable and a claimant will then have to consider claims against ISSPs or search engines.

---

[1] See the illuminating discussion of the issue in Tugendhat and Christie, *The Law of Privacy and the Media*, 3rd Edn, paras 15.09 to 15.16.

CHOOSING THE CAUSE OF ACTION

Introduction

9.13   If, having considered the factors mentioned above, a claimant wishes to bring a claim in respect of material published on the internet the first question that arises is what type of claim should be brought: what cause or causes of action should the claimant seek to rely on? This will depend on the nature of the claimant and the nature of the material published online.

9.14   In relation to companies the position is relatively straightforward:

- If the information is true then the only available claim will be for breach of confidence.
- If the information is false then the only available claims will be for defamation or malicious falsehood.

9.15   In the case of individuals there is a substantial degree of overlap between the available causes of action:

- If the information is false and concerns an individual then there are potential claims for defamation, malicious falsehood, misuse of private information, harassment or under the Data Protection Act 1998.
- If the information is true and concerns an individual there are potential claims for breach of confidence, misuse of private information, harassment and under the 1998 Act.

Defamation

9.16   Defamation is about false allegations – not about factual errors. The published statements must be analysed to determine:

- Whether they refer to the claimant;
- Whether they convey defamatory allegations about the claimant – this involves an analysis of the meaning of the words complained of (see para 5.16ff).

9.17   If, having considered the publication, it makes a defamatory allegation about the claimant it is then necessary to consider whether the publication has caused or is likely to cause serious harm to the claimant's reputation (see paras 5.29–5.36).

9.18   Where the claimant is an individual a number of considerations are relevant:

- The nature and seriousness of the allegation being made. The more serious the allegation, the easier it will be to infer serious harm to reputation.

- The extent of the publication – the number times the words were published. The more publishees, the easier it is to establish serious harm. The number of times that a particular article or post has been viewed is something which can usually be precisely determined – although this requires the cooperation of the defendant so cannot be done at the outset of an action.

- The nature of the publishees – the more influential the publishees (for example, readers of specialist blogs or websites) or the closer their relationship to the claimant (for example, members of the same profession) the easier it will be to establish serious harm to reputation.

- Whether or not there are specific individuals who can give evidence that they have seen the publications and have been influenced by them. In general, it is difficult to obtain evidence of this kind.

9.19 Where the claimant is a company or other body trading for profit then it is necessary to prove "serious financial loss". The body will need to consider whether it can show that it has suffered a loss of profit as a result of the publication of the libel. This is likely to involve accountancy evidence but, in practice will be very difficult to demonstrate because of the many factors that influence profitability (including, for example, non-defamatory adverse publicity). It is possible that "serious financial loss" could be established by showing that money had been spent on mitigating the loss – by, for example, employing a PR consultant to deal with the problem, or for the cost of investigating the identity of the wrongdoer or removing republications from the internet, or from "damage to goodwill" or "wasted management time" but these are controversial issues and have not been explored in the cases (see para 5.36).

9.20 If the words used referred to the claimant, were defamatory and have caused serious harm to reputation (or financial loss), it is then necessary to consider the available defences. No claim should be brought until these have been carefully considered. In the context of online publication the following defences are likely to be the most important:

- Truth: is the defendant likely to be able to establish the substantial truth of the allegation made? (see generally, paras 5.38–5.43).

- Honest Opinion: are the words used an expression of opinion (and expression which covers an obvious deduction or inference as well: see generally, paras 5.44–5.46). Words used on online forums or social media are more likely than traditional media publications to be interpreted as being "opinion".

- Public interest: is this an allegation in the public interest which the defendant reasonably believed it was in the public interest to publish? (see paras 5.47–5.59).

9.21   In many cases the answers to these questions will be obvious and will not require substantial analysis. False allegations of involvement in terrorism, child abuse or fraud are likely to satisfy all the relevant tests and be actionable in defamation. At the other end of the scale, even strong and intemperate expressions of opinion or criticism of a person's conduct (particularly if that person is a public figure) are unlikely to be actionable (unless they lack any conceivable factual foundation). In between these extremes difficult questions of analysis will arise which should be thought through before any defamation claim is threatened.

Malicious falsehood

9.22   A claim in malicious falsehood has the advantage that it is not subject to the "serious harm" test in the Defamation Act 2013, s 1 (see para 5.76) or to the "single meaning rule" (see para 5.78). However, such claims face formidable hurdles in that

- The claimant must prove that the factual statement being made is false. This may involve the difficult exercise of proving a negative.
- The claimant must prove that the defendant was "malicious" – that is knew that the statement was false or was reckless as to its truth or falsity. This proof must relate to the factual statement that the defendant understood s/he was making (see para 5.80). In practice, there must be positive evidence of malice – evidence of carelessness or incompetence will not be enough. Any complexity or ambiguity in the statement complained of is likely to make this task very difficult.
- That the statement has caused damage to the claimant or is likely to cause such damage (see paras 5.82–5.83 above). In practice this is likely to be a similar test to that in s 1(2) of the 2013 Act (relating to bodies trading for profit).

9.23   These hurdles are high and mean that outside the context of calculated commercial attacks on trading rivals, malicious falsehood claims are rare. In practice, they should only be contemplated in the very clearest of cases.

Harassment

9.24   A claimant must establish a course of conduct, targeted at the claimant, which is unreasonable and has caused alarm and distress (see paras 5.85–5.87).

9.25   The paradigm case of harassment is the physical "stalking" of the claimant. Many online harassment cases involve individuals who have followed or approached a person who they are obsessed with and have then posted material about them on the internet. If the element of "physical approach" is present then it is straightforward to rely on online postings as part of the same "course of conduct".

9.26   A purely online harassment claim will usually be more difficult to establish. In practice, it will usually require a substantial volume of online material. Such cases may, for example, involve a number of "sock puppet" accounts on Twitter or Facebook, and online comments posted in places where it is clear that they are likely to be drawn to the claimant's attention. However each case will depend on its own facts and it is possible for a harassment claim to be brought in relation to one single internet publication on a prominent website if the publication is continuous and would inevitably come to the claimant's attention on more than one occasion and on each occasion cause them alarm and distress.[2] Claims based on a few upsetting or offensive postings are likely to face considerable difficulties if framed in harassment.

9.27   If the claimant can identify what appears to be an "oppressive course of conduct" that includes online publications it is then necessary to consider whether the defendant can establish a defence under the Protection from Harassment Act 1997, s 1(3) (see paras 5.94–5.99). The defendant has to establish that the conduct is "reasonable" or pursued for the purposes of "preventing or detecting crime".

Breach of confidence

9.28   If a company or other body corporate complains that an individual is threatening to publish or has published true information relating to its affairs on the internet then it may have a claim for breach of confidence. It will have to show that (see paras 6.4–6.8):

- The information has the necessary quality of confidence; and
- It had a "reasonable expectation of confidentiality" in the information – this could be because of the circumstances in which the publisher

---

[2] *Coulson & Ors v Wilby* [2014] EWHC 3404 (QB) at [49].

obtained the information or because s/he has been told that the information is confidential.[3]

- There is no "public interest" in publication.

9.29   If there is a threat to publish then the claimant may wish to seek interim injunctive relief (see para 8.3ff). If the information has already been published then it may have lost the "necessary quality of confidence" – but this depends on how easily accessible it is.[4] Once the information has become public the claim is limited to a claim for damages against the original publisher because the republished information is no longer confidential.

Misuse of private information

Introduction

9.30   If the potential claimant is an individual and the information is private then s/he may have a claim for misuse of private information. There are two issues to consider (see para 6.16ff):

- Does the claimant have a "reasonable expectation of privacy" in relation to the information in question?
- Does the balance between ECHR, arts 8 and 10 (and/or, if appropriate, other Convention rights) favour publication?

First issue

9.31   In relation to the first issue, although this involves looking at all the circumstances (see para 6.22) some kinds of information are obviously private and will be likely to form the basis of a claim – for example, sexual (including potentially information as to the fact of a sexual relationship), medical and financial information. Information about what takes place "behind closed doors" in a person's home is likely to be treated as private. Information about criminal investigations and arrests (before charge) is also likely to attract a reasonable expectation of privacy.

9.32   Careful consideration needs to be given to whether and to what extent the "private" information complained about is already in the public domain. If it has been made widely available on the internet then it is unlikely that an interim injunction will be granted. However, if there is a "qualitative difference in intrusiveness and distress" likely to be involved as a result of

---

3 *Vestergaard Frandsen A/S & Ors v Bestnet Europe Ltd & Ors* [2013] 1 WLR 1556 at [23]–[25].

4 *Barclays Bank Plc v Guardian News and Media Ltd* [2009] EWHC 591 (QB) at [22].

threatened publication by the English media in hard copy as well as on their own internet sites then it is possible that an injunction could still be granted[5].

9.33 Information about things that have taken place in public or semi-public places is more complex. Photographs of children taken in public places are likely to attract a reasonable expectation of privacy. However, it seems that under English law, without more, a photograph of an adult in public going about his or her ordinary business is unlikely to be regarded as private (see para 6.23).

9.34 Conversely, there are activities which are generally regarded as essentially public – whether or not they are known to substantial numbers of people. For example, the events which take place in open court at a trial will (in the absence of reporting restrictions which will only be made when "strictly necessary") be treated as public. Certain events are the subject of public records and cannot, in general, be treated as private – for example, a marriage or the birth of a child. Events at public meetings are unlikely to attract a reasonable expectation of privacy.

9.35 False private information can also attract a reasonable expectation of privacy (see para 6.20). This means that if the information that has been published is a mixture of the true and the false the claimant does not have to give details of which parts are true and which are false – such details would potentially assist a defendant who wished to publish material about the claimant's private life. But a claimant should exercise caution – if all the private information is false a court is likely to take the view that defamation (or malicious falsehood) is the most appropriate cause of action. A "repackaging" of a defamation claim as being one for false private information may be treated as an abuse of the process, aimed at avoiding the operation of the rule in *Bonnard v Perryman*[6] or the 1-year limitation period in libel actions (see para 8.29).

Second issue

9.36 The second issue involves looking, in turn, at the strength of the ECHR, art 8 and other Convention rights of the claimant (and other relevant individuals such as the claimant's children and family members) and the art 10 rights (and/or other relevant convention rights) of the defendant.

9.37 The following matters are likely to be of particular importance when looking at the balance:

---

[5] *PJS v News Group Newspapers Ltd* [2016] AC 1081 at [35].

[6] [1891] 2 Ch 269.

- Whether the information concerns "core" privacy rights (sexual, medical, intimate communications) – the closer to the "core", the stronger the art 8 right.
- Whether there is evidence that the privacy rights of children or other family members are engaged.
- Whether art 10 rights engaged are "core" expression rights – the extent to which the publication relates to a matter of public interest and contributes to a debate of general interest.
- Whether the claimant holds public office or is otherwise a "public figure".

9.38   The exercise is fact sensitive. However, the question as to whether the information discloses wrongdoing or clear hypocrisy is likely to be central. Another key factor is the status of the claimant. Politicians and other public officials are likely to find it particularly difficult to restrain the publication of "non-core" private information.

Data protection claims

9.39   Claims under the 1998 Act can only be brought by living individuals. There is, however, no geographical limitation – anyone whose data is processed by a data controller established in the EU has data protection rights (see generally para 6.38ff). The term "data processing" has the widest possible meaning and anyone who deals in any way with electronic data will be processing it for the purposes of the 1998 Act (see paras 6.45–6.46).

9.40   There are two key questions to be answered in relation to any proposed 1998 Act claim:

- Is the information in question "personal data"? The term is a wide one and certainly covers anything "significantly biographical" about an individual that would include, for example, address or other personal identifying information, photographs or information concerning a person's whereabouts or activities on a particular day.
- Is the defendant a "data controller"? Anybody who determines the purposes for which data is processed and who is established within the EU (see para 2.6) will qualify. In practice this means anyone based in the EU who operates a website or a blog or who posts personal data on any website that is generally accessible to the public. Anyone based in the EU who posts personal data on a publicly accessible social media site is likely to be held to be a data controller (see para 6.47).

9.41   If the defendant is a data controller who is processing the claimant's personal data then potential claims arise if:

- The processing is causing or is likely to cause the claimant substantial and unwarranted distress or damage (s 10, see paras 6.55 and 8.69–8.71).
- The data is inaccurate (s 14, see paras 6.57 and 8.72–8.73).
- The claimant has been caused distress or damage by any contravention of the provisions of the 1998 Act – (s 13, see paras 6.58 and 8.53–8.56). This would include, for example, breach of the data protection principles (see para 6.48–6.52).

CHOOSING THE DEFENDANT

Introduction

9.42   In any internet publication case there are a range of possible defendants. These include

- The author of the publication.
- The provider of the website on which the publication appears, for example, Facebook or Blogger.
- The operator of a search engine which includes the offending material in search results.

The author

9.43   In general, the first choice as defendant will be the author of the publication who is the "primary wrongdoer". This person not only bears primary responsibility for the wrong but there are also good practical reasons for suing them if they can be identified. If a remedy is not obtained against the author they can simply repost the same or similar material on a different website. Action will then have to be taken against this website. The new publication will have a different URL and so any "delisting" request will have to be repeated.

9.44   There are, however, often practical difficulties with an action against the author. It is sometimes impossible to identify the author. Many will be using false identities and operate via web services which are based in the United States or elsewhere. A *Norwich Pharmacal* order can be sought from the web service provider in an attempt to identify the author. However, the increasing use of proxy registrant services and other devices to conceal identity means that such court orders can be ineffective (see para 3.38).

9.45   If the defendant cannot be identified then consideration can be given to bringing what is known as a "Persons Unknown" action. The claim is brought against a defendant identified by description rather than by name. It is necessary for the unknown persons to be identified by description, in such a way as to identify with certainty those who are included within it and those who are not. For example, in the leading case[7] the claim was issued against

> "The person or persons who have offered the publishers of the Sun, the Daily Mail, and the Daily Mirror newspapers a copy of the book 'Harry Potter and the Order of the Phoenix' by JK Rowling or any part thereof and the person or persons who has or have physical possession of a copy of the said book or any part thereof without the consent of the claimants."

9.46   If an action is brought against "Persons Unknown", the court can grant an interim injunction to restrain those persons from carrying out acts such as the misuse of private information or harassment.[8] Such an interim injunction can be served on third parties and takes "*Spycatcher* effect" (see paras 8.15–8.17).

9.47   The court can also grant a final injunction[9] or make an award of damages[10] against "Persons Unknown". Although it is unlikely that any damages or costs will be recovered in such a case, the final court order can be served on a website or ISSP and should lead to the material being taken down.

Operators of websites

9.48   The operator of a website has a defence under s 5 of the 2013 Act if it can show that it did not post the statement on its website. If the author can be identified and served the operator will have a complete defence. If the author is anonymous, the website operator will have the option of following the s 5 procedure set out in the Defamation (Operators of Websites) Regulations 2013 but it can only keep publishing the content complained of and still rely on the defence if:

- The poster consents to be identified to the complainant; or

---

[7] *Bloomsbury Publishing Group Plc & Anor v News Group Newspapers Ltd & Ors* [2003] 1 WLR 1633.

[8] *Stone & Anor v "WXY"* [2012] EWHC 3184 (QB), and *Kerner v WX* [2015] EWHC 128 (QB).

[9] *Novartis Pharmaceuticals UK Ltd & Ors v Stop Huntingdon Animal Cruelty & Ors* [2014] EWHC 3429 (QB).

[10] *Brett Wilson LLP v Person(s) Unknown, Responsible for the Operation and Publication of the Website www.solicitorsfromhelluk.com* [2016] 4 WLR 69.

- The poster provides full contact details (including a postal address) to the website operator which can be disclosed pursuant to a court order.

In all other circumstances, unless the website operator decides that it wants to advance a defamation defence it will need to remove the content complained of and be careful to adhere to the complex web of time periods set out in the Regulations.

9.49   An internet intermediary is likely to have a "safe harbour" defence (see Chapter 7) so, before any action is brought notice must be given in accordance with the Electronic Commerce (EC Directive) Regulations 2002. If the internet intermediary fails to take down the offending publication then proceedings can be issued against it. It will be necessary to give notice to the intermediary setting out full and proper details including the full name and address of the claimant, the URL for the material complained about and full and proper details of the unlawful nature of the material in question (see generally, Chapter 7).

9.50   In many cases it will be necessary to obtain permission to serve the proceedings out of the jurisdiction (see para 4.16ff). However, Facebook in the EU is operated by Facebook Ireland Limited, which is based in Dublin and which can be served under the Recast Brussels Regulation (see para 4.57ff).

Search engines

9.51   One of the main ways in which individuals obtain information from online publications is through the use of search engines such as Google or Bing. A "delisting" request can be made under Google's *Costeja* procedure (see para 2.18ff). If that is unsuccessful then an application can be made to the ICO or proceedings can be issued under the 1998 Act. The operator of the Google search engine is Google Inc, which is based in California and permission must be obtained to serve the proceedings on Google Inc out of the jurisdiction.

PREPARING AND ISSUING THE CLAIM

Introduction

9.52   Once a claimant has identified the possible cause(s) of action arising out of the publication of material on the internet and the potential defendant(s) it is then necessary to consider whether to seek interim remedies. These are dealt with in the next section.

9.53   There are a number of steps that need to be considered before a claim is commenced:

- Letter of Claim and Response;
- Application for anonymity order;
- Preparation of claim form and particulars of claim;
- Choosing the Court; and
- Issues concerning service.

Letter of claim and response

Introduction

9.54   Under the modern approach to litigation a letter of claim is essential. If, however, an urgent interim remedy is required then letter of claim may not be appropriate. The notification of the claim will take place when the injunction application is served (or, if an injunction is obtained without notice, when the injunction itself is served). In other cases, however, a letter of claim should be sent to the defendant using whatever contact details are available.

9.55   In cases involving internet publications it is essential to gather evidence at all stages, including the very early stages, as websites can be amended and the evidence lost. Screen grabs or hard copy print outs should therefore be obtained that demonstrate precisely what was being published, when, and to whom.

Defamation

9.56   The Pre-Action Protocol for Defamation ("PAPD") sets out the requirements for a letter of claim in a libel action (PAPD, para 3.2). Such a letter should include the following information:

- name of claimant;
- sufficient details to identify the publication or broadcast which contained the words complained of;
- the words complained of and, if known, the date of publication; where possible, a copy or transcript of the words complained of should be enclosed;
- factual inaccuracies or unsupportable comment within the words complained of; the claimant should give a sufficient explanation to enable the defendant to appreciate why the words are inaccurate or unsupportable;
- the nature of the remedies sought by the claimant;

- Where relevant, the letter of claim should also include:-
  (i) any facts or matters which make the claimant identifiable from the words complained of;
  (ii) details of any special facts relevant to the interpretation of the words complained of and/or any particular damage caused by the words complained of.

9.57   In addition, the claimant should, in the letter of claim, identify the meanings he/she attributes to the words complained of (PAPD, para 3.3).

9.58   The defamation pre-action protocol letter is an important document which should be prepared with care. The relevant "factual inaccuracies" should be identified and the true position fully explained (with evidence if appropriate). This is important where there is online publication, as after a defendant has been put on notice of the falsity of the allegations, it will be much harder to defend any continuing publication. The defendant is likely to lose the benefit of any "public interest" defence which s/he might have had (see para 5.56). The "meaning complained of" should also be carefully worked out. If, as often happens, a very expansive meaning appears in the letter and a much narrower version in the particulars of claim this will, inevitably, damage the claimant's case. Guidance on the contents of defendants' letters of response is provided in paras 10.10–10.11.

Other causes of action

9.59   There is no specific pre-action protocol for misuse of private information, breach of the 1998 Act or harassment but a claimant should follow the guidance set out in the Practice Direction on Pre-Action Conduct. This provides (in para 3) that before commencing proceedings, the court will expect the parties to have exchanged sufficient information to:

    (a) understand each other's position;
    (b) make decisions about how to proceed;
    (c) try to settle the issues without proceedings;
    (d) consider a form of Alternative Dispute Resolution (ADR) to assist with settlement;
    (e) support the efficient management of those proceedings; and
    (f) reduce the costs of resolving the dispute.

9.60   Such steps will usually include (para 6):

    (a) the claimant writing to the defendant with concise details of the claim. The letter should include the basis on which the claim is made, a summary of the facts, what the claimant wants from the defendant, and if money, how the amount is calculated;

(b) the defendant responding within a reasonable time – 14 days in a straight forward case and no more than 3 months in a very complex one. The reply should include confirmation as to whether the claim is accepted and, if it is not accepted, the reasons why, together with an explanation as to which facts and parts of the claim are disputed and whether the defendant is making a counterclaim as well as providing details of any counterclaim; and

(c) the parties disclosing key documents relevant to the issues in dispute.

9.61   In the case of internet publications a claimant will often want to prevent the continuing publication as well as claim damages for the past publication; it is therefore important to set out in the letter of claim why and how the publication is misusing private information and/or harassing the claimant and/or is in breach of the data protection principles, including details of the harm that is being suffered by the claimant. This will put the defendant on notice and make it more difficult for them to defend the continuing publication.

9.62   A claimant who is relying on the 1998 Act should always include a notice under s 10 of the 1998 Act if the facts justify it. This notice requires the defendant to cease processing their personal data if such processing is causing them or likely to cause them, or another, substantial damage or distress and that damage or distress is unwarranted; it could apply, for example, in the case of the online publication of an article containing inaccurate data. It starts time running and a defendant must reply within 21 days.[11] If the defendant fails to comply with the request properly it also allows the claimant the option of complaining of a breach of the sixth data protection principle.

Application for anonymity

9.63   Ordinarily a claim form must include the full name of each party[12], however in a misuse of private information case a claimant will wish to consider whether or not to apply for an "anonymity order". Such an order can be made under CPR 39.2(4) which provides:

---

[11] S 10(3) of the 1998 Act.

[12] CPR PD 16, para 2.6.

"The court may order that the identity of any party or witness must not be disclosed if it considers non-disclosure necessary in order to protect the interests of that party or witness".

9.64 An anonymity order is a derogation from open justice and must only be ordered where that is necessary, and only to the extent that is necessary. The procedure for making an anonymity application is set out in *CVB v Mirror Group Newspapers Ltd*.[13] An application should be made, without notice, to a High Court Master in the Urgent and Short Applications List, supported by a witness statement explaining why anonymity is necessary on the facts of the case. An order made by the Master will then permit the issue of anonymised proceedings – although this will not be an injunction preventing the naming of the claimant. When an anonymity application is being made, an application can also be made for an order protecting hearing papers and documents from public inspection under CPR 5.4C and CPR 31.22(2).

9.65 There is no requirement under the Human Rights Act 1998, s 12(2) or CPR 23.4 to give notice to an intended defendant or anyone else of such an application. Any person affected by an order for anonymity (or an order for the protection of hearing papers) made without notice can apply to discharge the order. Such an application is not required to be within any time limit. This gives to non-parties an effective means to enforce their rights under ECHR, art 10[14].

9.66 A claimant must carefully consider his or her claim at the outset to ensure that, as far as possible, they rely on the correct causes of action and relevant factual matters. Future amendments to add parties or causes of action to the Particulars of Claim after service will require an application to Court if the other parties refuse to provide written consent[15]. Even if successful, a claimant is likely to have to pay the costs of and occasioned by any amendment.

9.67 In defamation claims statements of case should be confined to the information necessary to inform the other party of the nature of the case he has to meet. Such information should be set out concisely and in a manner proportionate to the subject matter of the claim.[16] Other specific points in respect of defamation claims include:

- The claim form must identify the publication that is the subject of the claim (CPR PD 53, para 2.2(1)). The particulars of claim must set out

---

[13] [2012] EMLR 29.

[14] *CVB v Mirror Group Newspapers Ltd* at [53].

[15] CPR 17.1(2).

[16] CPR PD 53, para 2.1. See too *McPhilemy v Times Newspapers* [1999] 3 All ER 775.

the meaning of the words complained of and, if an innuendo meaning is relied on, the relevant extraneous facts (CPR PD 53, para 2.3).

- A claimant will now be required to set out why and how, with supporting facts and matters if appropriate, the serious harm test under s 1 of the 2013 Act is satisfied.

- In cases where a claimant has gathered evidence which demonstrates serious financial loss then a special damages claim can be pleaded.

- It is particularly important for a claimant to set out their libel claims fully in their particulars of claim as the defendant making an offer of amends will only be held to have made that offer on the claim as notified in that statement of case.

- If the claim includes a special damages claim for removing the repetitions and republications of the defamatory statement on the internet, the claim should refer to whether or not the task is an ongoing one (i.e. continuing loss); give proper particulars of the republications relied on; set out the basis on which the s 1 serious harm requirement is satisfied; and set out the discrete cost of dealing with each republication[17].

9.68 In misuse of private information and breach of confidence cases consideration should be given as to whether an anonymity and protection from hearing papers order needs to be obtained before the claim form is issued (see paras 9.63–9.65). Private or confidential information can be set out in a confidential schedule to the particulars of claim. While such schedules are less common in data protection and libel claims they can also be used in appropriate cases. Parties using such confidential schedules for statements of case and other documents that are referred to in public hearings should obtain an order under CPR 5.4C and/or CPR 31.22(2) to prevent them from being publicly inspected without an order of the court; any such application for an order by a third party should be on reasonable notice to the parties concerned.

9.69 In cases involving internet publications on different "platforms" (for example, newspapers that are accessible both via their website and via iPhone or Android apps) it is important for a claimant to include all such platforms in their claim as this can have a significant impact on the scale of publication.[18]

9.70 In all cases a claimant needs to value their claim for the purposes of determining which band it falls into for the issue fee. However if too low a value is given it seems clear from CPR 16.3(7) that this does not limit the

---

[17] *Lisle-Mainwaring v Associated Newspapers Ltd & Anor* [2017] EWHC 543 (QB) at [179].

[18] Ibid, at [50].

power of the court to give judgment for the amount it finds the claimant is entitled to recover. Thus in *Harrath v Stand for Peace Ltd & Anor*[19] Sir David Eady awarded the claimant £140,000 even though the claim form indicated that the claimant expected to recover no more than £10,000.

9.71 In cases involving foreign language publications on the internet consideration should be given as to whether a claimant can also rely on the English translation of the article as a result of Google translate or an equivalent application[20].

Choosing the court

9.72 If the case includes a claim for defamation it must be brought in the High Court.

9.73 Claims for breach of confidence, misuse of private information, harassment and breach of the 1998 Act can be brought in either the High Court or the County Court. In practice, internet publication cases are usually complex and are brought in the High Court.

Issues concerning service

Defendant in England and Wales

9.74 If the defendant is domiciled in England and Wales a claimant should serve the claim form using one of the methods set out in CPR 6.3, which include personal service and first class post. If a defendant resides or carries on business within the UK and has given the claimant that address for the purposes of being served with the proceedings, the claimant may serve the claim form using that address (CPR 6.8(a)). If the defendant does not give an address at which they may be served, CPR 6.9 applies and the place of service will depend upon the nature of the defendant; for example an individual must be served at their usual or last known address and a limited liability partnership must be served at the principal office of the partnership or any place of business of the partnership within the jurisdiction that has a real connection with the claim.

9.75 If a defendant's solicitor has notified the claimant in writing that they are instructed to accept service of the claim form on behalf of the defendant at a

[19] [2017] EWHC 653 (QB).

[20] *Ahuja v Politika Novine I Magazini DOO & Ors* [2016] 1 WLR 1414 at [8] and [65].

227 | ONLINE PUBLICATION CLAIMS: A PRACTICAL GUIDE

business address within the jurisdiction the claim form must be served at the business address of that solicitor (CPR 6.7(1)).

Defendant in EU

9.76 A claimant may serve a claim form out of the jurisdiction on a defendant in Scotland or Northern Ireland without the permission of the court in the circumstances provided for in CPR 6.32. In proceedings where the claim does not fall within CPR 6.32(1) or (2), service of the claim form on a defendant in Scotland or Northern Ireland may be possible with the permission of the court under CPR 6.36 subject to the special considerations stated in CPR 6.37(4).

9.77 If a defendant resides or carries on business within another EEA state and has given the claimant that address for the purposes of being served with the proceedings, the claimant may serve the claim form using that address (CPR 6.8(a)).

9.78 A claimant serving a claim form out of the jurisdiction where permission is not required must file the Form N510 (Service out of the jurisdiction) when filing and serving the claim form (see para 9.80).

Defendant outside the EU

9.79 CPR 6.33 sets out the circumstances where the claim form can be served outside the United Kingdom without permission of the Court. A claimant will need to show that their claim falls under one of the four different contexts where the English courts have power to determine the claim and, in relation to each, satisfy other additional conditions. The four contexts are the following:

(1) under the Civil Jurisdiction and Judgments Act 1982 or the Lugano Convention (CPR 6.33(1));

(2) under the Judgments Regulation (CPR 6.33(2));

(3) under the 2005 Convention (CPR 6.33(2B)); and

(4) under other legislation notwithstanding the fact that the defendant is not within the jurisdiction and the facts giving rise to the claim did not occur within the jurisdiction (CPR 6.33(3)).[21]

9.80 A claimant serving a claim form out of the jurisdiction where permission is not required must file the Form N510 (Service out of the jurisdiction) when filing and serving the claim form (CPR 6.34(1)). If this form is not filed with

---

[21] *In re Harrods (Buenos Aires) Ltd* [1992] Ch 72.

the claim form, the claim form may only be served once the claimant files the form or if the court gives permission (CPR 6.34(2)).

Service on a defendant outside EU – applications for permission to serve out

9.81   A claimant must make an application for permission to serve out on the basis that the claim falls under one of the "gateways" set out in CPR PD 6B, para 3.1 (see para 4.16ff).

Service by an alternative method

9.82   Where it appears to the court that there is a good reason, it may authorise service of a claim form, or any other document, by a method or at a place not otherwise permitted by the rules (CPR 6.15 and 6.27). A court may order that steps already taken to bring a claim form or document to the attention of the other party is good service (CPR 6.15(2)). An application for an order under this provision must be supported by evidence but may be made without notice (CPR 6.15(3) and CPR PD 6A, para 9). This provision can be used prospectively to permit alternative service in a service out case – provided that this is not contrary to the law of country where the defendant is to be served.[22]

9.83   In an online publication case, permission may be obtained to serve by email on an email address used by the defendant or via social media. Service has been permitted under this provision:

- By email on defendants in the United States – although the judge noted that evidence should in future be put before the court as to whether that method was permitted by local laws (because if it was, alternative service would be unnecessary).[23]
- To the "contact" emails for a proxy registrant service.[24]
- Via an identified defendant's Facebook account.[25]
- Via an unknown defendant's Twitter account.[26]

---

[22] *Abela v Baadarani* [2013] 1 WLR 2043 at [20] and [24].

[23] *Bacon v Automattic Inc & Ors* [2012] 1 WLR 753.

[24] *Brett Wilson LLP v Person(s) Unknown, Responsible for the Operation and Publication of the Website www.solicitorsfromhelluk.com* [2016] 4 WLR 69 at [11].

[25] *AKO Capital LLP v TFS Derivatives* (HC, 21 February 2012); see http://www.telegraph.co.uk/finance/newsbysector/mediatechnologyandtelecoms/9095489/Legal-claims-can-be-served-via-Facebook-High-Court-judge-rules.html.

[26] *Blaney v Persons Unknown*, (HC, 5 October 2009); see https://www.out-law.com/page-10419.

INTERIM REMEDIES

Introduction

9.84   In any online publication case a claimant will want to consider whether to apply for an interim injunction and, if so whether this should be on notice to the defendant or "without notice". Interim injunctions are likely to be most important in actions for breach of confidence, misuse of private information and harassment. In practice, they are very difficult to obtain in defamation and data protection cases. The law is dealt with above (see para 8.3ff), practical issues are considered in this section.

9.85   Before seeking an injunction a claimant should normally contact the defendant to explain why the publication would be unlawful and inform the defendant that if they do not confirm that no publication will take place the claimant will seek an urgent injunction. Failure to provide such notification can only be justified, on clear and cogent evidence, by compelling reasons, for example where the defendant is a blackmailer and there is a real prospect that alerting them to the fact that an injunction is going to be sought is likely to result in them publishing the information.[27] This may well apply if the defendant is an internet based organisation, tweeter or blogger; but where the defendant is a media organisation there will rarely be compelling reasons that would justify a "without notice" application, either on the grounds of secrecy or urgency.[28]

9.86   If contact has been made and the defendant fails or refuses to respond, or the defendant states that publication is still intended and does not provide good reasons justifying the publication, then steps should be taken to seek an injunction. The speed at which the injunction is sought will depend upon the likely time of any threatened publication. Internet publications could take place at any time and applications will therefore often be sought on the same day or very shortly after the claimant discovers about the threatened disclosure. Notification should be given to the defendant that an injunction is being sought and details of the hearing provided to them.

Preparation for the hearing

9.87   If there is time a claimant should prepare:

- An application with a draft order;

---

[27] *ASG v GSA* [2009] EWCA Civ 1574 at [3]; *DFT v TFD* [2010] EWHC 2335 (QB) at [7].

[28] Practice Guidance: Interim Non-Disclosure Orders, para 22.

- A supporting witness statement or statements justifying the need for an order;
- A claim form; and
- A skeleton argument.

These documents are explained in more detail below.

The application and draft order

9.88 Applications for injunctions can be made before proceedings are issued.[29] If the application is made before the claim form is issued the order should state in the title after the names of the applicant and the respondent "the Claimant and Defendant in an intended Action"[30]. The draft order should contain a penal notice and notice to anyone who is informed of the order under the title. In privacy and breach of confidence cases consideration should be given as to whether an anonymity order, a private hearing and/or restrictions of access to hearing papers is needed (see para 9.63ff). A claimant will be required to give an undertaking in damages to the defendant. A version of the model order for an interim non-disclosure order in *Microsoft Word* can be found in the "Resources" section on the Inforrm's blog.

9.89 The injunction should clearly set out what the defendant, as well as any third party served with the order, must or must not do. If it relates to private and/or confidential information, the details of the information should be set out in a confidential schedule to the order.

The evidence

9.90 The witness statement should, if at all possible, be from the claimant, however if this is not possible the claimant's solicitor can make the statement on instructions. The witness statement should explain the background to give details of the threatened publication; why publication should not be allowed (e.g. explanation that the information is private and/or confidential and only known to a very limited number of people; and the harm that any publication would cause to the claimant and their family/children). Private and/or confidential information should be set out in a Confidential Exhibit to the witness statement and this should be explained in the main body of the statement. If none of the parties connected to the private information (e.g. in relation to an extra-marital affair, those having the affair and their spouses)

---

[29] CPR 25.2(1)(a).

[30] CPR PD 25A, 4.4(3).

want the information published it is useful to serve short witness statements from each explaining their position.

9.91   If the application was made without notice the evidence must set out why notice has not been given[31]. Without notice applications are only justified where "secrecy is essential".[32] On a without notice application, the claimant has a duty of "full and frank disclosure". The application notice and witness statement must be filed with the court on the same or next working day or as ordered, together with two copies of the order for sealing[33].

The claim form

9.92   If the application has been made before the issue of a claim form, unless the court orders otherwise, either the claimant must undertake to the court to issue a claim form immediately or the court will give directions for the commencement of the claim. Where possible the claim form should be served with the order for the injunction.[34]

Practicalities and the hearing

9.93   During court hours the hearing will take usually take place in Court 37 in the Queen's Bench Division or before the interim applications judge in the Chancery Division. If it is not possible to arrange a hearing then telephone applications can be made between 10am and 5pm weekdays by telephoning the Royal Courts of Justice on 020 7947 6000 and asking to be put in contact with a High Court judge of the appropriate Division available to deal with an emergency application in a High Court matter. The appropriate district registry can also be contacted by telephone. In county court proceedings, the appropriate county court hearing centre should be contacted[35].

9.94   If an application is being made over the weekend or in the evening a claimant should call the Royal Courts of Justice on 020 7947 6000 and ask for the clerk to the Duty Judge; there is one clerk for the Queen's Bench Division and one for the Chancery Division. Injunctions will only take place over the telephone

---

[31] CPR PD 25A, 3.4.

[32] CPR PD 25A, 4.3(3).

[33] CPR PD 25A 4.5(4).

[34] CPR PD 25A, 4.4(1), (2).

[35] CPR PD 25A, 4.5(1).

if the applicant is acting by counsel or solicitors[36]. An *Out of Hours Application Form* [37] must be completed.

9.95 If the application is being dealt with after the issue of the claim form, where possible, the application notice, witness statement and a draft order should be filed with the court two hours before the hearing[38]. In other cases, time permitting, a copy of the papers, or at least the skeleton argument and the draft Order, should be sent to the judge prior to the hearing.

9.96 A full note should be taken of what is said at the hearing. If the defendant was not represented at the hearing, the note of the hearing must be provided with a copy of the order. If the order is granted then a claimant will normally immediately serve it on third parties to put them on notice so they are also bound by it (see paras 8.15–8.17 and the "*Spycatcher* principle").

The return date

9.97 If the witness statement filed for the original hearing was made by the solicitor rather than the claimant due to lack of time, then a statement from the claimant should be filed and served. If the defendant has served evidence in response, evidence from the claimant in reply can be served.

9.98 The return date is usually about 7 days after the original hearing. It is not necessarily before the same judge. The claimant has to apply for the renewal of an injunction until trial. The case will be heard without the same pressure of urgency, on the basis of fuller evidence and argument.

BETWEEN ISSUE AND TRIAL

Introduction

9.99 Once a claim has been issued and the particulars of claim are served, the matter will proceed to trial in accordance with the procedures set out in the Civil Procedure Rules. There are a number of particular procedural issues that arise in publication proceedings that will be considered in this section:

- Offer of amends procedure.
- Statements in open court.
- Strike out and summary judgment.
- Trials of preliminary issues.

---

[36] CPR PD 25A, 4.5(5).

[37] https://hmctsformfinder.justice.gov.uk/HMCTS/FormFinder.do.

[38] PD 25A, para 4.3(1).

- Disclosure and source protection.
- Expert evidence.
- Preparing for trial.

These will be considered briefly in turn.

Offer of amends

9.100   Chapter 10 contains guidance on the offer of amends procedure and explains the difference between a defendant's unqualified offer, which accept the claimants' defamatory meaning, and a qualified offer, where the defendant puts forward an alternative defamatory meaning. In practice, in most cases a claimant who receives an unqualified offer of amends must accept it as it is likely to be extremely difficult to prove that a libel was published maliciously. If the offer is "qualified" the question will be whether the claimant is going to be able to show that the words complained of bear a more serious defamatory meaning.

Statements in open court

9.101   A statement in open court can be made as part of a settlement in a claim for libel, slander, malicious falsehood, or misuse of private information or confidential information.[39] The statement may be a bilateral one made by both parties to the claim, or unilateral, made by one party.[40] Such a statement provides an opportunity for the making of a public apology and for the parties to explain how the action has been settled in their own words. Any statement can be reported by the media and will be protected by absolute privilege.

9.102   If a statement in open court is included as a term of settlement in a Part 36 offer or any other offer of settlement in a claim for defamation then the procedure in CPR PD 53, para 6 will apply. A party can apply for permission to make a statement in open court before or after they accept the Part 36 offer or other offer to settle.

9.103   The court will be expected to allow a statement in open court to be read unless there is some sufficient reason to cause the court to refuse it.[41] Judges considering whether to permit a statement to be read in open court must always consider whether the statement would be defamatory of third parties

---

[39] CPR PD 53, 6

[40] This is usually the claimant but can be a defendant, *CTB v News Group Newspapers Ltd & Anor* [2011] EWHC 3099 (QB).

[41] *Barnet v Crozier & Anor* [1987] 1 WLR 272, at 279–280 *per* Ralph Gibson LJ.

(if it is a statement agreed between the parties), and (if it is a unilateral statement by a claimant) whether it might also be defamatory of the defendant[42]. They should also consider whether it infringes the art 8 rights of any individual and, in determining whether or not to grant permission, weigh up the prejudice caused to that individual if the statement was published against the prejudice caused to the parties to the statement if that part was removed or amended.

9.104   An application for permission should be made to the Senior Master or, if not available, to the Master in the Urgent and Short Applications List.[43] Where permission is opposed then the matter will be listed before a judge.

Strike out and summary judgment

9.105   The claimant or the defendant may make an application to strike out some or all of the opposing party's statement of case (under CPR 3.4) or for summary judgment (under CPR 24). No special issues arise in relation to online publication cases.

Trials of preliminary issues

9.106   Trials of preliminary issues can be valuable in defamation cases. The court can make an early determination as to the meaning of the words complained of and whether they are defamatory.[44] In a number of recent cases there have been trials of preliminary issues as to "serious harm" under s 1 of the 2013 Act (see para 5.29ff) but, more recently, caution has been expressed as to whether this is an appropriate way of saving costs.

Disclosure and source protection

9.107   The rules governing the disclosure of documents are found in CPR 31. Claimants in internet claims are entitled to disclosure from the defendants of a wide variety of electronic documents that fall within the definition of standard disclosure, as well as any hard copy documents. "Documents" are defined in CPR 31.4 as "anything in which information of any description is recorded" and encompasses electronic documents, including email and other

---

[42] *Murray v Associated Newspapers Ltd* [2014] EMLR 23 at [28].

[43] Queen's Bench Guide, A Guide to the working practices of the Queen's Bench Division within the Royal Courts of Justice 2017, paras 19.4.1 to 19.4.4, pp.106–107.

[44] For example, the orders made in *Brown v Bower* [2017] EMLR 24.

electronic communications, word processed documents and databases, as well as documents stored on servers and back-up systems that have been "deleted" and metadata (see CPR PD 31A, 2A.1).

9.108   CPR PD 31B sets out the rules governing the disclosure of electronic documents. This explains, for example, that metadata may include the date and time of creation or modification of a word-processing file, or the author and date and time of sending an email (see CPR 5.7). This information is not always obtained or provided by defendants automatically in disclosure and, if relevant, claimants should highlight such areas in correspondence or their Electronic Documents Questionnaire.

9.109   Media or "citizen journalist" defendants will usually redact any documents to prevent disclosure of the identity of any confidential sources. The importance of protecting a source is recognised by the Contempt of Court Act 1981, s 10 and a right protected by ECHR, art 10. In order to come within the ambit of the protection the defendant must show that providing the disclosure would lead to a "reasonable chance" that the identity of the source would be revealed.[45]

9.110   s 10 provides that disclosure will not be ordered unless it is established "that disclosure is necessary in the interests of justice or national security or for the prevention of disorder or crime". It must be shown that disclosure is required by an overriding public interest. "Necessary in the interests of justice" means more than merely relevant to the issues in the litigation.[46] In practice, it is highly unlikely that an order for source disclosure will be made in the context of an online publication claim.

Expert evidence

9.111   Expert evidence is governed by CPR 35. The starting point is that expert evidence shall be restricted "to that which is reasonably required to resolve the proceedings". Expert witnesses have an overriding duty to the Court which has a general control over expert evidence and may limit the scope and cost of expert evidence and may direct that a single joint expert is instructed.

---

[45] *Richard v BBC* [2017] EMLR 22 at [40].

[46] *Maxwell v Pressdram Ltd & Anor* [1987] 1 WLR 298.

9.112   In online publication cases it is common for "technical issues" to arise about the operation of the internet or particular services on it such as "search" or particular social media platforms. As a result, parties are often given permission to rely on expert "computer" or "internet" evidence.

9.113   Examples from the case law in relation to matters specifically concerning online publication include expert evidence as to:

- The identification of the sender of anonymous emails.[47]
- The extent of publication of tweets[48] or of an online newspaper.[49]
- The technical and procedural measures that could be taken by a search provider in relation to search results or images.
- The technical operation of unfamiliar technologies, for example, BitTorrent.[50]

9.114   It is possible that a court may also permit "non-technical" evidence about the operation of the internet. In the Canadian case of *Baglow v Smith*[51] the Court appointed an expert in "internet social media, culture and communications" who gave evidence as to the nature of communication on the internet. It is not clear whether an English Court would be prepared to permit expert evidence of this kind.

Preparing for trial

9.115   The preparations for trial in an online publication case will not be any different from those in a "traditional media" case. If the case is proceeding in the Queen's Bench Media and Communications list then the guidance given in The Queen's Bench Guide should be followed. It is important to remember that the case may give rise to technical issues that may not be familiar to the court. It is important that these are clearly presented to the court. It might be possible to do this by agreement.[52] Otherwise it will be necessary for these matters to be explained either by expert evidence or in submissions.

---

[47] *Takenaka (UK) Ltd & Anor v Frankl* [2001] EWCA Civ 348.

[48] *Cairns v Modi* [2013] 1 WLR 1015.

[49] *Ahuja v Politika Novine I Magazini DOO & Ors* [2016] 1 WLR 1414.

[50] *AMP v Persons Unknown* [2011] Info TLR 25.

[51] [2015] ONSC 1175.

[52] For example, the agreed Appendix "How Twitter Works", attached to the judgment in *Monroe v Hopkins* [2017] 4 WLR 68.

ENFORCING INJUNCTIONS AND JUDGMENTS

Introduction

9.116   A High Court injunction or undertaking order can be enforced by means of what are known as "committal proceedings". In such proceedings the applicant complains to the Court that the respondent has failed to comply with a court order and seeks a "penal sanction" from the court. This can take the form of a fine, a sentence of imprisonment or "sequestration" of assets.

9.117   Committal proceedings can only be brought if the Court order that the respondent is said to have breached is endorsed with a "penal notice". Such a notice makes it clear that if the order is disobeyed the defendant may be held in contempt of court and "sent to prison, fined or have assets seized". If no penal notice is endorsed then the injunction cannot be enforced by committal proceedings (CPR 81.9).

9.118   Committal proceedings fall into two categories:

- Committal for breach by a defendant ("civil contempt"), dealt with in CPR 81, Part II.
- Committal for interference with the due administration of justice ("criminal contempt"), dealt with in CPR 81, Part III.

These will be considered in turn.

Civil contempt

9.119   In general, before civil committal proceedings can be brought, a copy of the injunction must have been served personally on the defendant (CPR 81.6). The Court may, however, dispense with service if it is satisfied that the defendant has had notice of the injunction by being present or by being notified "by telephone, email or otherwise" (CPR 81.8).

9.120   There are number of strict procedural requirements for an application for committal. The application must set out the full grounds on which it is made, setting out each act of contempt complained of and must be supported by affidavits containing the evidence relied on (CPR 81.10). Unless the court directs otherwise, 14 days' notice of the hearing must be given (CPR PD 81, 15.2). If the defendant is not represented the Court will usually adjourn the application to permit the defendant to apply for legal aid and obtain representation. The contempt of court must be proved "beyond reasonable doubt".

Criminal contempt

9.121 Where a third party who has had notice of an injunction has acted contrary to its terms then, under the *Spycatcher* principle (see paras 8.15–8.17) this constitutes a "criminal contempt". An application to commit for such a contempt requires the permission of the court (CPR 81.12(3)).

9.122 An application for permission to make such an application must be made by way of Part 8 claim form to a judge of the Court which granted the injunction (CPR 81.13). Such an application must be accompanied by:

- A detailed statement of the applicant's grounds for bringing the application.
- An affidavit setting out the facts and exhibiting the documents relied on.

9.123 The claim form and these documents must be served personally on the respondent (CPR 81.14). The respondent has 14 days to respond and the application must then be dealt with at an oral hearing. If the court gives permission it will give directions for a hearing of the application.

Applications for committal when the defendant is abroad

9.124 It is clear that CPR 81 has "extra territorial effect" and that an application for committal for contempt can be made against a defendant who is out of the jurisdiction.[53]

9.125 An application to commit for contempt (whether civil or criminal) is an application to commence proceedings for contempt and if the application concerns an interim injunction it is necessary to find a "gateway" for the purposes of CPR PD 6B to serve a committal application on a person outside the jurisdiction. An injunction is not a "judgment" for the purposes of CPR PD 6B, 3.1(10)[54] and it seems that no other gateway is available.

---

[53] *Dar Al Arkan Real Estate Development Co & Anor v Refai & Ors* [2015] 1 WLR 135.

[54] *Deutsche Bank AG v Sebastian Holdings Inc* [2017] 1 WLR 1842 at [19].

9.126   In relation to a final injunction it is not necessary to obtain permission to serve an application for committal on a defendant outside the jurisdiction due to the operation of the (Recast) Brussels Regulation, art 24(5). This provides that in proceedings concerned with the enforcement of judgments the courts of the Member State in which the judgment has been or is to be enforced shall have exclusive jurisdiction regardless of the domicile of the parties.[55]

---

[55] *Deutsche Bank AG v Sebastian Holdings Inc & Anor* [2017] EWHC 459 (Comm) at [21] to [26].

CHAPTER 10: DEFENDING A CLAIM, PRACTICAL ISSUES

CHAPTER SYNOPSIS

- The author and perhaps the primary publisher of a post may be able to advance substantive defences. In contrast, an ISSP will often know little or nothing about the underlying facts but may be entitled to rely on specific "intermediary defences".
- Addresses the practical issues that arise in relation to defending claims: initial considerations (e.g. is the claim addressed to the right person, are the elements made out, jurisdiction); defences and assessing the merits; practical considerations for intermediaries; interim applications; settlement and other procedures between issue and trial (offers of amends, preliminary rulings on meaning, Without prejudice and Part 36 offers, strike out and Summary judgment, disclosure and expert evidence).

INTRODUCTION

10.1   When a claim is made in respect of online publication there are different considerations depending on the nature of the claim and the role of the person against whom the claim is made. The author and perhaps the primary publisher of a post may be able to advance substantive defences. In contrast an Information Society Service Providers (ISSPs) will often know little or nothing about the underlying facts but may be entitled to rely on specific "intermediary defences".

10.2   Guidance on the legal defences available to publishers is contained in Chapter 5 (for defamation, malicious falsehood and harassment) and Chapter 6 (for breach of confidence, misuse of private information, and breach of the Data Protection Act 1998), while Chapter 7 deals with defences specific to ISSPs. This Chapter addresses the practical issues that arise in relation to defending claims, under the following headings:

- Initial considerations.
- Defences and assessing the merits.
- Practical considerations for intermediaries.
- Interim applications.
- Settlement.
- Between issue and trial.

INITIAL CONSIDERATIONS

10.3   In general the person to defend a claim should be the author of the post or article. That person has primary responsibility for the publication and will usually be in the best position to defend any claim made in relation to it. If the claim is addressed to someone who is not the author, then consideration should be given to passing the claim on to that person (if their identity is known). But another person may be liable once they have notice of the claim and will need to address it substantively.

10.4   Cases can often be resolved informally at an early stage. Sometimes a threatened claim is completely lacking in merit and a robust initial response will see it off. At other times a claim has merit but can be resolved quickly by an agreement to remove or correct a post, with or without an apology. An agreement to do these steps promptly may be sufficient to persuade a claimant not to pursue a potential damages claim or to accept a much lower payment than initially sought. It also minimises potential exposure to legal costs.

10.5   There are a number of initial questions to ask:

- Is the claim addressed to the right person?
- Is the claim made for a known cause of action?
- Are all the elements of the claim made out?
- Do English Courts have jurisdiction?
- Is the claim clearly formulated?
- What is the claimant actually asking for?
- Is further information needed?

10.6   A publisher will always consider whether there are any obvious defences. A post that does not identify the claimant at all (directly or indirectly) does not require subtle analysis. A publication may only have been read by a handful of people in England and Wales. A claim in defamation that relates to a publication that is not likely to cause any serious harm to reputation because it is trivial or there has been minimal publication is another example. But most cases are not so straight-forward.

10.7   Pre-action correspondence comes in all forms, from an email sent by a disgruntled reader without the benefit of any legal advice to a detailed letter of claim drafted by lawyers. The former may make a general complaint, for example, about the alleged inaccuracy of a post, but without identifying any specific cause of action. It cannot be assumed, however, that a claim lacks merit because it has not been properly formulated and it should also be remembered that individuals whose concerns are not addressed may then decide to instruct lawyers. Each claim needs to be evaluated on its merits, although sometimes it may be necessary to ask the potential claimant to provide further information to clarify the basis of his claim.

10.8   The Pre-Action Protocol for Defamation ("PAPD") emphasises the importance of the parties to a claim in defamation, acting in good faith, exploring the early and appropriate resolution of the claim (PAPD, para 1.3). The Protocol points out that defamation is different from most other civil claims as time is always "of the essence, the limitation period is (uniquely) 1 year, and almost invariably, a claimant will be seeking an immediate correction and/or apology as part of the process of restoring his reputation." (PAPD para 1.4)

10.9   It is important for both parties to follow the guidance in the PAPD. Guidance on the requirements for claimants in their letters of claim is provided in Chapter 9 (see paras 9.56–9.58). If any of that key information is missing, a defendant should seek that information from the claimant before providing a substantive response.

10.10   The PAPD states that a defendant should provide a full response to the letter of claim "as soon as possible" and that if they believe that they won't be able to respond within 14 days (or any shorter period set out on the letter of claim), they should write back and specify the date by which they will respond (PAPD para 3.5).

10.11   The PAPD provides the following guidance on the contents of the defendant's letter of response (para 3.5):

> "The Response should include the following:
>
> - whether or to what extent the Claimant's claim is accepted, whether more information is required or whether it is rejected;
> - if the claim is accepted in whole or in part, the defendant should indicate which remedies it is willing to offer;
> - if more information is required, then the defendant should specify precisely what information is needed to enable the claim to be dealt with and why;
> - if the claim is rejected, then the defendant should explain the reasons why it is rejected, including a sufficient indication of any facts on which the defendant is likely to rely in support of any substantive defence;
> - It is desirable for the defendant to include in the response to the letter of claim the meaning(s) he/she attributes to the words complained of."

10.12　There is no specific Pre-Action Protocol for misuse of private information, breach of confidence, breach of the Data Protection Act 1998 or harassment, however most of the above guidance for letters of response in defamation claims remains sound for those claims as well (although meaning is unlikely to be an issue). The Practice Direction on Pre-Action Conduct applies and provides some general guidance (see para 9.59–9.60). The guidance for defendant's letters of response is less detailed than that of the PAPD and any letter following the PAPD guidance would cover all of the most relevant points (the general guidance also refers to notification of counterclaims, which are relatively uncommon in publication cases).

10.13　A claimant may demand an immediate correction to, or withdrawal of, an online publication. In addition, a claimant in a data protection case may issue a s 10 notice, requiring a defendant to cease processing their personal data that is causing, or is likely to cause, substantial and unwarranted damage or distress (see para 9.62). A data controller is required to respond to a s 10 notice within 21 days and failure to respond gives the claimant a potential complaint of a breach of the sixth data protection principle.

10.14　Demands for immediate corrections or withdrawals of publications should be addressed promptly. The response is likely to be heavily influenced by the merits of the complaint or claim. Sometimes that assessment is straight-forward, for example, where an article has made a clear factual error, or where a post by a third party is obviously abusive and offensive on its face. But in many cases a more detailed evaluation will be necessary, requiring an assessment of the claim and potential defences. These issues are addressed in the next section.

ASSESSING THE MERITS

Introduction

10.15　Where a claimant has clearly formulated the claim – making it clear what precisely is being complained about and why – a defendant must then try to assess whether it has any merit. The person best placed to do this is, of course, the author but other potential defendants will have to engage in this exercise on the basis of whatever material they have available. While in the case of an online article published by a newspaper, the defendant can turn to the journalist for further information about the factual basis for the allegation, in the case of a posting by a third party on a user comment or on social media, the information will often be limited to the content of the post and the letter of claim, although the ISSP may be well-advised to seek comments from the poster (as Google Inc did in *Davison v Habeeb & Ors*[1] and *Tamiz v Google*[2]).

10.16   In broad terms, claims tend to fall into one of three categories:

(1)   Claims that are obviously weak, because for example they have not been formulated by reference to any recognisable cause of action, the claim is missing an essential ingredient, the allegation is trivial, or publication has been very limited. A claim of this kind probably does not require a detailed factual investigation and the defendant can reject the claim at the outset. If the claimant issues proceedings the defendant is likely to want to apply to strike out the claim, or for summary judgment (see para 10.92–94).

(2)   Claims where all the ingredients of the claim are made out and which appear to be meritorious on their face, where the prospects of success are likely to depend on factors which require further analysis and/or factual investigation to evaluate the claim itself or the strength of any available defences. These claims are the most complex and time-consuming.

(3)   Claims that are obviously strong and where it is clear from the outset that the defendant is unlikely to have any defence. Claims falling into this category would be cases where a defendant publisher has made a clear factual error that gives rise to the cause of action e.g. a defamatory allegation directed against the wrong person, or where e.g. a posting by a third party in user comments or on social media breaches the terms for users of the website e.g. by use of vulgar and sexist language or by making racist comments. Defendants will generally try to resolve these claims through an informal resolution at the pre-action stage and/or settlement of an issued claim.

10.17   However, different approaches need to be taken depending on the nature of the complaint and in particular (assuming that this is made clear) the cause of action relied on. Unlike a claimant who has the luxury of choosing the cause of action and how to formulate the claim (addressed in detail at para 9.13ff), the defendant must simply defend the claim that has been brought, relying on whatever defences are available to it. We will consider six causes of action in turn.

---

[1] [2012] 3 CMLR 6. HHJ Parkes commented that the oucome might have been different had Google not sought input from the poster.

[2] [2012] EMLR 24.

Defamation

Meaning

10.18   In a defamation case the fundamental issue is what the words mean: what defamatory allegation is being made by the publication? (see generally, para 5.16ff). Meaning is therefore of critical importance. If a publication does not bear a defamatory meaning then that is the end of the claim: factual inaccuracy is irrelevant.

10.19   If the publication bears a defamatory meaning the precise nature of the allegation is of critical importance for a number of reasons:

(1)   It will be highly relevant to whether that publication has caused, or is likely to cause, serious harm to the reputation of a claimant (see para 10.25ff);

(2)   Meaning dictates what facts a defendant has to prove in order to succeed in a truth defence (see para 10.31ff below).

(3)   Meaning is very relevant to public interest defences, as the more serious the defamatory allegation the stronger the public interest defence required to justify publication of that allegation (see para 10.37ff).

(4)   Meaning also has a major bearing on damages, being one of the two main factors (along with the scale of publication) that courts take into account when deciding on the level of compensation.

10.20   The assessment of the meaning of a publication is heavily dependent on the context and the means of the communication. The courts have recognised that a different approach to meaning is likely to be appropriate for online publications where members of the public make postings, such as bulletin boards, or postings on social media such as Facebook or tweets on Twitter, compared with traditional media such as books or newspaper articles where the authors are established writers or professional journalists.

10.21   As Eady J pointed out in *Smith v ADVFN Plc & Ors* (a case concerned with a thread on a bulletin board),[3] such threads are rather like contributions to a casual conversation, which people simply note before passing on; they are often uninhibited, causal and ill-thought out; those who participate know this and expect a certain amount of "give and take"; they are, in this respect, more like actions for slander than to the usual, more permanent kind of

---

[3] [2008] EWHC 1797 (QB) at [14]–[16]. See also *Clift v Clarke* [2011] Info TLR 13 at [36] (per Sharp J): "The postings are in reality, it seems to me, no more than 'pub talk'".

communications found in libel actions. Eady J also noted that readers do not often take a thread and go through it as a whole like a newspaper article; they tend to read the remarks, contribute if they wish to and think no more about it. As he put it:

> "From the context of casual conversations, one can often tell that a remark is not to be taken literally or seriously and is rather to be construed merely as abuse. That is less common in the case of more permanent written communication, although it is by no means unknown. But in the case of a bulletin board thread it is often obvious to casual observers that people are just saying the first thing that comes into their heads and reacting in the heat of the moment. The remarks are often not intended, or to be taken, as serious." [17]

10.22   Twitter has also been treated by the courts as "conversational medium" where an impressionistic approach to meaning is appropriate. As Warby J held in *Monroe v Hopkins*[4] when discussing meaning in the context of a defamation claim concerned with defamatory tweets:

> "The most significant lessons to be drawn from the authorities as applied to a case of this kind seem to be the rather obvious ones, that this is a conversational medium; so it would be wrong to engage in elaborate analysis of a 140 character tweet; that an impressionistic approach is much more fitting and appropriate to the medium; but that this impressionistic approach must take account of the whole tweet and the context in which the ordinary reasonable reader would read that tweet. That context includes (a) matters of ordinary general knowledge; and (b) matters that were put before that reader via Twitter." [35]

10.23   The same approach to meaning is appropriate for other forms of social media which allow members of the public to post comments online, such as comments to posts made on Facebook, or on YouTube, or comments made by members of the public following a comment piece on a newspaper's website.

10.24   From a defendant's perspective, the significance of this approach to meaning in claims concerning postings by members of the public on social media is that it makes it easier to argue that a case should be stayed on the grounds of *Jameel* abuse of process (see para 10.92), or to argue that the words bear a lower defamatory meaning than claimed (which is relevant to truth and public

---

4 [2017] 4 WLR 68.

interest defences), or, where liability is established, to argue that damages should be low to reflect limited harm to reputation.

Serious harm

10.25   The serious harm test was one of the major innovations of the Defamation Act 2013 and was intended significantly to raise the bar for claimant individuals and companies who wanted to bring a defamation claim (see generally, para 5.29ff). Guidance on the application of the serious harm test has now been provided by the Court of Appeal in *Lachaux & Ors v Independent Print Ltd* (summarised at para 5.31ff). Defendants should carefully scrutinise claims brought by natural persons to see if the material relied on in support of serious harm is likely to "seriously affect" their reputation and, in the case of companies, whether they have established that the defamatory publication has caused, or is likely to cause, serious financial loss.

10.26   There is a spectrum of harm. At one end there are cases involving trivial or low level allegations published to small numbers of people, where a claimant may struggle to establish serious harm and the claim is liable to be struck out. This happened in *Daryanani v Ramnani*,[5] for example, where there had been modest circulation of the minutes of a meeting recording allegations against a trustee that the recipients, who were his fellow trustees, would already have known about through attendance at the meetings.[6] However, serious harm is never simply a "numbers game" and there can be serious harm arising from publication of a really serious allegation to even one person e.g. an allegation of theft made against an employee to an employer.

10.27   At the other end are cases involving seriously defamatory allegations published on widely read websites, where the inferential case for serious harm is likely to be so strong that no evidence is required.[7]

10.28   In the middle will be cases where the seriousness of the allegation is itself contentious, or where the claimant and defendant put in conflicting evidence on serious harm, or where it is unclear what impact a given publication will have had on a particular readership. In these cases, of which *Monroe* is an example, careful consideration of all the circumstances of publication is necessary.

10.29   Where a claim has been brought and the evidence of serious harm to reputation appears to be weak or speculative, or the circumstances are such

---

[5] [2017] EWHC 183 (QB).

[6] [2017] EWHC 183 (QB).

[7] *Sobrinho v Impresa publishing SA* [2016] EMLR 12 at [47] (per Dingemans J); *Lachaux*, at [82(3)].

that serious harm to reputation is inherently unlikely (e.g., because the allegation was never likely to be believed, or the publication didn't tell the publishees anything new), then defendants should give serious consideration to applying for a ruling on serious harm and summary judgment. There is a substantial overlap between these applications and an application for a stay under the *Jameel* jurisdiction (which, unlike serious harm, is not confined to defamation claims) and these two options should be considered together.

10.30   A potential benefit to defendants of making an application on serious harm is saving the costs that would be involved in the claim proceeding to trial. However, a careful judgment is required on what such an application is likely to entail by way of evidence and argument from both sides. In a really weak case, the application is likely to save costs. In a middling case, there is a serious risk of costs spiraling and the Court of Appeal in *Lachaux* (at [82(4)]) has stated that courts should ordinarily be slow to direct a preliminary issue, involving substantial evidence, on a dispute about serious harm.

Defences

Truth

10.31   Whether it will be open to a defendant in an online publication case to advance a defence of truth is likely to depend in part on whether the defendant is the author or primary publisher of the defamatory publication.

10.32   If the publisher is a newspaper which has published an article online, its journalist will have gathered the relevant facts and the article is likely to have been reviewed by an in-house lawyer before publication to check that any defamatory allegation can be supported. In principle, therefore, it should be possible to advance a truth defence.

10.33   But the same is not likely to be true for ISSPs that are put on notice of postings by members of the public on social media such as Facebook, or Twitter, or YouTube, or where for example a defendant newspaper has published a comment from a member of the public about one of its articles. In these cases, the ISSP or media organisation will usually not have any knowledge of the relevant facts and so the possibility of advancing a truth defence is unlikely to arise. Usually the best the ISSP can hope for is to get comment from the poster, so that, faced with two competing accounts of the truth, they are not required to accept the claimant's allegation of unlawfulness[8].

---

[8] *Davison* [2012] 3 CMLR 6.

10.34　Where a truth defence is available, the considerations which apply in respect of online publications are substantially the same as those for other kinds of publication. A defendant will have to gather all the available evidence and examine it critically to see if a truth defence can be made out.

10.35　What a defendant has to prove is that the "sting" of the libel is substantially true. It is important therefore to focus on what facts can be proved to support the central defamatory allegation, putting out of consideration anything which is peripheral. Knowing that something is true and proving it are two quite different matters. There must be sufficient documentary or witness evidence or both to satisfy a court that it is more likely than not that the defamatory allegation is true. A defendant must be able to advance a strong evidential case for a truth defence to withstand the serious scrutiny that it will receive at trial.

10.36　In a case where there is some but not particularly strong evidence to support a truth defence, a defendant will usually have a better prospect of success by relying on another defence to a defamatory allegation of fact, such as the public interest defence in s 4 of the 2013 Act (see below).

Public interest

10.37　The public interest defence in the Defamation Act 2013, s 4 is dealt with at para 5.47ff. In practical terms, a defendant considering whether to advance this defence to a defamatory allegation of fact will have to look critically at all the circumstances of publication and ask itself:

(1)　Is the statement complained of on an issue of public interest? For a discussion of the concept of public interest, see 2.29ff above.

(2)　Did the defendant reasonably believe that publishing the statement complained of was in the public interest?

The issue of "reasonable belief" has two elements. The subjective element requires the publisher to show it did genuinely believe that publishing the information was in the public interest. The "reasonableness" element requires the publisher to establish that it behaved fairly and responsibly in gathering and publishing the information. This second requirement will place all aspects of the information-gathering and editorial decision-making process under close scrutiny.

10.38　In principle, it would appear to be open to a defendant ISSP that has made available an article through a third party posting or a search result to rely on the public interest defence. In these cases, an ISSP may be able to advance a public interest defence on the basis of information contained in the article, or which can be gathered from the public domain, or possibly through making contact with the original publisher. It seems likely that the public interest factors that an ISSP would rely on would be different from those of the original media organisation and that some of the "responsible journalism" factors would not be applicable for example whether a claimant was given an opportunity to comment. These issues remain open, as to date, there have been no English cases where a defendant ISSP has defended a defamation claim at trial on the basis of the public interest defence.

Honest opinion

10.39   This defence protects statements of opinion, or value judgments, as opposed to statements of fact. The opinion must have been honestly held, but this is interpreted generously: the defence protects any opinion that could have been held honestly, even if only by a person with prejudiced, exaggerated or obstinate views. The publication, must however, indicate the factual basis for the opinion and those facts must either be true or based on a privileged publication (dealt with in para 5.44ff). In practical terms, therefore, a defendant will have to prove that the facts on which the comment was based were true at the time of publication, or that they formed part of a privileged report published prior to the comment, such as fair and accurate reports of court proceedings.

10.40   The honest opinion defence is most likely to assist mainstream media organisations, or bloggers who publish their own content, in defending comment pieces published online. These opinion pieces will often contain honestly held opinion, indicate the factual basis of the opinion, and rely on facts which have been checked for their accuracy. The defence may also enable media organisations to defend comments published by readers in relation to their articles, as in this situation the factual basis for the comment is likely to be the article itself.

10.41   In the Canadian case of *Baglow v Smith*,[9] the claimant, who was a left-wing political commentator, brought a claim in defamation against the author of a right-wing political blog, who had referred to him as "one of the Taliban's most vocal supporters". The claimant asserted that this was an allegation of fact, not of comment. However, the court found that readers of the article would have been aware from the claimant's previous writings that he supported the repatriation from Guantanamo Bay to Canada of an alleged Taliban member, so the statement was held to be an opinion based on known facts. The fair comment defence (as it is still known in Canada) succeeded,

---

[9] 2015 ONSC 1175.

with the court finding that the defendant's "rant" was honestly held opinion. This case suggests that the defence may assist in defending online commentators who are known for expressing forthright views, on websites where members of the public seek out such views.

10.42   It may well be harder for an ISSP to be able to defend comments made by members of the public on social media, for two main reasons. First, the law requires that the comment is not free-standing, but must indicate the factual basis on which it is based. Many comments on social media will not meet this criterion – Facebook, for example, is full of people's comments on other people's comments, in many cases not referable to any clear facts. Secondly, even where opinions can be shown to be based on published facts, it is likely to be difficult for an ISSP to prove the truth of those facts, unless as in *Baglow*, the facts can be taken to be a matter of general public knowledge.

Website operators

10.43   The website operator defence under s 5 of the 2013 Act is described in para 9.48 and is available both to media organisations which allow third party postings and ISSPs which host social media websites. In summary, operators of websites have a defence to a defamation claim in respect of posts made by third parties on their websites. The defence is quite complex in its manner of operation but has the advantage that it may allow a defendant to continue to publish the article complained of, providing the poster is willing to be identified or provide full contact details to the complainant. However, if the poster's cooperation cannot be secured and a defendant wants to avoid liability by simply removing the article from its website, this can be done under s 5 for defamation claims (or alternatively under the Electronic Commerce (EC Directive) Regulations 2002, which applies to all types of legal liability).

Claims against foreign defendants

10.44   S 9 of the 2013 Act is not so much a substantive defence as another way in which defendants can challenge the jurisdiction of English courts to try a defamation claim (see generally, para 4.46ff).

10.45   Foreign defendants (defined as defendants who are not in the UK, the EU or any Lugano Convention state) can now challenge a claim brought against them by invoking s 9, which will result in the claimant having to establish that "of all the places in which the statement has been published, England and Wales is clearly the most appropriate place to bring an action in respect of the statement." This provision assists foreign defendants to challenge jurisdiction in cases where publication in the UK has been small compared to publication in another country with which the claim has a more substantial connection e.g. the United States. The small number of reported cases on s 9 suggest that it may be having the deterrent effect that was hoped for at the time it was enacted.[10]

Malicious falsehood

10.46 Claims in malicious falsehood are relatively rare because it is hard for claimants to establish the elements of the tort: see the discussion at paras 5.75ff and 9.22ff. Typically the tort (sometimes known as "trade libel") is concerned with one business publishing malicious statements about another business which are calculated to harm its rival. A business that publishes such statements on its website will not be in the position of an internet intermediary because it will be publishing its own content, so it will not be able to avoid liability by removing the statement and will have to defend the claim in the usual way.

10.47 Claims against media organisations for malicious falsehood in terms of their own content are very rare. However, ISSPs face significant risks in terms of malicious falsehood given the willingness of posters on social media deliberately to spread untrue information about other individuals. Such postings may well meet the high threshold required to establish malice, however in many cases they will not be likely to cause financial loss. Postings that involve false statements referring to individuals (but do not have malice or the likelihood of financial loss) may nonetheless amount to defamation.

Harassment

10.48 When faced with a claim in harassment, a defendant should ask itself:

(1) Does the evidence demonstrate a course of conduct on at least two occasions that was targeted against the claimant and was likely to cause alarm and distress?

(2) Was the conduct so unreasonable and oppressive that it would sustain criminal liability under the Protection from Harassment Act 1997?

(3) Does the defendant have a defence? (see generally, para 5.94ff).

10.49 In the context of online publications, harassment can take place where someone embarks on a campaign of offensive postings about another person, although there will usually have to be a significant number of such postings and they will have to be seriously offensive to cross the threshold in (2) above.[11] The rise in the use of social media has made it easier for individuals

---

[10] *Ahuja v Politika Novine I Magazini DOO & Ors* [2016] 1 WLR 1414.

[11] See *J20 v Facebook Ireland Ltd* [2016] NIQB 98.

to engage in online harassment, often under the cloak of anonymity, so ISSPs may find themselves as defendants to these claims if they do not act promptly to remove such postings once they are on notice.

10.50   While a course of conduct on at least two occasions is an element of the tort, the publication of names of individuals on a website in the knowledge that it will inevitably come to their attention on more than one occasion can amount to harassment[12] but such cases are likely to be unusual.

10.51   It is relatively rare for media organisations to find themselves defending harassment claims relating to their own publications, whether online or in hard copy. There is clear authority that the reasonable conduct defence must be interpreted liberally in relation to journalism and that before the media is held liable in harassment there must be some exceptional circumstance to justify such a serious interference with freedom of expression.[13]

Breach of confidence

10.52   In practical terms, a defendant receiving a claim for breach of confidence, or more commonly a threatened application for an injunction to protect confidential information, will ask itself:

(1)   Has the claimant established that the information is confidential, according to the relevant tests?

(2)   If so, is there a sufficiently strong public interest in the publication of the confidential information to outweigh the claimant's right to confidentiality? (see generally, para 6.2ff).

10.53   The English courts tend to be deferential to claims of commercial confidence, placing heavy weight on the public interest in the maintenance of duties of confidence and readily accepting assertions about the potential damage that might result from leaked information. Accordingly, where the confidentiality of the information has been established, media organisations have often failed to persuade the court that the public interest in publication of the information should prevail.[14]

10.54   Public interest factors to look out for which have been successfully deployed in previous cases include confidential information that was relevant to a public debate about the safety of convictions (based on the use of unreliable

---

[12] *Law Society v Kordowski* [2014] EMLR 2.

[13] See the cases cited at para 5.91ff.

[14] For example *Northern Rock Plc v Financial Times Ltd & Ors* [2007] EWHC 2677 (QB); *Barclays Bank v Guardian News and Media Ltd* [2009] EWHC 591; *Brevan Howard v Reuters* [2017] EWCA Civ 950.

breathalysers)[15] and a confidential report that was relevant to a public debate about the value-for-money of a controversial public-private partnership[16]

Misuse of private information

10.55   A defendant faced with a claim for misuse of private information must focus on two questions:

(1)   Does the claimant have a reasonable expectation of privacy in relation to this specific information?

(2)   If so, is the claimant's right to privacy outweighed by the public interest in publication of this information?

(See generally, para 6.16ff).

10.56   Often it will be obvious that the claimant has a reasonable expectation of privacy in relation to the information, if it relates to a core aspect of their private and family life, such as their sex life, relationships with other family members or children, their finances or their medical information. If the information comes from confidential communications such as letters, emails or voicemail messages, there is very likely to be an expectation of privacy in relation to it; likewise if it relates to activities which took place in a private place. Children and other vulnerable persons get strong protection for their privacy, even in relation to activities which have taken place in public.[17] If disclosure of the information has caused the claimant serious anxiety or distress, that is also regarded as highly relevant.

10.57   At the other end of the spectrum, the activities of public figures are accorded a lower degree of protection, as they must be taken to have accepted a high degree of public scrutiny. That is particularly the case for politicians who have stood for elective office, but the principle is not confined to them and extends to all people in the public eye, whether in politics, business, finance, the professions, sports, or the arts, particularly if they can be regarded as "role models".[18] If the information in question relates to the exercise of any public function or position, it is unlikely to attract a reasonable expectation of privacy.[19] Nor is there likely to be a reasonable expectation of privacy for everyday activities carried out in public places. If a claimant has consented to

---

15   *Lion Laboratories v Evans & Ors* [1985] QB 526.

16   *London Regional Transport v Mayor of London* [2003] EMLR 4.

17   *Weller & Ors v Associated Newspapers Ltd* [2016] 1 WLR 1541.

18   *Ferdinand v Mirror Group Newspapers Ltd* [2011] EWHC 2454 (QB).

19   *Axon v Ministry of Defence* [2016] EMLR 20.

something that would otherwise amount to an infringement of his privacy e.g. filming inside his home, he will have a greatly reduced expectation of privacy if he later changes his mind.[20]

10.58 In between these two extremes there is a whole range of cases which will be highly fact-specific and require difficult judgment calls. For example, private activities sometimes take place in public places; does a claimant then retain their expectation of privacy, or has it been lost? What if a claimant has themselves been responsible for publicising one aspect of their private life in the past; do they then lose the right to complain about if in future the media wants to publish more private information about them? To what extent should the court take into account the impact of disclosures on family members, who may be victims of the claimant's discreditable behaviour?

10.59 The second stage of the analysis involves balancing the claimant's right to privacy against the public interest in publication of the information. Public interest factors to look out for which have been successful in previous cases include

- correcting a public figure's false image of marital fidelity;[21]
- allegations about a prominent businessman's misuse of company resources and manpower to assist his partner;[22]
- publication of the fact of a sexual relationship between a prominent banker and his more junior female colleague, as part of the debate about powerful men engaging in such relationships;[23]
- a story about an England under-16 rugby player having failed a test for banned steroids;[24] and
- a story about a businessman having a second family, which was relevant to a widely reported dispute about allegations he had used company resources for personal ends.[25]

Data protection

10.60 If the defendant is a media organisation or any other entity that has processed personal data for the purpose of journalism, then the obvious defence will be

---

[20] *Tobe Hayden Leigh v Nine Lives Media* [2017] EWHC 1564 (QB).

[21] *Ferdinand v Mirror Group Newspapers Ltd* [2011] EWHC 2454 (QB).

[22] *Lord Browne of Madingley v Associated Newspapers Ltd* [2008] QB 103.

[23] *Goodwin v News Group Newspapers Ltd* [2011] EMLR 27.

[24] *Spelman v Express Newspapers* [2012] EWHC 355 (QB).

[25] *Hutcheson v News Group Newspapers Ltd* [2012] EMLR 2.

to rely on the journalism exemption under s 32 of the 1998 Act (see generally, para 6.61ff). It should be noted that "journalism" for this purpose has been defined broadly and that enterprises engaged in communicating information to the public are likely to meet the definition.

10.61   A defendant seeking to rely on s 32 will need to establish that the data is processed only for journalism (or art or literature), with a view to publication of some material, and that it reasonably believed that publication was in the public interest, and that it reasonably believed that compliance with the data protection principles would be incompatible with those purposes. In addition to this exemption from the principles, s 32(5) prevents a claimant from getting an interim injunction on data protection grounds where a defendant is holding journalistic material with a view to publication (see para 6.70).

10.62   If the defendant is not engaged in journalism, the applicable defence will depend on whether the personal data being processed is personal data or sensitive personal data (defined at paras 6.43–6.44). The most likely candidate for personal data is the defence in para 6 of Sch 2 to the 1998 Act (processing that is necessary for the purposes of legitimate interests pursued by the data controller). In relation to sensitive personal data, none of the categories in the Data Protection (Processing of Sensitive Personal Data) Order 2000 is of obvious application to a defendant publishing information to the public on a matter of public interest.

PRACTICAL CONSIDERATIONS FOR INTERMEDIARIES

10.63   Internet intermediaries that qualify as "information society service providers" under the E-Commerce Directive benefit from the exemptions from liability established under the Directive (see Chapter 7). The most relevant of these for providers of content authored by third parties (for example, a media site with comment facilities and social media websites) is the hosting exemption. "Hosts" are protected from liability for damages arising from any civil claim in the circumstances set out in the Directive and Regulations (see para 7.34ff).

10.64   The safe harbour only exists however, if an ISSP (1) "does not have actual knowledge of unlawful activity or information" (which means it must not be aware of facts or circumstances from which unlawful activity would have been apparent) and (2) acts promptly to remove or disable access to the information, upon obtaining such knowledge.

10.65   There is an irony to the way the safe harbour operates with regard to the moderation of user comments. If ISSPs engage in moderation and seek to filter out unlawful information before notification, they risk depriving themselves of the hosting safe harbour for any "unlawful information" that slips through. However, for most ISSPs the question is academic because the scale of postings is such as to make pre-moderation impossible. A middle way between moderation of all content and no moderation at all is to allow members of the public to flag inappropriate content and to focus any review on those comments – most newspaper websites function in this way.

10.66   A second area of potential difficulty arises from notifications which are intended to trigger actual knowledge but which are formulated in vague terms. This is a matter of difficult judgments. On the one hand, ISSPs are entitled to require complainants to provide "details of the location" and "details of the unlawful nature of the information in question". European case law demonstrates that the information must be "sufficiently precise and sufficiently substantiated", while UK cases highlight that the information must enable the ISSP to make a meaningful evaluation of whether information is unlawful. So ISSPs should feel justified in pushing back on vague complaints.

10.67   On the other hand, ISSPs that rely too heavily on claimants to make out their claims with clarity risk being found liable on the basis that should have known the information was unlawful as "diligent economic operators" (see para 7.53).

10.68   ISSPs should consider taking a "generous" approach, seeking to analyse the material complained about and forming an independent assessment of unlawfulness, without strictly confining themselves to the terms of the complaint. A failure to do so carries significant risks.[26]

INTERIM APPLICATIONS

Injunctions

10.69   Applications for interim injunctions are very important in breach of confidence and misuse of private information cases, as they are often dispositive of the claim. There is usually little to be gained for either party in proceeding to trial after an injunction hearing. If the injunction has been granted, the claimant will have substantially obtained the relief sought: the prevention of publication. The defendant will have had the counter-arguments considered and rejected by the court, applying the same test as would be applied at trial (albeit without detailed testing and consideration of the evidence). If the injunction is refused, the claimant's arguments will have

---

[26] *CG v Facebook Ireland & Anor* [2017] 2 CMLR 29.

been rejected and once publication has taken place the information will be in the public domain.

10.70 Applications for interim injunctions sometimes come "out of the blue" and often come on with urgency. One of the dilemmas facing a defendant who intends to publish a news story but faces an urgent application is whether to insist that the injunction application is brought on as soon as possible, or whether to allow the claimant more time to prepare. A swiftly heard application will often suit editorial demands, but may mean that the defendant struggles to prepare in time for the hearing, particularly if evidence is required.

10.71 Injunction applications can be made to a judge, either in Court or (if necessary, out of hours on the telephone). Unless there are truly exceptional circumstances where hearing the application on notice would undermine the purpose of the hearing (e.g. in a blackmail case where giving notice may result in a defendant deliberately thwarting the application through pre-emptive publication), applications should always been on notice to the defendant (see para 8.10). If an application is made without notice when it should have been on notice, or if the claimant has not adhered scrupulously to the requirement of "utmost good faith" – presenting the case with candour and, in particular, drawing the judge's attention to any weaknesses in the evidence or adverse authorities), this can in itself be a ground for getting the injunction set aside.[27]

10.72 Assuming the application is on notice to the defendant, it is often in the interests of both parties to agree a "holding position" that allows the orderly preparation of a contested application to an agreed timetable rather than forcing a rushed application before the Duty Judge.

10.73 Typically, a "holding position" takes the form of an agreement or an undertaking. An agreement involves a broadcaster or other defendant publisher agreeing not to broadcast a news story without giving the other party a certain amount of advance notice (the idea being that if notice is triggered the applicant has sufficient time to make an urgent application). Such an agreement is typically made by an exchange of letters. Agreements not to publish will usually be acceptable to claimants if they come from a reputable publisher, but may be harder to negotiate for less well-established publishers, or publishers outside the court's jurisdiction.

10.74 The more formal alternative is for the defendant to give undertakings to the court (which can be formalised in e.g. the preamble to a consent order), that it will not publish the story before the injunction application has been heard.

---

[27] For example *Andresen v Lovell* [2009] EWHC 3397 (QB) at [26]–[29]; *YXB v TNO* [2015] EWHC 826 (QB).

Breach of such an undertaking would be likely to amount to a contempt of court.

10.75　The Practice Guidance puts the onus on the claimant/applicant to adhere to a range of important procedural safeguards for defendants/respondents (see para 9.84ff above). Particular points for defendants to watch out for include

- whether notice has been properly given; if not, whether that was justified;
- whether a without notice application was presented with the utmost candour (applicants are required to serve a note of the hearing);
- whether all the required documentation has been provided;
- whether it is strictly necessary to have a private hearing (which applicants always want and is usually not strictly necessary); if not strictly necessary, the application should proceed in open court, with appropriate protections for confidential information.

BETWEEN ISSUE AND TRIAL

10.76　In a claim where the focus is not exclusively on injunctive relief, for example because the claimant is also seeking damages, a claim relating to an online publication will proceed towards trial in the normal way. From a practical standpoint the issue for a defendant will be deciding whether it wishes to settle or to defend the claim.

10.77　If settlement is favoured, a number of options should be considered including making an offer of amends in a defamation case or making "without prejudice" or Part 36 offers in all other cases. If the claim is to be defended, consideration should be given to whether to make an interim application – for a ruling on meaning, or for strike out or summary judgment – that may be able to narrow down, or dispose entirely, of the claim.

Offer of amends

10.78　The offer of amends procedure is a potentially useful way of settling a defamation claim or creating a defence to a claim where otherwise one might not exist, where the defendant knows that it does not want to defend the claim but has been unable to agree on a correction, apology and compensation with the claimant. It is particularly helpful where a defendant knows it wants to bring the claim to an end but is concerned that the claimant is not actively pursuing settlement and that the legal costs are mounting.

10.79　The "offer of amends" procedure is set out in the Defamation Act 1996, ss 2–4. A defendant can, at any time before serving a defence make an "offer of amends": either an "unqualified offer" – in relation to meaning pleaded by the claimant – or a "qualified offer" – in relation to a specific defamatory meaning which it is accepted that the publication bears (s 2(2) of the 1996 Act). Such an offer is to make a suitable correction and sufficient apology, to pay compensation and costs (s 2(4)).

10.80   It is very hard for a claimant to refuse to accept an offer of amends, particularly where it is unqualified and there is no on-going dispute about meaning. If an offer of amends is accepted then the parties will seek to agree on the steps to be taken by way of correction, apology and compensation. If agreement cannot be reached the Court will determine the appropriate amount, taking into account the steps taken in fulfilment of the offer (s 3). The defendant will receive a substantial "discount" on the figure which would otherwise have been awarded by way of libel damages and additionally is likely to have made a major costs saving, compared to having allowed the claim to progress further.

10.81   If an offer of amends is not accepted it provides a complete defence to an action for libel (s 4(2)) unless it is shown that the defendant published the libel maliciously (s 4(3)). It is very difficult for a claimant to establish that a defendant has published a libel maliciously, as the claimant must show that the defendant has acted in bad faith.[28]

10.82   Where an offer of amends is accepted, the defendant can expect to obtain a significant discount on the damages that would otherwise be payable. Factors that the court will take into account in deciding the level of discount include whether the offer has been made early, whether the defendant's apology is late or off-hand, whether an ill-founded defence has been raised in correspondence, whether the defendant made clear how it would conduct its defence including in relation to attacks on the claimant's character and whether the defendant's overall attitude in correspondence has aggravated the claimant's hurt feelings.[29] Discounts in the cases have ranged from 10% to 50%.[30]

Rulings on meaning

10.83   One potential weapon in the defendant's armoury is to apply to the court for a preliminary ruling on meaning. The procedure is set out in the Defamation Practice Direction, which allows a court to decide, at any time:

---

[28] *Milne v Express Newspapers* [2005] 1 WLR 772.

[29] *Lisle-Mainwaring v Associated Newspapers Ltd & Anor* [2017] EWHC 543 (QB).

[30] Ibid, at [118].

(1)   Whether a statement complained of is capable of having any meaning attributed to it in a statement of case;
(2)   Whether the statement is capable of being defamatory of the claimant;
(3)   Whether the statement is capable of bearing any other meaning that is defamatory of the claimant.[31]

10.84   In procedural terms, such an application can be made at any time after service of particulars of claim, but should be made promptly.[32] The application must state that it is an application for a ruling on meaning made under the Practice Direction, and the application notice or supporting evidence must identify precisely the statement and the meaning attributed to it that the court is being asked to consider.[33] The court may also exercise the power to rule on meaning on its own initiative.

10.85   In principle, a ruling on meaning can be helpful in a clear case where a claimant has pleaded a meaning that is unsustainably high, as it may allow a defendant to advance a truth or public interest defence that can succeed on a lower meaning. However, defendants should think very carefully before seeking such a ruling. Evaluating the meaning of a defamatory allegation is often not straightforward as words are inherently ambiguous, lending themselves to different interpretations depending on the precise context in which they are used. In addition, rulings on meaning have been described as "an exercise in generosity, not in parsimony" and the threshold for excluding any given meaning is high.[34] As a consequence, the law reports are littered with cases where judges on appeal have disagreed on the meaning of a defamatory allegation, between themselves, or with the first instance judge, or sometimes both.[35] Accordingly, defendants are advised to invoke this procedure only in the clearest of cases and to consider alternative, less risky options, such as a *Jameel* abuse of process application.

Without Prejudice and Part 36 Offers

10.86   Some cases are defended as a matter of principle, because the claim is weak or unmeritorious, or the claimant is a rogue, or because settling the case would have knock-on implications for many other cases. But in cases where liability

---

[31] Defamation Practice Direction, para 4.1.

[32] Defamation Practice Direction, para 4.2.

[33] Defamation Practice Direction, paras 4.3, 4.4.

[34] Brown LJ in *Jameel v Wall Street Journal Europe Sprl* [2004] EMLR 6.

[35] For example *Lewis & Ors v Daily Telegraph* [1964] AC 234; *Skuse v Granada Television Ltd* [1996] EMLR 278; *Mapp v News Group Newspapers Ltd* [1998] QB 520; *Bennett v News Group Newspapers Ltd* [2002] EMLR 39; *Jameel v Wall Street Journal Europe Sprl* [2004] EMLR 6.

is likely to be established, the commercial case for settlement is usually a strong one. Costs in online publication cases are ordinarily high, as they are charged at commercial hourly rates.

10.87   In addition, in some cases there are the added costs created by conditional fee agreements providing for success fees, as well as deferred insurance premiums. Even if the parties are quite far apart in terms of their valuation of the compensation due to a claimant, that difference will often be dwarfed by the legal costs that will be saved by settling the claim at an early stage. Where the primary issue between the parties is compensation, it therefore makes good sense for defendants to make an offer to settle to protect themselves on costs.

10.88   Defendants have one of two choices when making an offer to settle. The first is to make an offer that is "without prejudice save as to costs", also known as a Calderbank offer. The effect of making the offer in such terms is that it cannot be disclosed until the conclusion of the trial, when costs are decided. At that point the judge will apply CPR 44 and if the claimant has not done significantly better than the defendant's WP offer, the claimant will usually be ordered to pay the defendant's costs from that point of time onwards.

10.89   The second choice is to make an offer under CPR 36. Part 36 is a self-contained procedural code for the settlement of claims. Part 36 offers also operate as WP offers (i.e. they cannot be disclosed), but they must adhere to certain formalities and they carry specific costs consequences. A claimant who accepts will be entitled to costs up until the point of acceptance. A claimant who rejects the offer and then fails to beat the offer at trial, will be liable for the defendant's costs from the last date for acceptance (which is ordinarily 21 days after the offer was made).

10.90   A generous settlement offer on damages made under Part 36 therefore creates a very strong incentive for a claimant to settle the claim. The choice is then between guaranteed, generous compensation and having his legal costs met, versus the substantial risk of failing to beat the defendant's offer and becoming liable for the defendant's costs. This is a grim prospect, as the defendant's costs will almost certainly exceed by a significant margin any damages awarded to the claimant at trial, leaving the claimant substantially out of pocket.

10.91   In terms of the choice for defendants, a "without prejudice" offer is more flexible as it does not necessarily involve agreeing to pay the claimant's costs. In a weak case, a WP offer can be made on a "drop hands" basis (in other words, there is no order for costs) or for a set amount of costs (say 50%). A Part 36 offer, however, is always an offer to pay the claimant's costs up until acceptance. On the other hand, the Part 36 regime creates a particularly strong incentive for claimants to settle, because of the automatic adverse costs consequences of failing to beat an offer (although the court does retain a discretion to make a different order if the normal order would be unjust).

Strike Out and Summary Judgment

10.92   These are two important powers that may provide defendants to online publication claims with a quick way to dispose of weak claims. In cases where there has been minimal online publication within this jurisdiction, a court may be persuaded to strike out the claim on the basis that there is no real and substantial tort. The case of *Jameel v Dow Jones and Co Inc* [36] established the court's power to strike out a claim on this ground, which is a form of abuse of process. The Court of Appeal held that defamation proceedings will be struck out where there is no realistic prospect that they would yield any legitimate advantage that outweighs their cost and expense, where, in its words, "the game is not worth the candle."[37] This doctrine has been applied in a number of cases involving ISSPs.[38]

10.93   In claims brought by individuals, there is a significant overlap between the grounds which will support a strike out on the basis of *Jameel* abuse of process and those which will support a strike out arising from a claimant's failure to establish serious harm. In the case of companies, an additional ground for strike out would be a failure to establish that publication has caused, or is likely to cause, serious financial loss.

10.94   An application for summary judgment can be used to obtain judgment in respect of a claim as a whole or a particular issue, where the claimant has no real prospect of succeeding on that claim or issue. In addition, in defamation claims, there is a specific power of summary disposal under the 1996 Act. These applications would be relevant where the claimant has advanced a weak claim, for example, a breach of confidence claim where confidentiality has been lost as a result of prior publications, or where a defendant has a defence, for example a journalism exemption in a data protection case, to which the claimant has no real answer.

---

[36] [2005] QB 946.

[37] Ibid, at [57].

[38] *Kaschke v Osler* [2010] EWHC 1075 (QB); *Davison v Habeed & Ors* [2012] 3 CMLR 6; *Tamiz v Google* [2012] EMLR 24.

Disclosure

10.95 Defendants to online publication claims are entitled to disclosure from claimants in the usual way under CPR 31. The documents to which defendants are entitled are defined broadly so as to include hard copy documents and electronic documents of all kinds including email and other electronic communications such as text messages and voicemail messages, word-processed documents and databases and documents stored on portable electronic devices.[39] Defendants are also entitled to disclosure of electronic documents that have been deleted and to the metadata in documents.

10.96 Disclosed documents are subject to the prohibition on collateral use in CPR 31.22(1), which means that a defendant can only use the documents for the purpose of the proceedings and that otherwise they remain confidential. If a document is read to or by the court, or referred to at a hearing that takes place in public, however, the prohibition on collateral use ceases to bind, unless the receiving party undertakes otherwise or the claimant obtains an order that the restriction continues to apply.

10.97 Defendants providing disclosure in online publication claims will be alive to the need to protect a journalist's sources. The protection of sources is a fundamental principle under ECHR, art 10 and is governed by the Contempt of Court Act 1981, s 10, which defines the limited circumstances in which an overriding public interest may permit an order for source disclosure. While a defendant must disclose the existence of a document that might reveal a source, the defendant may claim privilege from inspection for the whole or part of such a document.

Expert evidence

10.98 Claimants quite commonly rely on expert evidence in online publication claims. Typically this will happen where evidence is required about a technical issue that the court needs to understand, or there is a dispute between the parties about how a given technology works, or what technological solutions are available to a defendant. One of the potentially difficult issues that ISSPs may confront when faced with this evidence is how to respond to it and whether to seek to adduce expert evidence of their own.

10.99 ISSPs may have good reasons for not wishing to disclose details of how their technologies work, or what limitations they operate under, or what potential

---

[39] CPR PD 31B, para 5(3).

technological solutions may be available to them, for reasons of commercial confidentiality or otherwise.

10.100   One of the ways to avoid having to reveal too much about potentially sensitive technological issues is to analyse the claim and consider whether admissions can be made to narrow the scope of the issues in dispute. If a given matter is admitted, evidence on the point is not going to be required.

10.101   If notwithstanding the admissions there remain matters in dispute, then evidence will be required, but defendants should think through carefully exactly what evidence is needed to make out their case. What distinguishes expert evidence is an expert's ability to give opinion evidence, but a party always requires the court's permission to adduce expert evidence. Where the evidence can be confined to essentially factual issues it can be given by a non-expert witness and a party has the right to put such evidence before the court without seeking permission.

INDEX